GRAHAM NORTON
REVEALED

GRAHAM
NORTON
REVEALED

ALISON BOWYER

ANDRE
DEUTSCH

This edition published in 2013 by
Andre Deutsch
an imprint of the Carlton Publishing Group
20 Mortimer Street
London W1T 3JW

First published in 2002

Text © Alison Bowyer 2002, 2009, 2013
Design © Carlton Publishing Group 2013

The right of Alison Bowyer to be identified as the author of this work has
been asserted by her in accordance with the Copyright, Design and Patents
Act 1988.

A CIP catalogue record for this book is available from the British Library.

ISBN 978 0 23300 389 4

The publishers would like to thank the following sources for their kind
permission to reproduce the pictures in this book:

First plate section
Getty Images: / Dan Wooller/WireImage: 8t; PA Photos: /William Conran:
3b; Rex Features: /Tim Anderson: 5, 6t, 6b; / Araldo Di Crollalanza: 7b; /
Edward Hirst: 4b; /Julian Makey: 4t; /Ken McKay: 7tl; / Martin Stenning: 8b;
/Richard Young: 7tr

Second plate section
Rex Features/Tony Larkin, 2. Rex Features/Richard Young, 3. Getty Images/
Dave M. Benett. 4. Getty Images/Oleg Nikishin/Epsilon, 5. Getty Images/
Dave M. Benett, 6. & 7. Rex Features/Ken McKay, 8. & 9. Press Association
Images/Ian West/PA Wire, 10. Getty Images/Eamonn McCormack

Every effort has been made to acknowledge correctly and contact the
source and/or copyright holder of each picture, and Carlton Books Limited
apologises for any unintentional errors or omissions which will be corrected
in future editions.

Printed and bound by CPI Group (UK) Ltd, Croydon, CR0 4YY

CONTENTS

ACKNOWLEDGEMENTS

The author would like to thank the following people for their help and assistance: Paul Scott, Judith Chilcote, Scott Michaels, Noel Giles, Niall MacMonagle, Nicholas Parsons, Steve Lount, Colin Bateman, Niall Power Smith, Julie Forrester, Billy Forrester, Harry Moore, Yvonne Shorten, Noreen Lynth, Professor Colbert Kearney, Maura Betty, Eileen Maquire, Karen Koren, Mark Goucher, Pepi Lemer, Tris Reid-Smith, Stephen Scott, Jon Rogers, Martina O'Carroll and T.J. from Bandon Tourist Office. Thanks also to the team at Carlton Books.

1 FROM BANDON TO DOLLYWOOD

May 13 2001, the showbusiness night of the year. The great and the good of the UK film and television industry had gathered at London's Grosvenor House Hotel in Park Lane to celebrate the very best of British talent.

The Baftas – the annual awards ceremony of the British Academy of Film and Television Arts – is the most eagerly awaited event in the showbusiness calendar. The UK's equivalent of the Oscars, it is an opportunity for everyone in the industry to eat, drink and be merry while giving themselves a collective pat on the back.

The famous faces had been arriving for hours, posing for the battalion of press photographers waiting outside and occasionally signing autographs for the fans who had queued to watch the glamorous arrivals. Anybody who was anybody was there: soap stars, actors, comedians, producers and directors, all dressed up to the nines and wondering who would be awarded the prestigious accolade of a Bafta. The celebrated bronze mask can make a career and cement an already successful one and, in a profession notorious for its here-today-gone-tomorrow fickleness, there is enormous competition to win one.

The night of the 2001 awards was to belong to one man: Graham Norton. One of the most outrageous performers on TV, the camp presenter caused a sensation by winning not one but two Baftas, beating the two most successful shows on the box, *The Weakest Link* and *Who Wants To Be A Millionaire?*

This was no small feat. The BBC's *Weakest Link*, fronted by self-styled 'Queen of Mean' Anne Robinson, was a runaway success, regularly attracting millions of viewers. On the opposite channel, ITV's *Who Wants To Be A Millionaire?* was *the* programme everyone was talking about. Hosted by the Capital Radio DJ and TV presenter Chris Tarrant, it was the first television quiz show to offer a genuine jackpot of one million pounds.

The two shows were deemed to have revolutionized prime-time television and their formulas had been sold around the world. Media watchers were convinced the gong for Best Entertainment Programme would be a two-horse race but, in the event, they were both non-runners as Norton snatched the prize for his risqué late-night Channel 4 programme, *So Graham Norton*. Rushing on stage to accept the award, he spoke for many of the people there when he said, 'I can't believe we beat *The Weakest Link*! How mad is that?'

But he should have had more faith. While *Millionaire* and *Weakest Link* regularly pulled in more viewers, they had the benefit of being on the two main channels. To those in the industry, Norton's Friday night show was considered to be at the forefront of 21st-century entertainment. His popularity was sealed when he won his second Bafta of the evening for Best Entertainment Performance, the second year running that he'd won that category. And in 2002 he was to make it a hat-trick, prompting speculation that the award should be renamed the Graham Norton Award for Best Entertainment Performance.

Norton's double whammy in 2001, following the £4 million deal he had signed three weeks before to stay at Channel 4, confirmed him as Britain's hottest television talent and the next day's papers were full of his victory. In fact Channel 4 swept the board at every level, winning 11 trophies. Its executives couldn't resist a smile as they savoured the triumph of trouncing the competition. The BBC had a particularly poor night with just seven awards.

The BBC contingent could have been forgiven for feeling bitter that Graham had done so well for Channel 4. Just weeks before, the BBC had tried to poach him from the station, apparently offering £5 million to lure him away from the channel that had made him. But Graham, who likes to describe himself as 'that shiny poof off the telly', decided to stay put. His decision was partly to do with loyalty – a quality he values very highly in himself and others – and partly because he was concerned that the BBC would want to tone down his material. A wise choice, believed many in the industry, given the BBC's tendency to lob huge amounts of money at stars without knowing what to do with them once they've lured them away from commercial television.

At Channel 4 – the station launched in 1982 with a remit to cater for a young, cosmopolitan audience – Graham could get away with featuring a woman who could fire out a ping-pong ball from between her legs. At the BBC, answerable to the licence payers of Middle England, the opportunity for such things would be seriously curtailed. As the television presenter Vanessa Feltz pointed out in her column in the *Express*: 'At Channel 4, he can be as iconoclastic, irreverent and spontaneous as his prodigious wit allows. What was in store for him at the Beeb? *Blankety Blank*. Trust your instincts Graham, never quit the hit.'

The BBC did eventually get their man, but they had to wait another couple of years. In the meantime Graham decided that he would rather stay with his avant-garde Channel 4 chums in Covent Garden than chance his hand with the corporate suits and accountants that rule Television Centre. The BBC's desire to have him on their schedules was entirely understandable. A massive hit with viewers, particularly the young, upmarket audience that television companies so love to target, Graham had the Midas touch. His show regularly attracted four million viewers and won loads of awards, including an International Emmy.

In fact it seems that everyone loves the engagingly flamboyant star. He consistently tops magazine reader polls on such diverse subjects as My Dream Neighbour, Fantasy Dinner Guest, Ideal Boss and Ideal New Best Friend. His fans far outnumber his detractors, with much of his appeal lying in the fact that his humour – quick and sharp – is seldom cruel. Graham encourages people to laugh at themselves while he and the audience openly laugh at them. But such is his particular blend of charisma and charm that he usually manages to do so without hurting anyone's feelings.

His particular skill is the ability to get people to admit to the most outlandish acts of behaviour – things you'd imagine no sane person would confess, even to their closest friend. His reaction to these revelations – usually one that implies he has never *ever* heard of such goings on – is so funny that when the audience laughs it is often more in response to him than to the original confession. As well as getting people to reveal their deepest, darkest secrets, he is able to induce the most unlikely people to do the wackiest things. Who else but Graham could persuade the late MP and former Labour Northern Ireland minister Mo Mowlam to conduct a marriage ceremony between two dogs? Or elicit from Judith Chalmers the admission that she wasn't wearing any knickers?

Graham's secret lies in the fact that, crucially, he never belittles the people who appear on his show. He is unfailingly charming and polite to his celebrity guests, many of whom were his childhood idols. The only exception so far has been the actress Raquel Welch, whom he called 'a grumpy old bitch' before cutting her satellite link. 'She was just being so annoying and the audience turned against her,' he said unapologetically.

It was no accident that *So Graham Norton* was given the late-night slot usually occupied by *Eurotrash*. It may have seemed a natural progression to replace one outlandishly near-the-knuckle programme with another, but in fact Graham's show was far less offensive. Instead of the porn-dressed-up-as-comedy format favoured by *Eurotrash*, Norton's humour harks back to a different era. He is what one television critic has referred to as 'A 21st-century Larry Grayson with access to the web', an old-fashioned entertainer at heart, repackaged for an anything-goes generation.

Crude and rude though he can undoubtedly be, Graham carries it off with such wit and charm that little old ladies can laugh along – remarks about oral sex seemingly going blissfully over their heads. He has got away with the most bizarre sexual voyeurism by treating everything as a harmless joke. With anyone else it would be perceived as tasteless but with Graham it is somehow just fun. 'We don't claim it's rocket science,' he said in the show's defence. 'We just take a childish delight in things.' It is Graham's unthreatening personality that enables members of the more conservative older generation to giggle at the most smutty innuendo. As he puts it, 'Patently, I am not a sex object. I am just a friendly, poofy chappie.'

His overwhelming popularity meant that in spring 2002 Channel 4 decided that Graham had what was needed to take on the biggest challenge of his career and go five nights a week – the so-called Holy Grail of television. The five-times-a-week format, perfected by the hugely successful and much-copied American host David Letterman with his CBS show, has become the bench-mark in nightly TV chat, and it is the ambition of virtually every DJ and television presenter to follow in his footsteps. Graham was no exception. Like Russell Harty, Terry Wogan and Jonathan Ross before him, he coveted the kudos and status that a high-profile nightly show would bring him. In May 2002, a month after his 39th birthday, he achieved the dream with his new show *V Graham Norton*.

He won his first major award at the 1997 British Comedy Awards, stealing the gong for Best Comedy Newcomer from under the nose of Channel 5 chat-show host Jack Docherty. Docherty, who had been sufficiently confident of winning to have penned an acceptance speech, was shocked to hear Graham's name read out instead, an announcement made harder to bear by the fact that Norton had been his holiday stand-in on the show. Few who witnessed Graham proudly accepting his award that night could have realized just how long the wait had been for the Irish-born star. For most of his 39 years he had been a frustrated failure – an unsuccessful actor turned stand-up comic, forced to wait tables to make a living.

But life as a waiter and barman gave him the opportunity to hone the witty remarks and camp putdowns that have become his stock in trade. Drinkers asking for a glass of wine or beer found themselves on the receiving end of a barbed remark – and loved every minute of it. Encouraged by his popularity with the customers, Graham performed material he had written himself in a room above one of the pubs where he worked. But success was to elude him for many years. 'One of the reasons Graham is enjoying his fame so much now is because it was a long time in coming,' reveals his friend and mentor Niall MacMonagle. 'But he never gave up and he never complained. No one deserves it more than he does.'

And enjoying it he most certainly is. The boy who grew up in the small West Cork town of Bandon and spent much of his childhood glued to American television programmes, now rubs shoulders with the very celebrities he once idolized. He got on so well with country singer Dolly Parton when she appeared on his show that she invited him to her Tennessee theme park Dollywood, and he flew to New York on Concorde to attend Liza Minnelli's wedding. No party, it seems, is complete without Graham. When David and Victoria Beckham threw their 2002 pre-World Cup party to raise money for the NSPCC it was Graham whom they invited to host the charity auction. His transition from barman to A-list celebrity was complete. No wonder he remarked as he introduced *The Proclaimers*, one of his favourite bands, on his show: 'I love my life!'

In the space of a relatively few years he has managed what many of his contemporaries can only aspire to, and become a household name. With four Baftas under his belt and – since 2004 – a high-profile multi million pound contract with the

BBC, he has succeeded in making it to the very top of his profession.

While his particular brand of humour may not be everybody's cup of tea – the *Sunday Times* once declared him an 'Enemy of the People' – for millions of fans he is the brightest star on TV. Certainly as far as the BBC is concerned, the millions who tune into programmes such as *Any Dream Will Do* and *I'd Do Anything* means that Graham Norton is worth every penny of his rumoured £7 million contract. And when ITV comes knocking at his door again, as they already have, the BBC will no doubt put up a fight to hang onto one of its most popular stars.

2 SMALL TOWN BOY

Graham Norton was born Graham William Walker on April 4, 1963, at 48 St Brigids Road, Clondalkin, the family home just outside Dublin.

Number 48 was a modest three-bedroom semi-detached house built in 1952, in a pleasant residential street. Clondalkin is now part of the urban sprawl surrounding Dublin but at the time of Graham's birth it was a small village on the outskirts of the city.

The night of his birth is remembered vividly by neighbour and family friend Rachel Horan. 'Graham was born in the back room of number 48 and I was in the house the night he was born,' she recalls. When Graham's mother went into labour Mrs Horan walked the few yards from her own house at number 28 to keep his father company as he paced back and forth downstairs, anxiously awaiting the new arrival.

Graham was delivered safely by the doctor who afterwards, following with the Irish tradition, went downstairs to wet the baby's head with the proud father. However, as the night progressed so did the merriment, none of which apparently went down too well with Graham's exhausted mother Rhoda. 'I spent the night at the house with Billy Walker and Rhoda said afterwards that she was awake and could hear us,' says Mrs Horan, a former schoolteacher. 'The doctor stayed on and had a drink and Rhoda was very annoyed because she was in some pain afterwards.'

Billy and Rhoda already had a daughter, Paula, born two years earlier, and Graham's arrival completed the family. They moved from Clondalkin a few months later.

Graham's parents had met and fallen in love in the mid-fifties. William George Walker, known as Billy, was a farmer's son from Carnew, County Wicklow. He had been brought up on a farm until his early twenties but chose not to follow in the footsteps of his father George and went into the brewery business in Dublin instead. A keen biker, he had driven all over Europe on his motorbike before his marriage and loved to recount stories of his travels.

Rhoda Marie Graham, a painter and decorator's daughter from Belfast, had also travelled. She had lived for a while in Canada, where she worked in a bank, but at the time of her wedding she was working as a typist in Belfast. Both Protestants, they were married on September 2, 1957, at the Parish Church of St Nicholas in Belfast. Billy was 30 and his bride five years younger. They were to later name their son Graham, after Rhoda's maiden name, and William after his dad.

The family was destined to move around a great deal because Billy's job as a sales rep for Guinness took him all over Southern Ireland. They were in Clondalkin for a couple of years and then moved to Windsor Park, a 35-minute drive away. From there the family went south to Waterford, to the nearby coastal town Tramore, and on to Kilkenny.

This meant a succession of schools for the young Graham, an unsettling experience for any child. Just when he got used to one school and made friends, the family would up sticks and move somewhere else and he would have to start all over again. 'I didn't ever feel traumatized by being the new kid at school, but I didn't like it that much,' he later admitted. On one occasion he recalls being virtually dragged to school by his mother, who smacked the back of his legs in frustration at his stubbornness. But in small town Ireland nothing went unnoticed. 'One day she went to some Mothers' Union meeting and these women said someone had seen a mother abusing her child on the way to school,' Graham laughed. 'Mum was mortified.'

Lacking the company of lots of siblings, Graham's childhood, although not unhappy, was somewhat lonely and uneventful. As a youngster he would spend his spare time sat at home, glued to the television. 'Every time a year went by I just thought, "Great, that's another one",' he would later recall. 'It sounds like a wretched existence but, in fact, I was a happy child in a loving family and the isolation just gave me time to watch more TV.'

Graham loved watching television, particularly the American programmes that dominated British and Irish television at the time. He developed an obsession with America and dreamt of going to the States where 'they drove big cars and had a fantastic life'. He idolized Hollywood stars like Joan Collins and Sophia Loren and with the effortless diligence of the true aficionado, became an expert on film and television trivia. 'Graham was always talking about television, but he would talk about it in a factual way,' says his brother-in-law Noel Giles. 'He knows the subject inside out because he has absolutely lived it.'

Graham attended primary school in Kilkenny but in 1975 the decision was made to enrol him and his sister at a private boarding school in the West Cork town of Bandon. It was common practice among Protestants to send their children to boarding schools, which were often some distance away, as Protestant schools were few and far between. Youngsters would usually be sent to board in Dublin for a few years before going to grammar school, which would generally be a boarding school too.

Bandon Grammar School was a small, fee-paying co-educational school that had been established in 1641 by Richard Boyle, Earl of Cork. The school was set in 30 acres of land, part of which was a working farm. The boarding accommodation, which housed around 100 boys and girls in separate residences, was situated a short walk away from the main school building, overlooking a field of grazing cattle. Graham was to share a small dormitory with eight other boys, sleeping in a bunk bed and with his possessions kept in a locker.

Bandon itself is a market town 19 miles south west of Cork city. Situated in a fertile river valley, agriculture is the main occupation of the people who live there, although a significant number of them work at Schering Plough, a chemical company just outside Bandon. Built as a garrison town in 1604, its population currently numbers 6,500 – a significant number of whom are Protestant.

There is a well-known saying about Bandon that goes: 'Bandon, where the pigs are Protestant,' explains Graham's former English teacher Niall MacMonagle. 'The people there are Church of Ireland and it means that it's such a little pocket of Protestantism that even the animals are Protestant. It would be seen as a very Protestant town.'

In selecting Bandon Grammar for their children, Billy and Rhoda appear to have made a good choice. It was as far removed from the stereotype of the grim English public school as is possible to be. Beatings and bullying were not part of life at Bandon Grammar School. Instead the school's philosophy was to value its pupils' right to be different and to excel in different ways. It prided itself on its strong Christian ethos, teaching tolerance and understanding of others' beliefs and opinions. The perfect place, therefore, for someone like Graham.

'It was one of the happiest places I have ever been,' says Niall MacMonagle, who taught there for four years. 'And very open-minded. Small is beautiful and there was something wonderfully wholesome about it because most of the kids were from the countryside.'

Graham was 12 years old when he started at the school, which nowadays charges £1,000 a term for boarders. One of the first boys he met was Niall Power Smith, a quantity surveyor's son from Dublin. 'At that stage there were between 40 and 50 boys who were boarders, and about the same number of girls,' he recalls. In the classroom with Graham by day and sharing a room with him at night, Niall got to know Graham very well. 'He coped with boarding school the same as any of us did really,' he says. 'We weren't really homesick because it was a very nice school and everyone got on well. It wasn't a very upmarket school, it was middle of the road with a mixture of people. A lot of them were farmers' children from the surrounding area, some, like Graham, were from the town, and a few of us were from Dublin.

'It was middle class in the Irish sense; meaning that it would be slightly better off people who went there. Not everyone at

21

the school was Protestant; there were a few Roman Catholics, including myself, but there was no problem with tolerance. Most people there were generally extremely nice and so were the teachers. It was actually grand and I would send my own kids there.'

Graham; however, has said that much of school bored him and that he couldn't wait to leave. 'I just thought I had to do it but I could never understand why we weren't paid to go there,' he said. 'Maybe I would have enjoyed it more if I'd had a social life. But I didn't. I just watched TV all the time.' But in truth he appears to have thrown himself wholeheartedly into school life. He was heavily involved in drama and debating and, as Bandon Grammar was a liberal establishment, he was allowed to skip the more physical aspects of school life. 'You didn't have to do rugby if you didn't want to,' explains Power Smith. 'I suppose the only difference between us and Graham was that we were big into sport and he wasn't. But nobody held that against him or had a problem with it.'

Sport held absolutely no interest for Graham. He did win a medal for cross-country running but that was only because he was on the team. He actually came in last, 'many, many hours later,' as a friend recalled. Rugby was a particular horror and Graham and classmate Billy Forrester would avoid playing it whenever they could. Instead the two friends would sit on the touch-line eating their sandwiches and chatting. 'Some of my best memories of Graham are from that time,' says Billy. 'Graham was such a clever one with words and stories.'

Graham did play cricket, but as school friend Colin Bateman points out, 'only under duress'. He remembers him cross-country running and, 'He wouldn't have shone at it,' he laughs.

'It wouldn't have been his thing at all – utter purgatory! He was in the tennis team though.'

Graham by far preferred the intellectual life to that of the playing fields. 'There was a whole group of us who used to spend sports classes in the library,' explains school pal Julie Forrester, sister of Billy. 'We were the library bunch. Graham also got out of woodwork and did art. We didn't do embroidery or anything like that at our school – art was considered girlie enough. Boys would have been laughed at if they'd done art; the only person who could have got away with it was Graham.'

In other circumstances a non-sporty, slightly effete boy who chose to hang around with girls in the library instead of getting muddy on the rugby field might have found himself picked on for being different. He might have found himself on the receiving end of a spot of bullying from the more macho boys in the school; teased and ridiculed for his bookish ways. But happily Graham was to escape unscathed. 'There wasn't really much bullying going on at school,' says Power Smith. 'There might have been a slight bit but it was frowned upon. There was a slight divide between the sporty set and the arty set but there was no animosity. Everyone was very friendly.'

What also protected Graham from being a potential target for bullies was the extraordinary wit and charisma he possessed even then. 'Everyone liked Graham,' explains Niall Power Smith. 'He was very well respected and always had a good sense of humour.' Colin Bateman agrees. 'Graham was always very gregarious,' he says. 'He was obviously a little different because his talents lay in a different direction to the rest of us, who just wanted to beat each other up on the rugby field. He was a great character.'

'Graham was just accepted, always, for what he was,' says Julie Forrester. 'He always had a niche for himself and everybody appreciated that niche. That's not to say that our class was particularly enlightened or anything, it was just that he was able to make a comfortable place for himself. It came more from him than from any of us.

'There were certain things you'd ask Graham and certain things you'd ask somebody else. He was the one who was good at drama and talking. He was able to tag along with us in all the girls' subjects; he was an honorary girl really. He was much more comfortable in female company than in male company. There was a fair amount of not very nice stuff going on at school and people did get bullied, but as far as I know he was immune.'

In 1979, when Graham was 16, a new teacher arrived at Bandon Grammar School who would become a major influence on his life. His name was Niall MacMonagle and he was a 26-year-old Irishman who was passionate about English literature. Different to any of the teachers Graham had had before, Niall MacMonagle would become a mentor and friend to Graham for many years to come.

'Niall was the best English teacher we ever had and he was certainly an inspiration for Graham,' says Billy Forrester. 'He was so excited about literature and interacting with the students that he used to get into trouble because he didn't spend enough time in the staff room at coffee time; he would rather be talking to his pupils. Instead of talking about Kavanagh or Yeats, he would talk about Ian Dury. He'd come in with a photostat of a bit of poetry, or it might be a song by Ian Dury, and he'd distribute it as fast as possible to get a quick reaction. He was revolutionary.'

Graham had always enjoyed English. Before Niall

MacMonagle joined the school he had been taught by Miss O'Callaghan and was one of her most enthusiastic students. 'Miss O'Callaghan and Graham were both quite strong characters,' recalls Colin Bateman. 'Graham sat in the front of her class and caused no trouble but made lots of noise! He was a star in waiting. I think he already knew which direction he was heading in with his acting and everything.'

If anything, with the arrival of Niall MacMonagle Graham now enjoyed his lessons even more. Years later he was to describe in an interview how important Niall's classes had been to him. 'He was the one who really inspired me,' he said. 'He made me realize how exciting it could be to read a novel. He would take us on with so much energy.' He recalled how the teacher would bring in bags of books and give them out. The first one he gave Graham was *The Bell Jar*, the poet Sylvia Plath's largely autobiographical novel about a young woman's descent into madness. It had been published the year Graham was born. 'I was so blown away by it, I loved it in a way I'd never loved a book before,' he once recalled. 'He also gave me *Memoirs of a Survivor* by Doris Lessing. I wonder how much reading those books at an early age changed me. Maybe if I had read them as a jaded adult they wouldn't have had that impact. Would I have collided with them in the same way?'

Significantly for the effeminate Graham, he considered Niall MacMonagle to be different from the rest of his teachers in other ways too. 'Niall was rather fey looking and that was quite exotic as well,' Graham said. 'On top of the feyness it was his interest in the subject that stood out. He really did make me read books in a different way; it is, kind of, as if he tried to take me beyond the idea of the plot.'

MacMonagle, who now teaches at Wesley College, Dublin, is equally effusive about his former pupil. 'Graham was incredible in the classroom,' he says. 'He was just so alive to everything we ever did. He was one of 24 but he stood out because he had such energy and an upbeat optimism about him. He was as talented and wonderful as he is now.'

A born entertainer, Graham excelled in school plays and when he forgot his lines, ad-libbed confidently. 'We put on several productions and he was just marvellous in them,' says MacMonagle. 'We put on a thing called *Engaged*, which is a Victorian melodrama by W.S. Gilbert of the Gilbert and Sullivan duo. And Graham played Ernest in *The Importance of Being Earnest*. When he forgot a line he would out-Wilde Wilde. He ad-libbed with such style and panache that nobody noticed!'

Niall Power Smith shared the spotlight with Graham in *The Importance of Being Earnest*. 'We would have been in the fifth year, which would have made us 16 or 17,' he says. 'I remember the production quite well.'

Graham was also an excellent mimic. His sister Paula recalled how her brother's natural ability to entertain was evident right from the very beginning. 'He has always made people laugh,' she says. 'He's naturally witty and from a very young age could imitate people perfectly.' Julie Forrester recalls how, like all good mimics, Graham would carefully study people. 'One thing I have noticed about Graham is that he seems always to be looking out, rather than looking in,' she says. 'It is very much a put on expression; some kind of pose for effect. At school, you never saw him disappearing into reverie. There was always something about his eyes that seemed to say, "I'm looking at you, you're not looking at me".'

Boarding-school life followed a predictable, if boring, pattern. There were classes from 9am until 10.30am, when there would be a break for morning tea, and then more classes until lunch. The afternoon lessons finished at 4pm. 'At four o' clock you could do your own thing; play sport or attend a club or whatever was going on,' says Niall Power Smith. 'We used to walk into Bandon but you had to ask permission to do that if you were a boarder. Our uniform was grey trousers with either a blue or white shirt, grey sweater, black and silver striped tie and a black blazer. It was quite a nice uniform but you had to wear it all the time, except on Saturdays.'

Weekends at Bandon Grammar School were even more boring than weekdays. 'A lot of people were weekly boarders who went home for the weekend so there might only have been 20 people left at school,' explains Niall. 'Graham would have gone home most weekends. On Saturdays you could go downtown, with permission, but you would have to sign out and sign back in.'

'Downtown' was hardly an exciting prospect. 'There was very little to do in Bandon,' says Niall. 'It has come on a hell of a lot from those days, but then it was a very quiet, sleepy country town that hardly had a supermarket. We would go in and walk around and do the odd thing. There might have been one or two coffee shops. Cork had more to offer but we couldn't really get there. I was rugby captain and the great thing about playing sport was that you did get away for matches; that was one of the big attractions of sport for a lot of us.

'If you were into sport there was always plenty to do. And there were things organized, like plays and stuff like that. On Sunday there was church in the morning and then Sunday

27

lunch. The food was always very good at our school, excellent in fact. Other teams who came to play us always looked forward to the food.'

A couple of years after Graham started at Bandon Grammar, his parents moved to the town to be with their children. Guinness was offering people voluntary redundancy and, as Billy had worked for the company for a number of years, the sum on offer was quite substantial. He decided to take it and with the money he and Rhoda were able to afford a large bungalow with a garden, right next to the school.

This meant that Graham and his sister no longer had to board, which was welcome news for Graham on several levels. As well as enabling him to return each day to the bosom of his family, he once again had free access to his beloved television set. As a boarder, he had been dismayed to hear that he would only be allowed to stay up and watch one television programme a week. 'And that, for a reason I don't know, was *Charlie's Angels*, and it just filled us all with excitement,' he said. 'I adored the show. Mind you, you watch it now and it makes *Magnum* look like *Henry V*. Even at the time we knew it was froth. I didn't like *The Avengers*, it looked too much like Ireland. *Charlie's Angels* didn't. There were no hedges, just dusty roads and go-faster stripes. It was very sexy.'

Once he was back living with his parents, Graham could resume his love affair with the TV set uninterrupted. Noel Giles first met Graham when he was 12 years old and remembers his obsession with television even then. Noel, who was 18 years old and dating Graham's sister Paula, liked his girlfriend's kid brother and was keen to find common ground between them.

This, however, proved to be something of a challenge. Noel

was a man's man who was set to take over the family farm just outside Bandon. 'Graham wasn't remotely interested in farming,' he recalls. 'I knew he liked comedy and as I was into *The Goons* I tried to get him to take an interest in them. But I don't think it was quite his type of comedy. Some people are interested in football, some people are interested in pop music, Graham was interested in television. He was interested in it as a factual, knowledgeable thing, not just as something to watch.'

If Graham was happy to be back living at home, his parents were equally delighted to have their family together under one roof. Rhoda Walker, a stalwart of the local Mother's Union, was a proud housewife and mother – a fact that was immediately apparent as soon as one looked at her son. 'When Graham arrived in school every morning he just looked so clean and well cared for,' recalls Niall MacMonagle. 'His school uniform was always spotless and he was always very well turned-out. His home life was just so stable and supportive. He was very well loved by his parents and that gives a child great confidence.'

This self-assurance was never more in evidence than when Graham was involved in a debate. He shone at public speaking and went on to represent his school at senior level in an all-Ireland debating competition. Speaking for the motion that 'the rights of man are a myth', he won praise for his 'competent presentation of well researched material' and sense of humour. And in a portent of things to come, he was singled out for his 'confident handling of interruptions from the audience' – a skill which would pay dividends when he later embarked on a career as a stand-up comedian.

'I can remember him debating and he was very good at it,' recalls Power Smith. 'I was involved in debating as well but

Graham was always the key man. He was very, very good on his feet and always stood out.'

'Graham was terrific at debating and public speaking,' agrees Niall MacMonagle. 'When I first met Graham Walker, as he was then, he was studying for his Leaving Certificate, which is the equivalent of A levels. He was in a fifth year class and it was the most wonderful group. There was a gang of them that hung around together and there was a really good dynamic within the group. They were all very able and gifted intellectually and were very involved in writing.'

When MacMonagle started up a school magazine, called *School Bag*, Graham was a keen contributor. 'Graham wrote some wonderful short stories for the school magazine,' he recalls. 'They really were strange, wonderful pieces. I remember one short story, I think he called it 'Northern Fruit', and it began: "Eddie's son loved the lightbulb." It was a play on Edison. It was about this guy Eddie, who was a taxi driver, who lived with his wife and child in New York City.

'Graham charted the great change in their lives from struggle and hardship to great affluence. And without labouring the story or giving off a kind of sledgehammer moral, he spoke about how the son grew up to be very like the father; discontented and uneasy. At the very end the father had moved out of the city and the son was moving back in. It was a very well-made piece. I was very impressed.'

And when the town's picture house burned down in 1980 the 17-year-old Graham wrote a touching tribute in the school magazine. Entitled 'Requiem for a Cinema', he wrote, 'During the summer a fire stole from us a dear old friend – Bandon cinema. We will miss it.' He went on to describe its 'glamourous

[sic] interior, with its slimy, condensation covered walls, its lino covered floors and its faded, decrepit chairs.' The monotony of many a dull film was relieved, he wrote, 'when a row collapsed or the little man with his trusty torch threw somebody out.'

Despite the lack of scintillating films on offer, the cinema had been a major attraction for Graham and his friends. In fact, it had been a major attraction for the whole community. As he pointed out, 'In a town like Bandon where each night is a non-event, the cinema provided a valuable service.'

Graham's story about the cinema gives an insight into the unrelenting boredom that was everyday life for youngsters in Bandon. The town had a good golf club and angling was a popular pasttime, and that was about it. Neither activity held much interest for the teenage Graham. Bandon, he has said, is either the gateway to West Cork or the escape hatch from it, depending on your point of view.

Niall Power Smith explains how isolated they were living in Bandon. 'We were so terribly innocent back then,' he says. 'We were a long way removed from things in Dublin, like drugs for example. We'd never heard of them. They didn't exist down there, which is probably one of the reasons my parents sent me to Bandon. It was a different world. We did smuggle in cider, the odd bottle – if we could get away with it, and mostly we did – but that was very minor. We were quite well supervised because we were in a house and there was a housemaster there all the time. There wasn't that much opportunity to get into mischief.'

Misdemeanours, if they were discovered at all, didn't carry much of a penalty. 'There wasn't any corporal punishment,' explains Niall. 'If you did something wrong you had to do what they called "impositions". You would have to sweep the tennis courts or clean out the showers. Or pick up stones at the farm – that was the worst one! I can't remember if Graham had to do any impositions; I'm sure we all did.'

School holidays didn't provide much let up from the tedium either. With expensive continental holidays beyond their reach financially, Graham's family spent their annual summer break at a little rented caravan in Dunworley, West Cork, which was all of 12 miles away.

It was while staying at Dunworley that Graham lost his heart for the first time. 'I remember the first summer we stayed. I was aged about seven and I fell in love with Dolly the horse,' he recalled. 'Well, she was actually a foal. Anyway, I cried buckets when we had to go home, but I got over it quite quickly: you see I was shallow at even such a young age. She had been sold by the time we returned the next year.'

The summer vacation was much like being at home, in that basically there was nothing to do. 'In the evenings we would go to the pub, which I think was actually called The Pub, because you couldn't sit in a caravan all night, could you?' he said. 'I would try and make an orange juice last three hours. There would be singing, and an old man played the accordion. My party piece was Cliff Richard's "Power to all our Friends".'

Later on, his father's redundancy money enabled the family to venture further afield and they would travel in Billy's car to England and France. 'I would sit in the back of the car and listen to my parents argue,' said Graham. 'Because roundabouts are very rare in West Cork and there are lots in France… and they are all backwards.'

With such little on offer in the way of excitement, Graham and his friends were thrilled when Niall MacMonagle began taking them into Cork City for nights out. Although it was only 19 miles from Bandon, Cork was a world away in terms of what it had to offer. It had cinemas and theatres, restaurants and bars; things noticeably lacking in Bandon at the time.

These evening outings to see films and plays were done at the young teacher's own expense. 'Niall was just an amazing teacher, one of those teachers you only come across now and then,' says Graham's classmate Yvonne Shorten. 'He'd take us out to see really new plays in Cork, off his own bat. He was a really creative man, he was just brilliant.'

Unlike most of their teachers, Niall MacMonagle treated the teenagers like adults. But although they were 17 and 18 at the time, they were essentially kids from a small town and were easily impressed. 'I remember going to see a movie on a Sunday night and being so enthusiastic about it that I brought four or five of them up on the Monday night to see it,' Niall recalls. 'I was living in Cork at the time and afterwards I brought them back to the flat for a cup of coffee. My brother John was there, wearing a pair of black leather trousers, and this caused a sensation! They thought it was the ultimate in sophistication. Graham was full of excitement at meeting someone who wore black leather trousers.'

Like many of his school friends, Graham couldn't wait to leave Bandon and head to the bright lights of Cork or Dublin. They talked about going to university and travelling the world. When the school arranged job interviews at the local bank in Bandon, Graham went dutifully along, even though he had no intention of taking one. 'They sent us down en masse and I can vividly remember sitting there in my brown check sports jacket, waiting to be seen,' he recalled. 'Thank God, I didn't get the job.'

'We used to talk about our plans and one of Graham's big dreams was to be on Gay Byrne's *Late, Late Show*,' says Yvonne Shorten, who is now a fitness instructor living in London. 'Bandon is a small market town, which is one of the reasons I left myself. It is quite provincial. It's great to go home to but when you're a teenager you think "there's a big wide world out there." We both felt a bit like that.'

However, not all of Graham's classmates felt that way. Many were more than happy to stay in Bandon and make their life in the town. For whilst undeniably lacking the excitement on offer in big cities, Bandon is situated in a particularly beautiful part of Ireland. Virtually unspoilt and close to the sea, the town is surrounded by lush green meadows and hedgerows teaming with wildlife.

This dichotomy within the class was very apparent to Niall MacMonagle. 'I remember talking about the excitement of going to the city and many of the kids in the class said they had no interest in going to the city,' he says. 'They were so self-assured and self-contained that they weren't dazzled or drawn by the bright lights or the excitement of urban living. I thought it admirable of them really because most of us when we are in our teens, especially when you are living in a place like Bandon where you've got to get a bus to get a bus, are tempted by the city.'

Graham was popular at school with both boys and girls and his former classmates admit that many of them never considered that he might be gay. 'To be honest, we were all a bit naïve in those days and it was not really something we thought about,' says Yvonne Shorten. 'I led a very sheltered upbringing. I only realized things were like that when I came to London. But in retrospect I wasn't surprised because his humour was quite camp and his demeanour was quite camp as well.'

Graham – whose first proper crush had been on David Cassidy at the age of seven – has admitted that he had girl-friends at school, but only 'in the way that all Irish boys at that time had girlfriends. You would be asked who you were going out with and you would point – her, over there,' he explained. 'Graham didn't know he was gay when he was at school,' says Colin Bateman. 'He wouldn't have had a clue and I remember him dating one or two of the young ladies. We all were; it was quite normal behaviour.' There was one girl in particular that Graham went out with for quite a while. Her name was Belinda Watson and she was from England. 'She was his girlfriend but they were just going out, as you do at school,' says Colin. 'Graham would have been about 15 or 16 at the time. We were all ducking and weaving back then. It was all innocent stuff – terribly innocent by comparison to what kids are up to now.'

Elaine O'Driscoll, who is one of the ones who stayed put in the area and who is now a solicitor in Cork, says that Graham was something of a school heart throb. 'You wouldn't believe it now, but a lot of the girls fancied Graham,' she says. 'He was lovely.' Julie Forrester guessed the truth about Graham's sexu-ality, however, and once even challenged him about it. 'I think we all knew that he was gay even though he didn't,' she says. 'We knew before him. I just knew that he was different; he wasn't like the other boys. I remember in sixth class telling him that he was gay and him denying it completely. As a group we were talking about it and I said, "Well you're gay Graham, aren't you?" and he categorically denied it. He said, "I'm not, I'm not." '

Graham's denial was probably rooted part in genuine uncertainty and part in fear. It was to take him several more years before he would discover the truth about his sexuality, but he suspected he might be gay and was terrified of what it might entail. He had no positive role model to identify with; at that point in his life the only camp person he had any knowledge of was the television presenter Larry Grayson. That he might in any way be like the simpering Grayson was a notion that filled him with horror.

He once recalled how, as an 11-year-old child, he was watching Grayson on the television and recognized aspects of himself in the star's demeanour. Not surprisingly, he admits that this somewhat freaked him out. 'I knew that on some level I was like him, but I didn't want to be like that,' he said. 'I remember thinking, "Oh God, if I'm gay does that mean I am going to grow up to be like him?"' Little wonder then that at school Graham chose to avoid discussions about his sexuality.

When he was a boarder Graham would join in with the other boys when talk turned to girls. 'He was a good-looking lad and very funny,' says Niall Power Smith, who is now a property developer in Dublin. 'We would talk about girls in the dormitory and Graham joined in, but it was all very innocent – extremely so when I look back at it! We didn't know anything, we never did anything and Graham never discussed his sexuality. At that stage he wasn't perceived as being different from anyone else. It never crossed our minds that he was gay.'

Graham's family did think it a little unusual that by the age of 18 he had not yet brought a girlfriend home, but according to his brother-in-law Noel, they didn't give it too much thought at the time. But, as Julie Forrester explains, the signs were there if you

36

wanted to read them. 'He was always camp at school: the way he acted and the way he spoke, the way he moved his hands and the expressions he made with his face were exactly the same as the ones that you see on the television,' she says. 'We were watching *Are You being Served?* on the TV but Graham never minced like John Inman; he was just extravagant with his gestures.'

She recalls how Graham, who was obsessed with the way he looked and would scrutinize his appearance in the mirror, even made believe he was black. 'He always used to pretend that he was of African descent because of his facial features,' she says. 'He was always looking for the exotic. He definitely wasn't the small town Bandon boy.' Julie also remembers that Graham's famous sense of humour could occasionally manifest itself in cruelty as he experimented with the effect his remarks had on people. On his show he is seldom seen to humiliate guests but at that stage in his development he had not honed his humour quite so carefully.

'He put could you down if he wanted to, but in an experimental way rather than a very nasty way,' she says. 'I remember once he brought the art teacher an apple. He was the only boy in the art class because all the boys did woodwork. He brought her an apple and it wasn't meant to be a nice thing; it really was for the entertainment of the class. He wanted her to feel uncomfortable and to have a laugh at her expense. We loved it; we lapped it up. We thought it was great, but I bet she didn't like him very much.'

Living in a country where 98 per cent of the population was Catholic, Graham and his Protestant school friends were very aware of being different. 'You are part of a very small minority and there is a somewhat warped view with the majority as to what you're about,' explains Colin Bateman, who is now a farmer on the outskirts of Bandon. 'You are perceived as belonging to the landowning class. If you are living in a Protestant environment like Bandon Grammar School it is fine, but if you are transcending it then there will always be under-currents. Protestant friends of mine who went to Catholic schools had quite a hard time.'

'Bandon was a very strange town to grow up in because of the Protestant thing and the separation,' agrees Julie Forrester. 'It was hard to mix in those days because of which camp you belonged to and all that stuff. I remember escaping from school to try and mix but you always stood out like a sore thumb because your skirt was six inches shorter than the other girls'. There is a permanent divide that seems to have settled on Bandon because of the huge mixture of Protestant people. It's not so much bad feeling; it's just very separate. I thought it was really funny when an interviewer asked Graham if he was aware he was gay and he said, "No, I just thought I was Protestant." I thought that was great!'

By 1981, Graham was about to leave the stifling confines of Bandon for life in the outside world. Together with his friends Yvonne Shorten and Julie and Billy Forrester, he would depart without a backward glance, in his case never to return to live in the town.

If he had any regrets at all about leaving, it was that it meant saying goodbye to Niall MacMonagle. As a farewell gift the group presented their favourite teacher with a commemorative plate, made by Julie Forrester, whose family owned a pottery in the town. 'They wrote "To Uncle MacMonagle" and signed their names on it,' says Niall. 'But Graham, the devil, wrote Grahm and then he put a little arrow and put in the missing "a" and then wrote in the margin "sp", imitating my little marks on his homework.'

In the event, goodbye turned out to be merely adieu. MacMonagle, who keeps the treasured plate in the hall of his home in Dublin, was destined to be an important person in Graham's life and in later years the two would rekindle their acquaintance and become good friends. But in 1981 Graham was on the brink of an exciting new life and the next few years were to prove eventful to say the least.

3 LIFE BEGINS!

Graham left school without much idea of what he wanted to do next. Ever since he was a young boy it had been his ambition to go to drama school and become an actor, but this was an aspiration that for some reason he considered unattainable. 'I really wanted to be an actor but I thought, "That's an impossible dream,"' he said. Whether this defeatist attitude was to do with his own lack of confidence, or the more likely knowledge that acting would not be considered a serious career goal by his parents and teachers, Graham had convinced himself that his dream would remain just that.

He then entertained the notion that he might become a journalist because he had seen *The Mary Tyler Moore Show* on TV and thought it 'seemed very glamorous.' The show, a massive hit in America during the early seventies, starred Tyler Moore as unmarried, thirty-something television journalist Mary Richards. It looked a pretty good life to Graham and with the limited experience he had had – writing film reviews for his local newspaper, *The Examiner* – he decided to apply for a place at journalism college. That ambition suffered an early setback, however, when he failed to get in.

In fact, at the time he left school Graham's prospects were far from rosy. He had not done well in his exams – in his own words he had 'bombed'. Classmates remember him being able enough, but at the end he hadn't achieved the grades he could or should have. 'Graham always did quite well in his exams,' says classmate Niall Power Smith. 'He wouldn't have been top of the class but he wouldn't have been bottom either. He was very good at things like English and French and history. He wasn't a brain box or anything but he was an intelligent guy. He could coast along. He was probably the kind of guy who was just looking for his niche in life.'

At 18, Graham had yet to find that niche. He couldn't really see which career path he wanted to take. He didn't think that becoming an actor was a realistic goal and his parents agreed with him. Billy Walker had done an ordinary job all his life and, although he had worked hard, his aspirations had remained the same: to earn enough money to put food on the table and provide a decent standard of living for his family. Like many working class parents of their generation, he and Rhoda couldn't imagine how acting could be in any way described as a proper job. They wanted stability for their son and the kind of security that came with a steady job. 'I think they would have been happy if I had gone into the bank, but I couldn't see that,' Graham said. 'Happily, nor could the bank.'

Even his holiday job had been a disaster. He had been given a job, his first proper employment, working in a local pottery. 'I was supposed to be making ceramic brooches but I was so hopeless they took me off that and I ended up peeling apples for £1 an hour,' he revealed sheepishly.

So it was that, in the absence of anything better to do,

Graham enrolled at Cork University to study English. 'I went to university thinking, "I'll somehow become a journalist," but I never, ever wrote an article all the time I was there,' he confessed. Niall MacMonagle had instilled in him a love of English literature and this was the only subject he really wanted to do at Cork. But in their first year students had to do four subjects and, put off by the 9am geography lectures, Graham opted for French, history and Greek and Roman Civilization. This latter subject was apparently deemed impossible to fail. 'It was the only reason anybody did it,' Graham said. 'It was fantastically popular and hundreds did it in their first year but no one carried on with it.'

Undoubtedly the best thing about going to university was the opportunity it presented to get out into the world. Cork may have been less than 20 miles from Bandon but to Graham and his friends it felt like a thousand. Graham craved the city and would later say that his life started when he turned 18. He was not in the slightest bit sad to be leaving home; for a small town boy, the comforts of a warm clean home and parents who doted on him could not compete with a crummy rented flat and freedom.

'It was only people with a lot of money who had a car who were able to commute home,' says Graham's school friend Yvonne Shorten, who studied English with him at university. 'Most of us rented rooms in Cork. The digs were pretty basic and they weren't cheap either.'

During his first term at University College Cork (UCC), Graham shared a place with his old school pal Billy Forrester. 'It was a fairly grotty flat in Wellsley Terrace, Cork,' Billy recalls. 'But we had just finished school and it was our first adventure away from home. I think it was a party time for everybody. Getting out of school and moving away from Bandon to a university town with cinemas and cafes was very exciting. Even in the early eighties there was quite a lot going on in Cork.'

Graham loved his first year at UCC. Free from the restrictions and timetables imposed by school, and given the option of attending lectures or not, he savoured freedom for the first time. This wasn't simply the freedom of not having to get up at a certain time or having to wear a uniform; it was a spiritual freedom too. Surrounded by like-minded people he began to feel more at ease with himself and less like the square peg in a round hole that he had been in Bandon. 'I felt I had come home,' he was to later say in an interview with the *Guardian*. 'I met people I really liked – funny, intelligent, nice people – it opened up a whole world to me.'

Billy Forrester was one of Graham's best friends during the first months he spent in Cork. 'It was the time in our life when we were closest,' he says. 'Graham taught me how to make omelettes. We spent the first term of our first year together, but then we drifted apart. I was doing science and he was doing arts and I'd do my thing with my crowd while he was very much involved in drama and the art set.'

During his first year at UCC Graham concentrated more on his social life than he did on his studies. He considered going to drama school to be a hopeless fantasy, but that didn't take away his love of the theatre. He joined the university drama club, UCC Dramat, and was in a couple of plays. 'I often went to see Dramat productions and I remember Graham distinctly,' says Martina O'Carroll. 'He was very funny and lively and colourful and he had a very happy bunny face! He really did stand out as one who could communicate very well. All the conversations with him at that time were almost like a chat show.'

Martina, who now manages the Everyman Theatre in Cork, recalls being particularly impressed when she saw Graham in a production of Samuel Beckett's *Waiting for Godot*, at The Granary Theatre, Cork. He and his good friend Jeremy Murphy played the two tramps Estragon and Vladimir. It wasn't so much Graham's performance in the play that impressed Martina – she says he was only 'quite good' – but his guts at tackling it at all. 'There is another side to Graham that isn't evident when you watch him on television,' she explains. 'He was always the lively one but at the same time he took the time out to do Beckett. Beckett at 18! To me, Beckett is a mature reader's piece.

'It was very ambitious because Beckett wasn't as popular then as it is now. It is trendy to read him now because it is synonymous with your "wonderful arty Dublin writer," but at that time it was considered heavy drudgery. Graham was bright and intelligent and he had a great vocabulary. He was very well read and he wasn't afraid to take on something like Beckett.'

If going to university widened the horizons for Graham, it also brought the matter of his sexual orientation to the foreground. His sexuality, a subject that had troubled him greatly as a young teenager and which, as a result, he had pushed to the back of his mind, now became an issue. At school there had not been much opportunity to explore where his sexual preferences lay because, as his friends attest, they were all pretty naïve. But at UCC, with thousands of hormone-charged teenagers living away from home for the first time, sex was very much on offer. The big question for Graham was, would it be with men or women?

45

Although Graham suspected that he might be gay, he wasn't completely sure. In any event, it wasn't something he felt able to handle at that point. Like any 18-year-old, he was full of anxiety about his blossoming sexuality. But his problems were compounded on several levels. As well as the usual teenage worries about unrequited love and insecurity over one's appearance, Graham had to come to terms with the possibility that he was probably gay, and, what's more, that he was a gay man in southern Ireland. The implications of this were not lost on Graham.

In 1981, Ireland was still a rural country with a very conservative-minded population. In terms of social policy it was one of the most restrictive states in Europe. Many things were illegal: birth control, homosexuality – even divorce. The Catholic Church wielded enormous influence over people and its authority was seldom questioned. In a country that would not legalize divorce until 1996, being gay was a definite no-no. The Catholic Church considered homosexuality to be a mortal sin and although Graham was a Protestant, the Church of Ireland certainly didn't approve of it. 'Anybody who was gay would have been considered quite unnatural and abnormal,' explains Graham's schoolfriend Colin Bateman. 'But it wasn't really an issue. They just kept themselves to themselves. It was the same in the Catholic Church, with all the stuff that was going on in the priesthood back then. It was all kept really quiet so you didn't know what was happening. There was a cloak of silence and respectability over everything.'

Religion aside, the bald facts of the matter were that you could, in theory, find yourself in court for practising gay sex. It was a conservative country – and Graham was living in the most traditional part of all. 'It would have been very difficult to be gay in West Cork,' says Colin Bateman. 'It is a bit better now, but it would have been very difficult 20 years ago. Back then, being gay would have been thought of as completely weird and unnatural.'

It was not until a series of scandals in the early nineties that things started to change. Hard on the heels of revelations that paedophiles were operating within the Church came the Casey scandal. It was discovered that Dr Eamonn Casey, Bishop of Galway and one of the most senior Catholics in Ireland, had enjoyed a 20-year affair with an American woman and had a secret love child. The scandal gripped Ireland and the Catholic Church was plunged into a crisis from which it was never fully to recover.

When Casey's mistress Annie Murphy appeared on Irish TV on *The Late, Late Show*, virtually every household tuned in. Half the viewers saw Murphy as an evil hussy sent by the devil to destroy the Catholic Church; the other half were hooting with derision at the Church's misfortune. Youngsters were seen wearing t-shirts bearing the slogan 'Wear a condom – just in Casey.' The Bishop resigned on May 11, 1992, and went to work as a missionary in Central America. Homosexuality was legalized the following year, in 1993, with the age of consent put at 17, the same for men and women.

But sexual progression was still light years away when Graham was in Cork and he was under no illusions about what being gay would entail in terms of social vilification. Apart from contending with centuries of prejudice and, in the eyes of his Catholic compatriots, the not inconsequential matter of eternal damnation, there was the more fundamental problem of where

47

to go to meet people. Even in decadent London, at that time, there was very little in the way of a gay scene and outside of the cities in rural Ireland there was nothing at all. Twenty years on, Cork is a thriving place with a vibrant club scene. 'They are even talking about having a Gay Pride march next year,' says Graham's friend Billy Forrester. 'But when we were at UCC gay bars would have been very underground. There might have been one or two, but I don't recall them at all.'

That Cork, stronghold of Republicanism, should be the setting for a Gay Pride rally illustrates just how much the country has altered since Graham was a student. 'Ireland has changed so much,' says Graham's friend Julie Forrester. 'When we left Cork you couldn't buy a red pepper, people didn't know there was any such thing. The kind of changes that have happened since the eighties are just mind-boggling. The whole culture thing is so radically different. People have come back from abroad and brought different things with them. Nobody goes to Mass any more; only a very small minority go. The whole atmosphere is so different. I wouldn't say it's better, but it has changed completely.'

Against such a backdrop, it is hardly surprising that Graham would be cautious about his sexuality. This uncertainty would not resolve itself until the mid-eighties and while he was in Cork Graham experimented with love affairs with both men and women. He formed a close relationship with a male fellow thespian from UCC Dramat, and in his first year he also dated one of the female lecturers from the university.

'I remember Graham going out with a French woman when we were at uni,' says Yvonne Shorten. 'I saw her a couple of times and she was definitely his girlfriend. She was a little bit older than him.' Julie Forrester and another university friend, Mia Leahy, also remember her. 'She was a lecturer,' says Julie.

Graham didn't introduce either his boyfriend or his lecturer girlfriend to his family however. Indeed his brother-in-law Noel remembers him leading a very separate, almost secretive life at that time. 'We didn't meet the lecturer,' he explains. 'When Graham was in college at Cork he led a very divided life. It wasn't as if he was coming down to Bandon with his friends and buddies, and as far as I know his mother and father never went up and met him for coffee with his friends. There wasn't that kind of thing happening.'

Trying to 'find himself', and enjoying his new-found freedom, it was perhaps inevitable that Graham neglected his studies. He has admitted that he did no work but managed to do 'bizarrely' well in the first year exams. Buoyed up by having got away with it, at the end of his first year at UCC Graham headed to France with his lecturer girlfriend for the summer holidays.

But not long after they arrived in France, their relationship hit the rocks. 'It didn't work out with Graham and his teacher and when it fell apart he was left stranded,' recalls his friend Mia Leahy. 'He didn't have any money to get back to Cork and he ended up working outside the Pompidou Centre in Paris, mimicking people. He would walk behind them, impersonating their walk and copying their mannerisms. He was really good at it and that's how he made his money that summer.'

Graham, who Mia says was 'brilliant' at French, also took a job in a Parisian boutique to supplement his earnings. But his career as a salesman was to prove remarkably short-lived. Like one of the awful stories Graham would one day elicit from his audience, he later told his friends how that particular job was a complete disaster. 'At the end of his first day Graham went back to the place he was staying and the next day he couldn't find the shop, so he lost his job,' laughs his friend Harry Moore.

After France, Graham went to London to stay with Harry and Harry's then girlfriend Julie Forrester for a while before returning to Cork. 'Graham got a job working at a hamburger joint next door to the Rock Garden in Covent Garden,' says Harry. 'He was always energetically describing what it was like when he came back from work. He was just like he is on the television now; he doesn't look any different now to how he did then, except he had vaguely longer hair. He was still very loud, very camp and expressive.'

Upon his return to Ireland, things suddenly didn't seem so rosy anymore. Compared to London and Paris, Cork appeared boring and parochial. London especially, with its cosmopolitan acceptance of homosexuality, had made Graham see just how restrictive life in Cork was. Any thoughts he had of 'coming out' appeared totally unrealistic in the cold light of day.

He also realized that he would have to buckle down and study if he was to do well in his second year exams. His success in the first year papers now proved to be something of a double-edged sword because the lecturers expected him to keep up the good work. If his first year had been about settling in and getting a feel for university life, year two would be about applying himself to some serious hard work. He was not there to have fun, he was there to do a degree in English and French. None of which filled Graham with much excitement.

He was restless and simply wasn't enjoying the course any more. 'When I came back to Cork it wasn't quite the same,' he admitted. While Graham had been in Paris and London, his friend Billy Forrester had spent the summer in New York. He too felt disillusioned and they both began to think about jacking it in. 'I had the same experience as Graham,' says Billy. 'It was initially thrilling to get away from small town provincial life but by the second year Cork seemed dull. I dropped out and went to England. I didn't meet up with Graham again until much later in London.'

Even English, a subject Graham loved, seemed to have lost its appeal for him. Ironically, Graham felt that this was partly the fault of his former teacher Niall MacMonagle. 'He was one of the reasons I dropped out of university,' he said. 'That sounds bad but the reason is that a lot of the things I would have learnt there, I learnt with Niall. What he wanted us to do in essays and discussions was very university based. He was an intellectual short cut. And much more than that.'

Without the inspirational teaching he had experienced from his mentor, Graham could muster little enthusiasm for his studies. Stressed out by the demands he felt were being made on him, he started skipping lectures – but this only exacerbated the worry. 'They knew that I wasn't coming to tutorials and lectures,' he said. 'I felt pressurized and it wasn't so much fun. I was so miserable, I just wanted to do something else.'

His old friends could see how unhappy he'd become. 'I think he was a bit of an angst soul at times at university,' says Yvonne Shorten. 'He was very unsettled and I felt he wasn't happy with himself. He always put on a very good front; he wouldn't say that he was depressed or anything, he would just turn it into a laugh. But you could tell he wasn't happy with his situation. I just don't think he had found his niche.

'He was very involved in the dramatic society and he really

enjoyed that, but I don't think he enjoyed the academic side of things. I think he found it stuffy; academics can be a bit like that. A lot of the English lecturers were quite stuffy and I imagine the French ones would have been the same: lots of learning the language by rote.'

Graham's aversion to the serious side of studying had not escaped the notice of his lecturers, one or two of whom had started to realize that the academic life might not be for him. 'The tiny awareness I have of him was of somebody who seemed to be very, very bright but not at all committed,' says his English professor, Dr Colbert Kearney. 'Some students look as if they want to gobble up the course, but he didn't. I would have thought he could have been interested in drama or poetry or writing – he had that kind of presence – but he showed no signs of being totally dedicated and focused on full study.'

In a very short period of time Graham became very unhappy indeed. 'I went doolally,' he was to later admit in an interview with the *Sunday Times*. 'I remember sobbing in the office of a French professor.' One of his French lecturers, who did not want to be named, clearly remembers Graham's angst at this time. 'I knew that he hadn't found his niche,' she says. 'He was the wrong sort of person for UCC. He wasn't interested in what was on offer here. He had a lot of mockery where academia is concerned, which to a huge extent I sympathized with. The drama society was much more up his street.

'There are people who go to UCC because they feel that's what they are supposed to do but they probably shouldn't be there. Graham was academically confident but he had other difficulties on his plate. He was going through a difficult time.

He did confide in me and I was very sympathetic to where he was coming from.'

The stress that Graham felt over his studies was compounded by the turmoil he felt over his sexuality. 'I would say Graham was very conscious of being gay at that time and it was very hard for him,' says Martina O'Carroll. As things began to get on top of him, he would stay in his flat in Washington Street, Cork, crying and, bizarrely, collecting dead flies. It is a time in his life that he has since described as a 'psychotic episode'. 'I lived in this building that was more or less derelict,' he said. 'There were rats, and people would break in to have sex downstairs. It was total misery.'

Although a couple of his close friends could see he was depressed, Graham kept the full extent of his unhappiness hidden from his parents. It was only years later, when they read about it in a newspaper interview Graham had given, that the family realized how unhappy he must have been. 'I'm fairly certain that it was a surprise to all the family when we read about it in the paper,' says his brother-in-law Noel Giles. 'Often if there had been something in the paper about him he would say to his sister Paula, "Oh I just said that to get in the paper!" But he didn't say any of that about the psychotic episode.'

It therefore came as a bolt out of the blue for his parents when, towards the end of his second year at Cork, Graham announced that he was quitting university. 'I told my parents I was going away for the summer,' said Graham. 'That was my unsubtle way of breaking it to them.'

'He pulled out before the summer and I remember thinking, "That was a bit fast," ' says Noel. 'Maybe his father and mother knew something and they just didn't say anything to Paula. But my opinion is that it was a big surprise to everybody. And it was only when we read it in the paper years afterwards that we found out what had actually happened.'

Graham had decided to abandon his degree. 'I was so miserable, I just wanted to do something else,' he said. 'I couldn't take any more of that misery. I hated it. I just wanted to leave Cork, so I did.' He still had no idea of a career, he just knew that he wanted out.

More radically, Graham had also determined to leave Ireland. He knew that he was never going to make a future there. 'Ireland was an impossible place to be gay,' he said. 'Why would you be gay there? It would be like, "Now I'm gay, drinking my water in my gay way." Being gay is about sex, and there was nobody to have sex with. I would have been left dancing around my own handbag.' If he had stayed, Graham would have been an outsider in more ways than one. As a Protestant, he was aware of the mistrust with which he was viewed. 'There is always an undercurrent, a bit of tension,' says Colin Bateman. 'Things get said. You get used to it, but it's always there in the background.'

Graham didn't feel his time at university had been entirely wasted, however. In fact it was probably going to UCC that gave him the courage to pursue his objectives. 'It taught me to be less intimidated,' he said. 'It made me feel less of a misfit. I felt I didn't have to aspire to be like others.'

'I wasn't really surprised when Graham dropped out because a lot of people did,' says Yvonne. 'I dropped out myself for a year but I went back and finished my degree.' Graham, however, would not return to complete his. 'I'd met enough people to think, "Who cares if you've got a degree?"' he said.

'And with Cork University you could just put that on your CV and no one's going to check. It's not like a double first from Oxford.'

Graham later reflected: 'I think it went completely unnoticed that I had gone.' He was correct in his assumption. 'I probably didn't even notice,' admits Professor Kearney. 'In a lecture room you might have 120–140 students. Unless they are particularly brilliant or they come to you with problems, you don't get to know them. He never confided in me. If he had not become such a celebrity on television I probably would have forgotten him by now.'

So it was that in the summer of 1983, with just £200 in his pocket, Graham left Ireland. He was headed for America and, like many young gay men before him, his destination was San Francisco: the 'gay capital of the world'.

4 OFFER BEAUTIFUL OMENS

San Francisco in the early eighties was just about as far removed from Ireland as was possible to be. Home to a multitude of races, religions and cultures, and famously the birthplace of free love and Gay Pride, the city was the polar opposite of Cork. Where Ireland was predominantly white, old-fashioned and conservative, San Francisco was cosmopolitan, modern and, above all, tolerant. And while Ireland's climate was dominated by mist and rain – it wasn't for nothing that it was known as the Emerald Isle – San Francisco was bathed in almost year-round Californian sunshine.

Its laid back attitude was legendary. Ever since it was transformed during the Gold Rush of 1849 from a hamlet with 812 people into a city with 20,000 residents, San Francisco had prided itself on being different to anywhere else in the world. The variety of nationalities who had chosen to make their home there over the years had ensured an acceptance of many different religious beliefs and lifestyles. And who could think of San Francisco without simultaneously thinking of the hippies and flower children of the sixties.

In the mid-sixties, a group of people modelling themselves on the English Bohemians of the twenties, established a community in Haight-Ashbury, the neighbourhood around the intersection of Haight and Ashbury Streets. They believed in peace and harmony and nuclear disarmament and were opposed to the war in Vietnam. Famously labelled beatniks by *San Francisco Chronicle* columnist Herb Caen, by 1966 there were 7,000 of them living in the neighbourhood's spacious but rundown Victorian homes. Communal living was all the rage and they were happy to open their doors to anyone who shared their ideals.

There was a flourishing music and drugs scene in Haight-Ashbury, and the beatniks smoked marijuana and dropped acid while dancing to local bands like The Grateful Dead. It was one of the most happening places in the world – even The Beatles wanted to play there. While marijuana was illegal in the US, in the early sixties LSD was not and its use was widespread. Even when it was outlawed in October 1966, following claims that it caused chromosome damage, many people enthusiastically carried on taking it.

The word 'hippie' had first been used by journalist Michael Fellon to describe the young Bohemians in an article he wrote in September 1965, but the term did not catch on until two years later with the so-called 'Summer of Love'. In 1967 San Francisco found itself at the centre of the hippie explosion when thousands of young people descended on the city from all over America. Holding flowers and wearing garlands around their necks, they preached 'flower power': peace and love and understanding. The Scott McKenzie song 'San Francisco (Be sure to wear some flowers in your hair)' was released and became a massive hit. The Monterey Pop Festival led to stardom for many of the San Francisco-based bands and the hippie audience got happily high on whatever substances were passed their way.

People had started to descend on Haight-Ashbury around Easter time, although the Summer of Love didn't officially kick off until the summer solstice on June 21. By the time it finished, three months later, the district's hippie population had grown from 7,000 to 75,000. This didn't go down too well with some of the original hippie residents. Known as the Diggers, they had wanted to keep the neighbourhood out of the limelight and blamed the shop owners for wanting to 'turn on the world' and inviting the crowds in.

A natural progression of the tolerance and open mindedness practised by the hippies was an increased demand for equal rights for homosexuals. Even in the fifties San Francisco had been known to be a pretty friendly place for gays, and in the seventies it became the centre of the gay and lesbian liberation movement. Most of the action was focused on the Castro, a quiet, working-class neighbourhood that became an international symbol of gay liberation virtually overnight. It was not tyrannical regimes or political oppression that its mostly immigrant residents had fled, but – like Graham – intolerant communities back home. Once they had found themselves in the streets of the Castro they built a culture together, found political strength and became part of a movement that was sweeping America.

For the first time, gay people staked a claim to a neighbourhood. They didn't just want to be tolerated; they wanted somewhere where they could own businesses, buy properties, elect their own officials and feel free to walk down the street as a gay person. Until then, 'gay neighbourhoods' had been associated strictly with nightlife or prostitution. In 1977, a major milestone was reached when San Francisco politician Harvey Milk became America's first openly gay male to be elected to public office. His appointment was extremely controversial and seen as a major victory for gay rights. His assassination at City Hall the following year, along with that of the city Mayor George Moscone, was a devastating setback. The lightweight five-year sentence given to their murderer, former San Francisco politician Dan White, prompted the 'White Night Riots'. Thousands of demonstrators marched on City Hall, causing $1 million worth of damage.

The events in San Francisco were beamed around the world and if gay people felt they had a chance of being accepted anywhere, it was there. Graham was no exception. Although he didn't have any burning desire to become a flower child, the city's tolerance towards gays was a definite attraction for him.

Graham arrived in San Francisco in the summer of 1983. He was 6,000 miles away from home and as he got off the bus Cork must have felt like a lifetime ago. As luck would have it he arrived in the middle of a Gay Pride rally. He was 20 years old, but as he pointed out, this was 'an Irish 20, which anywhere else in the world is about 14!' With the £200 he had taken with him fast disappearing, he got a job as a waiter and set about finding somewhere cheap to stay.

In true San Francisco style he ended up in a commune. While times had changed in the city since the sixties, they hadn't changed that much and in the eighties communal living was still popular. Graham saw a newspaper advertisement offering rooms at a commune called Stardance and, intrigued, decided to apply. Stardance had been founded by hippie photographer Geoff Kozeny in 1978. It occupied a vast Victorian terraced house on three floors in Fulton Street, just a few blocks away from Haight-Ashbury. It was centrally situated; turning right out of the house led to City Hall; turning left would take you to the Golden Gate Park.

At the time Graham joined, the house was home to about 10 full-time residents as well as various visiting friends. Kozeny was a passionate believer in intentional communities, where people with the same ideals and beliefs chose to live together and work together for the good of their community. He spent a lot of his time travelling around the US visiting different communes, but Stardance had been his 'baby'. Most of the residents of Stardance were anarchists involved in green issues and environmental politics.

One of the first residents was a man called Thomas Colland who joined a month after it started. Although Geoff Kozeny was an intermittent resident at the house, Thomas Colland had been there more or less continually from the start. Dozens of people have come and gone in the time since Graham was there, but Thomas Colland vividly remembers the day he met the young Irish boy from Cork.

He has good reason to remember Graham – albeit as Graham Walker as he was in those days – because the two were to form an extremely close attachment. Graham, however, would have trouble recognising the name Thomas Colland because he knew him by an altogether different name. To Graham, he was Obo – or, to give him his full moniker, Offer Beautiful Omens.

The son of a wealthy stockbroker from New York City, Colland had majored in economics but, like Graham, had grown tired of university life. He decided to quit his studies, but unlike Graham – who took the route of least resistance and simply dropped out – Thomas gave it to his lecturers straight. 'I was disillusioned with the system and as I thought they would probably throw me out anyway, I just told them I was gay,' he explains. 'They said, "If you have the nerve to admit that you are gay, you can go out – that's it!" It was a horrible thing to say to someone but I also found it really funny because although I said I was gay, I wasn't actually.'

Having escaped the system, Thomas became a professional gambler for six months and spent his time 'trying to get really stoned and really high on drugs and knock myself out.' He decided to become an anarchist and in 1978 he moved to San Francisco to join a hippie commune. The members of that group, who called themselves Krista Village, had all taken on new names upon entering the commune. They had chosen their new names during a bizarre ceremony using an ouija board. 'When you joined that community most people would ask for a new name,' he explains. 'I'd been there for about two months when I asked for a new name. They were going to give me two choices. They came up with Obo first and I took it, then they gave me an acronym for Obo, which was Offer Beautiful Omens. They gave me a middle name, Day, and I took on the same last name as the rest of them, which was Help. So hence my name is Obo Day Help. That's my legal name now; it has been for 20 years.'

By the time Graham arrived in San Francisco, Thomas Colland had ceased to exist. 'Graham seemed shy and very unsure of himself when he first came here,' Obo reveals. 'We had him over to dinner and interviewed him to see if he was suitable for a place at the commune. The interview process usually starts with a phone call and if you get through the call you are invited to dinner. If you get through the dinner you are invited for a three-day stay and if that goes well you're in. It's a very democratic house and everyone has a say in who is allowed to move in. Graham's initial meeting with the house went very well. He said he had heard about us and he seemed to share some of our beliefs about the world. I think he was drawn towards being part of a community. Everyone was happy for him to move in and he lived here for about 12 months.'

Graham later said that he had never intended to live in a commune. 'I didn't have any big plan,' he said. 'I just wanted to get out of Cork. I wasn't a hippie, it was just cheap rent.' When he went to live at Stardance, he was asked to contribute what his wages as a waiter would allow. Residents who had jobs that paid well usually paid more than those in poorly paid work. And people who occupied the larger rooms on the first floor, particularly the sunny south-facing ones that looked out over the garden, also paid more rent. The rooms were all quite large and nearly all of the 20 or so bedrooms had a wooden sleeping platform suspended about a metre below the high ceiling to accommodate friends or visiting hippies from other communes. There were several bathrooms, which the residents shared, a couple of communal living rooms and a large, brightly painted farmhouse-style kitchen. French doors led out from a sitting room to a small veranda overlooking the garden several feet below. The hippies grew their own salad and vegetables for the house and were avid recyclers of household waste.

The commune prided itself on its family atmosphere and as

well as single people and couples there were sometimes children living at the house. Graham recalls feeling rather sad for the youngsters because he realized how they must stand out among their classmates. 'I always felt slightly sorry for the kids – they'd go to school and feel like aliens,' he said. 'They would come home with Barbie dolls and all they wanted was junk food like other kids, they had no interest in their parents' rebellion.'

At Stardance, as in most homes, the kitchen was the heart of the house. During the day, the members of the commune generally worked or pursued interests outside of the house but in the evenings they would try to sit down together as a family. Most evenings, therefore, Graham would eat with the other residents at a large wooden table in the brightly painted communal kitchen. 'The commune was fantastic,' he said. 'I worked during the day, then returned to the house where we had big pots of soup.' Where possible the commune would also make their own clothes and Graham also recalled how once in a cinema, when a man put his hand on his crotch, he encountered a completely impenetrable cat's cradle of string, which was what the commune used instead of zips.

On Wednesday evenings the residents would hold a meeting to talk about issues that affected the house. As well as discussing their long-running campaign legally to own the house as a collective, they would discuss any problems that had arisen between the residents. It was the policy of the commune to encourage people to talk openly about each other, even about very personal things. They called it 'direct talking' and it was valued very highly at Stardance. Graham, however, remembers it rather differently. 'It was meant to be healing, but it was just an excuse for a bitch!' he said afterwards.

Like all shared collectives, there was a kitty for food and bills and a strict democratic division of household tasks. After the chaos of the student flats he had lived in in Cork, Graham found the commune to be extremely well run. 'Graham fitted in here very well,' Obo recalls. 'He was obviously a nice guy. He was interested in everybody and had a good sense of humour. He was also very intelligent.'

Although not everyone in the house was vegetarian, most of the residents were and some were vegan. Consequently, the house followed a mainly vegetarian diet, with everybody expected to share the preparation of meals. 'We used to take turns cooking for the group,' explains Obo. 'Everyone would have a list of chores they had to do, like cleaning and shopping, and Graham was happy to do his share. But we would dread his cooking. He was a terrible cook! The only thing he could make was Irish stew and he cooked it every time it was his turn. Later on he got a job at a bakery and used to bring back stuff from there. At first it was great, but we were all soon sick of it.'

His lack of culinary prowess was not lost on Graham. 'I think they dreaded the nights I was on because my meal efforts were appalling,' he acknowledged. In fact, Graham's stew is just about the only thing that one long-term resident remembers about him. Arosa, a woman who has been at Stardance for almost as long as Obo, at first had difficulty placing him at all. But as she thought about it, it came back to her. 'There was an Irish boy here who always made stew,' she recalled tentatively. 'Yes, I remember, he made terrible stew!'

But while Arosa, being very much older than Graham, had very little to do with him, Graham and Obo soon became extremely close. Graham had found himself immediately attracted to the older man's confidence and laid back hippie charisma. For his part, Obo could sense that the naïve young Irishman was struggling to find his identity and he sympathized with his predicament. 'I could tell that Graham hadn't worked out for himself in his mind that he was gay,' says Obo. 'He didn't know what he was, but I did. I could tell straight away that he was gay. He was very effeminate and he told me that it had caused him a lot of problems in Ireland.

'He didn't feel accepted there and he had run away to be with people who would take him for what he was. I think he needed to be part of a family. He had suffered a lot in Ireland. He was very camp, but hadn't yet come out so it was tough for him. I also think he had been subconsciously attracted to San Francisco because it was the gay capital of the world.'

Living among the tolerant, liberal inhabitants of the commune, Graham tentatively found the confidence to be himself. Emboldened by Obo's easy-going attitude to sex, which was obvious to anyone with eyes in their head, Graham too began to lose his inhibitions. Obo, who was then aged 38, was the group's unofficial leader. He had had the kind of experiences that the young Graham could scarcely imagine, let alone contemplate himself, and Graham had never met anyone remotely like him before.

It was Obo who provided Graham with an authentic hippie experience by taking him to a famous hippie festival. The Rainbow Gathering, held every year, was a huge gathering of people who believed in intentional communities, non-violence and alternative lifestyles. Many of their traditions were based on those of the Native Americans, particularly the notion that they should respect and take care of the earth. Each year they gathered in the National Forests to pray for world peace. Many of the Rainbow contingent were smoking marijuana and Graham decided to give it a go. 'I did try dope, but I didn't really like it. I didn't know how to inhale,' he said. Referring to Bill Clinton's famous claim that although he had tried marijuana, he hadn't actually inhaled, Graham added: 'When President Clinton says he didn't inhale, I sympathize. I couldn't smoke dope, much as I persevered, because it used to irritate my throat.'

The genuinely committed hippies among them may have seen the festival as an opportunity to be at one with the earth; but to Graham it was all a bit of a laugh. 'We all got into a Volkswagen bus older than me and drove to Oregon for the Rainbow Gathering,' he recalled. 'There were thousands of people wandering on a mountain, drinking herbal tea and trying to shag each other. Bliss.'

It was probably inevitable that within a few months of arriving at the commune Graham developed an infatuation with Obo. Although he was almost twice his age, they began sleeping together. 'We started a relationship,' says Obo. 'I was bisexual at that time and we just sort of clicked. I think it was subconscious; Graham was just getting in touch with that side of himself and starting to come out. I guess that was one of the reasons he settled in San Francisco. It was at that time that he knew what he wanted to be. I think I was his first gay relationship.'

But Obo was more than simply a relationship to Graham. He was the first major love of his life. With the impetuousness of youth, he fell head over heels. The uncertainty and unhappiness that had characterized his life during the previous few years now evaporated and he allowed himself to follow his heart. However, in selecting Obo as the person to whom he would give his heart, Graham had not chosen wisely. He had been attracted by the romantic ideal of his lover's Bohemian lifestyle but, for an innocent abroad, the reality of the hippie life was hard to comprehend.

Obo was not, like Graham, someone who was merely playing at being a hippie by hanging out in a commune for a year or two before returning to normal society. He was the genuine article: a real-life hippie who smoked dope and believed in free love and free sex. A practising bisexual, he was routinely sleeping with men and women and was vehemently opposed to monogamy. He was married, but not in the conventional sense. To Graham's utter incredulity, he discovered that while Obo was a member of the Krista Village in the seventies, he had gone through a group marriage ceremony and had ten wives. And to Graham's extreme hurt, his lover made it abundantly clear that he had not the slightest intention of being faithful to him.

'Our relationship was not exclusive on my part,' admits Obo. 'During the time I was with Graham I was also having relationships with several other women and men. In those days I was interested in collective living and group marriage and I had been part of a group marriage at my previous commune. We took some LSD and then had a ceremony. There were 20 men and women and we shared a house and each other's beds. We were very much into free love. I have a daughter called Faith from that marriage and we were all fathers and mothers to the children. Krista Village lasted for 25 years and although I was only there for three months I was still heavily into the idea.

68

When I met Graham some of the original group were still living with me in the house.'

His lover's refusal to give up his bed-hopping ways was incredibly upsetting for Graham. 'Graham liked the idea of living in a commune, but he wasn't into group marriage or anything like that,' says Obo. 'It was all new for him. As well as Graham, I had five or six other relationships going on at the time and that didn't work out so good for him. He wanted more attention and he wanted a monogamous relationship with me.'

Graham tried to be free-thinking and tolerant about the situation but he knew deep down that it wasn't in him to accept such a set up. He has admitted that before he went to San Francisco he was 'incredibly conservative and judgmental' and that afterwards he was not. But he was to find it a great deal more difficult than he thought to shake off the values of his upbringing. He simply could not face sharing his new love with other people. But although Obo was sensitive to the effect his sexual proclivities were having on Graham, he was not about to change his way of life for him. The situation became a nightmare for Graham.

'Being in a relationship was obviously new for him,' says Obo. 'I think I was the first person he had become heavily involved with and he took it very seriously. He wanted us to be monogamous but that was just not the way I was at the time and it upset him. He found it difficult to come to terms with. It was very hard for him. But it was never going to work with me being with him exclusively. I was seeing women and I still had my ten wives from the group marriage.'

Obo's many partners meant that there were also serious health implications for Graham. In an interview with the

Observer in 2001, Graham appears to have given the impression that he was still 'very chaste' during his time in San Francisco. He makes no mention of his sexual relationship with Obo, or Obo's promiscuity. Graham may only have been having sex with one person, but through his lover he had links to literally dozens and dozens of people. This would be a risky business at any time, but in San Francisco in the mid-eighties it was akin to sexual Russian roulette.

In 1984, Aids was just beginning to decimate the city. From the first article about the disease published in the *New York Native* in July 1981, the San Francisco health department realized it had a serious public health problem on its hands. In 1982, when the syndrome was briefly known as Gay Related Immunodeficiency Disease – GRID – doctors had noticed a new phenomenon: many of the city's gay men were being struck down with pneumonia. Within months San Francisco was in the grip of a full-scale epidemic.

By 1983, the year Graham arrived in San Francisco, homosexuals and members of other high-risk groups were being urged by the Public Health Service to reduce the number of sexual partners. In May that year, just weeks before Graham turned up, thousands of gay men went on a 'Fighting For Our Lives' march in the city. Graham was also in San Francisco for most of the 'Bathhouse Crisis' of 1983 and 1984. Blaming sexual activity in the city's public baths for spreading the disease, the health department tried to make the baths off limits to people with Aids. Told by lawyers that this was not legally possible, there was then a move to close the baths completely. Other officials proposed that the city should outlaw sex in the public baths rather than close them.

In June 1984, Mervyn Silverman, San Francisco District Health Director, ordered bathhouse surveillance to detect unsafe sex. In October, 60 doctors from the Pacific Medical Center signed a petition calling for the baths to be closed. The city's baths and private sex clubs were duly closed, denounced as a 'menace' to public health. But the baths reopened within hours. In November, San Francisco Superior Court Judge Roy Wonder settled the matter by ruling that the baths could remain open providing they were monitored for safe sex practices every ten minutes.

Compared to other cities in the world, San Francisco was quick to respond to the Aids crisis. Early in 1983, Ward 86 was opened at San Francisco General Hospital, the country's first outpatient clinic dedicated to Aids. Community-based organisations sprang up quite early on to care for the sick and the dying. Within a few years of the onset of the crisis, a highly effective network of city and state agencies, hospitals, health care providers and community-based organisations had evolved. This unique network dedicated to helping people affected by Aids and HIV was so ground-breaking that it was to become known as 'the San Francisco model' of Aids care.

The 'gay capital of the world' was to be hit particularly hard by the disease and many thousands of people died. By March 2002, there had been almost 28,000 cases of Aids recorded in San Francisco. Of those, 19,000 had died. In a city with a population of just 750,000, this was a catastrophically high percentage. Throughout the eighties and nineties San Francisco was one of the three worst affected cities in the US, along with Los Angeles and New York City. In each of those places Aids became the leading cause of death among young men. Among San

Francisco's gay community the spectre of Aids hung over their heads like the death sentence it was. To put it bluntly, it was not a good time to be coming out – particularly in San Francisco.

Heartbroken and dispirited by the way his attempt at being in a gay relationship was going, Graham decided to have another go at being straight. Reckoning that sex with a woman might prove less complicated and a great deal safer, he struck up a friendship with a young middle-class American girl who lived nearby. Her name was Elizabeth and she and Graham would often talk about how great it would be to get married, not least because it would give them the right to live in each other's country. As the situation with Obo became more strained, Graham started to spend more time with Elizabeth.

She was not a member of the commune, although Graham did take her to the house on several occasions. Perhaps in an attempt to make his lover jealous, he introduced her to Obo as his girlfriend. He needn't have bothered. It was no skin off Obo's nose and, besides, Obo was certain that Graham was gay. 'He had a girlfriend called Elizabeth, I remember her very vaguely,' he says. 'She was the same age as him. I think their relationship was almost platonic – for him anyway. He was just coming out.'

Obo was in the habit of coming and going from the house when the mood took him, although he was never gone for long. 'I moved out for various love affairs and when they didn't work out I would come back,' he says. As the relationship with Graham got increasingly heavy, Obo took off again. 'Graham couldn't cope with the way I lived my life then. He wanted more than I could give him,' he says. 'He was very upset and there was tension between us. I went away to stay at another commune and when I returned to the house Graham had gone.'

Graham had decided he couldn't stay at Stardance a moment longer, seeing, as he would inevitably have to, the man he loved falling in and out of bed with other people. His experience with Obo had hurt him very badly and it was to be almost ten years before he would feel brave enough to trust anyone again. With a badly broken heart, Graham did what many people in his situation would do: he ran for home.

He later spoke briefly about his time at the commune, but did not go into any detail about his affair with Obo. In fact, his former love was relegated to a single mention. 'I remember the whole experience with great fondness,' he said. 'They all had strange names like Jam, Jem, Sac and Obo. I even recall vowing that I would never take the mickey out of poor hippies again; they were such a nice bunch. In fact, Obo was a very good friend and I still keep in touch with him. He's in his sixties now.'

Obo, who was in fact only in his early fifties when Graham made that remark, still lives at the turreted house in Fulton Street. It is now painted purple and lilac and has been renamed The Purple Rose Collective. He and Arosa are the only people who remain from Graham's time and the new residents, one of whom is a Brit, have no idea of the commune's famous former resident. Obo still owns the VW combi that he and Graham went to Oregon in, and continues to spends most evenings smoking marijuana and strumming his guitar. But one thing has changed. He is no longer bisexual and no longer promiscuous. Nowadays, he even manages to be faithful.

'Ten years ago I met a woman who is my current partner and I have been monogamous since then,' he says. 'We don't live together, but I feel like we are married.' At the age of 56, he admits his free love days are now behind him. 'I came to the conclusion that it was too much work and there are more important things in life that just filling my bed,' he adds. 'It takes a lot of effort and I spent years doing that. I just changed my priorities. I still don't like marriage. I feel like I'm married, but I don't want to get formally married. I'm into the relationship but I have seen so many people who are married and don't have a good relationship – including my parents. I think it says more to be together and not be married than to be married. That's my feeling.'

Krista Village is no longer in existence and much has changed since the heady days of group marriage and free love. Now it is more likely to be free education and free health care that the residents are passionate about. 'In those days we had a lot of the same values but now we are different,' says Obo. After two decades of battling through legal red tape, the collective finally owns the building in Fulton Street. 'We still have a meeting once a week to discuss the house and we still share food,' says Obo. 'But the atmosphere is different to how it was when Graham was here. The house was much less politically motivated then. In those days it was more a matter of lifestyle, now it is more political. We are all pretty much leftist activists and most of the people in the house now are anarchists.'

The collective bought the house for $90,000, but due to the increasing gentrification of the area around Haight-Ashbury, the anarchists now find themselves living next door to wealthy professionals. The dot.com explosion of the nineties put pay to the city's tradition of offering affordable housing to all income groups. The rocketing rents of the late nineties, when homes were steadily converted to high-rent loft-style apartments for newly-wealthy internet entrepreneurs, forced many people on lower and middle incomes out of the town. But Stardance is still there, albeit under its new name, and the neighbourhood is still proud of its hippie roots. It remains a lively centre for alternative arts, culture and lifestyles, despite the gentrification.

Years later, Graham would take his mother on a holiday to San Francisco to show her his old haunts. But significantly, he was not to take her to the commune and did not introduce her to Obo.

75

5 GRAHAM REINVENTS HIMSELF

Graham has admitted that he was running away when he left Ireland to go to America. Now he was running away again.

But just as he had done when he decided to leave university, he opted for the easy way out. Rather than tell his professors that he wouldn't be returning for his final year, he simply hadn't materialized at the start of term. As the weeks turned into months and there was still no sign of him, they were left to conclude that he wasn't coming back. Instead of explaining to his parents that he was going to America to find himself, he let them believe that he was merely going on holiday and would be back after a couple of months. In the event he was gone a whole year. And when his first serious love affair floundered, Graham didn't even tell his lover that he was leaving; choosing instead simply to slip away.

The end of his relationship with Obo had once again plunged Graham into uncertainty about his sexuality. He now knew that he had gay feelings, but if being gay meant having to contend with the promiscuous way of life favoured by Obo, and the perils of Aids and HIV, then he didn't want to be that way. Perhaps he had just been going through a gay phase, as the books he'd read had described. How much simpler his life would be if he could have a relationship with a woman instead. Perhaps with this in mind, Graham determined to make a go of his relationship with Elizabeth. She was a nice girl. She was from a respectable family in San Francisco. She was slim and pretty with blonde hair and she considered Graham to be excellent company. Why not marry her! She was someone he could be proud to introduce to his parents – unlike pot-smoking hippie Obo. In the throes of denial, and on the rebound, Graham asked her to marry him.

Graham would later dismiss Elizabeth's part in his life as simply 'a Green Card thing', referring to the much sought after US immigration card. He even mocked her by saying in an interview: 'We were going to live together. Isn't that so strange? As I say it, I find it hard to believe. How stupid was she?' But this is to gloss over his very real attempts at this time to be heterosexual. The official version of events has Graham returning from America alone, his sexuality as a gay man resolved. But in fact Graham left San Francisco engaged to be married, and took Elizabeth with him.

And so it was that when he arrived back in Ireland to visit his parents, he was accompanied by his 'fiancée'.

Graham's homecoming was a happy occasion for his parents. They were delighted to have him back. That he should turn up with a woman in tow was especially exciting for his family and if they were surprised to see him with a girlfriend after so long, they didn't show it. 'I don't think there had been any doubts about Graham's sexuality before then,' says his brother-in-law Noel. 'We certainly hadn't sat down and asked ourselves if Graham was homosexual. When he arrived with the American girl it was just an ordinary situation where a son brings home a girlfriend. Relatively normal at his age, except I think in Graham's case it was probably the first and last time it had ever happened.'

Curious to get a look at Graham's girlfriend, his sister Paula and her husband drove over to Rhoda and Billy's home to meet her. Noel recalls thinking that the pretty American girl seemed like quite a catch. 'She was quite attractive,' he says. 'She was slender; a good height and she had blonde hair. I have forgotten what she did for a living, or what her parents did, but it was all discussed and my memory of it is that it was all perfectly fine and normal. She gave the impression of being quite middle class. They were only over for a few days on their way back from America. They stayed at his parents' house, I would think in separate rooms.'

Billy and Rhoda were pleased with Graham's choice of girl-friend. And if they were harbouring any doubts about their son's sexual orientation, her arrival had firmly quashed them. 'I think they were chuffed,' says Noel. 'She seemed very nice.'

Now that he was back in Ireland, Graham's parents assumed that he would be returning to Cork to finish his degree. They were confident that the university would have him back; after all, he wouldn't be the first student to drop out for a year. But Graham had other plans. Although it had cost him dearly in terms of the emotional pain he would bear for years to come, Graham's time in San Francisco, and in particular the time he had spent with Obo at the commune, had given him the courage to chase his dreams. He now realized that if there was something he wanted to do badly enough, there was no reason why he should not do it. With this new-found confidence, he had resolved to pursue his original dream of becoming an actor.

That was bombshell number one. Number two was the news that he had no intention of staying in Ireland. Whatever uncertainties he may have had at that time, Graham knew there was no way he wanted to live in Ireland. He told his parents that he planned to make a life for himself in London and apply to drama school. This was disappointing news for his family on both levels but Billy and Rhoda were not the type of parents to rant and rave, or to interfere. 'It was the first time he had shown a real interest in any particular career, and we just let him get on with it and hoped he'd do well,' said his mother. 'He was far too proud to let us give him anything more than moral support. He never asked us for a penny.'

When Graham set off for England a few days later his parents undoubtedly worried about how he would fare in London with no money, no job and nowhere to live. 'When I left home I must have caused them so much concern,' he later admitted. 'They knew I had no money and I was determined not to ask them for any because I was pig-headedly self-reliant and I didn't want to give them the opportunity to tell me to get a proper job, which of course any sensible parent would have done.'

If Billy and Rhoda had known where their son was to end up living they would probably have been unable to sleep at night. Arriving in the capital with only a few pounds to his name, Graham picked up with some of his old schoolfriends from Bandon. Billy Forrester was living in London at that time, as was his sister Julie and her boyfriend Harry Moore. Yvonne Shorten had also moved to London. Stuck for somewhere to stay, Graham moved in with Julie and Harry at 96 Lilford Road, Camberwell – a rundown squat.

'After university I did not hear from Graham until he came back from America and was looking for somewhere to live in London,' says Julie. 'He came and lived with myself and Harry in various squats around south London. One of them was in Streatham, one in Brixton and another in Camberwell.' Graham was full of tales about his experiences in America, many of which Julie and Harry weren't sure whether to believe. 'He came back with stories of what he had got up to in America and was telling us about the hippie commune,' says Julie. 'With Graham, anything is a story to tell; to be embellished in whatever context he wants it to be. You always take everything that he says with a pinch of salt.'

Julie, who alone among Graham's school friends had realized him to be gay, was intrigued that Graham had a girlfriend with him. And she was even more surprised when Graham announced that they were going to get married. 'When he came back with his American girl I was very surprised,' she says. 'As far as I remember they were engaged. We thought she was very inappropriate for Graham. It was so odd to see him with that girl because she seemed so Middle America, so white middle class. She was not really posh, but she was so lacking in personality and straight, which none of us really were. We wanted adventure, we didn't want that kind of life.'

Although they had been pleased to see Graham, Julie and Harry did not take to his 'fiancée'. 'She was just so bland and uninteresting,' says Julie. 'She was blonde, although I'm not sure if it was real or dyed, and she wore high-heeled Wellington boots. That is what I remember most about her: the Wellington boots. We called her Sindy, probably because she was like a Sindy doll.' The American girl's views did not go down too well with the other inhabitants of the squat. 'We got into an argument with her,' recalls Harry Moore. 'We were vegetarians and she was saying that wearing fur was OK as long as the fur was grown on a mink farm and didn't belong to a bambi shot in the woods. She was a bit of a strange one. I got the impression that her thoughts on Graham were: "Oh he's very cute, what fun to be engaged to someone like this, ha, ha," and that he was just along for the Green Card.

'Graham wasn't out then. I would say that at that stage he was vaguely in denial,' adds Harry. 'He wasn't overtly gay in those days and he wasn't really effeminate. I assumed he was gay but I wasn't completely sure, particularly because we all dressed up and wore colourful clothes at that time. I was going around with blue hair – it was the eighties! I remember Graham had a pair of orange trousers made out of parachute silk which were very nice. I coveted those.'

Harry and Julie weren't certain about the status of Graham's relationship with his girlfriend. 'They shared a room, they had the front room,' says Julie. 'But I really couldn't tell if they were a couple or not. They certainly weren't always kissing or anything like that.' The pair were only at the house for a few weeks. Having come from a nice comfortable home in wealthy San Francisco, life in a dirty squat with Graham's bizarrely attired friends was simply too much for his fiancée to bear. 'They didn't stay very long,' says Julie. 'I suppose she thought the squat was dirty and didn't want to stay in it.' 'Our house would have been a bit of a shock for her,' agrees Harry. 'It was pretty run down at the time. Julie and I went to Amsterdam for a week and when we got back she was gone.'

When they next saw Graham, he was alone. It seemed that his engagement had ended as abruptly as it had begun. 'She didn't last very long over here,' says Julie. 'They came over to be engaged in the summer and I think she was back in America by the autumn. Graham was just starting a new life in London then, he was going to drama college and they went in different directions. As far as I know she just went home. But she left her boots behind. We inherited the funny wellington boots with heels!'

No one knew how the engagement had come to be broken off and Graham did not seek to enlighten them. 'He never said why it had ended,' says his brother-in-law Noel. 'Anything like that would be dealt with by a shrug.' But Graham later said in an interview that his relationship with Elizabeth ended because she fell in love with someone else. In contrast to the remark he made in another interview about her having been stupid not to realize that he was homosexual, he claimed their engagement had been phoney. 'She knew I was gay,' he said. 'We were really good friends and both wanted the option of living and working in Britain and America.' But in yet another interview he contradicted himself again, on that occasion claiming that he had been in love with her. 'I was in that phase of thinking that you fell in love with a person, not a gender,' he said. 'It sounds laughable now.' Elizabeth fell in love with an Iranian man and lost contact with Graham.

In the months that followed, Julie and Harry saw a fair amount of Graham. 'Julie and I were going to art school at the time and Graham stayed with us when he started drama school,' says Harry. 'We lived at different squats, including a house in South Norwood which was literally falling down – the front door was wedged closed because the wall was falling in on it.' To the young Irish exiles, life in gritty south London felt terribly exciting. Brixton had been the scene of major riots in April 1981, when black and white youths fought pitched battles with police in the streets to protest at what they considered heavy-handed policing. Over two nights the borough was set ablaze as hundreds indulged in an orgy of looting, vandalism and arson. The violence led to 213 arrests. More than 200 police officers were injured, as well as several newspaper and television journalists.

Each side blamed the other for the trouble. Metropolitan Police Commissioner Sir David McNee said that police–community relations were as good as could be expected and claimed that the riots had been started by outside agitators. He denied suggestions of police harassment of black youths and said the level of crime in Brixton necessitated a strong police presence. Black leaders rejected his comments and said the riots were an inevitable consequence of years of heavy-handed policing. The violence occurred as a direct result of 'Operation Swamp 81', a high intensity crackdown on street crime which flooded the area with police, making an already tense situation worse.

The scars inflicted on Brixton during the riots were to take a long time to heal, and to Graham and his friends the area had a tense atmosphere that they found thrilling. 'Brixton was quite raw then because it was just after the riots,' says Yvonne Shorten. 'We were both living in Brixton and I used to bump into Graham quite a lot.'

Graham's parents would no doubt have been horrified if they had seen the condition of their son's living accommodation, but to him and his friends the squat was just somewhere to live rent-free. 'It wasn't so much a culture shock as an invitation to experience different things,' says Julie. 'I don't think any of us were really fazed by it. The state of the squat didn't really matter to us at the time. I'm sure if I went into it now I would only be able to stick it for a couple of nights, but at the time it was a roof over our heads and a ticket to a more interesting life. It was very difficult to find anywhere affordable to live in London so we felt lucky and privileged to have such a palace!'

Faithful to his decision to become an actor, as soon as he arrived in London Graham applied for a place at the Central School of Speech and Drama. Based in north London, it was one of Britain's most prestigious drama establishments and a seemingly unending list of famous names had been through its doors over the years. Graham applied to do a three-year course and was on tenterhooks while he waited to hear if he had been accepted. When the news came that his application had been successful he felt that at last his life was taking shape.

Graham enrolled at Central on September 22, 1986. The day was to prove a major turning point in his life, marking the end of his old life and the start of a whole new identity. He said goodbye to Graham Walker, the aimless drifter who had no real idea what he wanted to do with his life, and instead became Graham Norton, would-be actor. He had made a conscious effort to take control of his life and shake off the dilatory mood that had dogged him since he had left school, but he had not envisaged having to change his name. When he arrived at Central, however, he was informed that there was already an actor called Graham Walker and he would have to choose another name for himself. The 'other' Graham Walker was already registered with the actors' union Equity and it was not possible for them to have two members with the same name. If Graham was serious about making a career for himself in the business he would have to register with Equity, so in the event he was left with no option but to change his name.

He chose Norton because it had been his great grandmother's maiden name and he liked the fact that it only had two syllables. He could have opted to be known as Graham Walker in other areas of his life and Norton professionally, but he decided to go the whole hog and 'become' Graham Norton. After 23 years of being called Graham Walker, this was something that took a lot of getting used to. 'I didn't feel like Graham Norton to start with,' he said some time afterwards. 'It felt awkward. But now I do feel like Graham Norton. Now it seems weird that I lived all my life as Graham Walker.'

Among the students in Graham's year at Central were Stephen Tompkinson, who later found fame in TV shows *Drop The Dead Donkey* and *Ballykissangel*; *House of Cards* star Susannah Harker; and Rufus Sewell, who went on to achieve Hollywood success. It seems hard to believe, but Graham's ambition then was to become a serious actor. One of his heroines was the respected film and television actress Fiona Shaw, who was born in Cork. 'He mentioned Fiona Shaw quite a bit, as somebody "up there" to be aspired to,' says his brother-in-law Noel.

Graham claims he had 'always wanted to be a serious person' and considered that being funny was a 'cop out'. Until he arrived at Central, he insists, he didn't even realize that he *could* be funny. 'It was there I first realized I was funny – or at least entertaining,' he said. 'In improvisations I would always go for the joke.' To start with, he says this would annoy him and he would think, 'Curses, curses, memo to self: must not do this!'

'I always wanted to find my hidden depth and so I fought against the funny stuff,' he explained. 'It was only at drama school that I discovered I couldn't do anything serious. When I tried to be serious, I looked like I'd stopped; my brooding silence was like someone had turned me off. I couldn't be serious and some people couldn't "do" funny. After a while I realized it was just as valid a skill.'

Graham was to describe his time at Central as 'three years of total self indulgence' and he threw himself into the seductive world of 'showing off and thinking only of me, me, me'. He wasn't just being self-deprecating when he described his level of self obsession at that time; his friend Billy Forrester remembers how living with a wannabe actor often proved somewhat tedious. 'I remember Graham's days at Central because there were a number of people in our set at the time who were going to drama school,' he says. 'I don't think any of them made it. They would come back to the squat having had these very gruelling self-analysis sessions – mind games of one sort or another. They would come back with a different voice or accent every day. It was a bit tiresome to be honest.'

Graham was a colourful character at the squat and chattered away non-stop about drama school, the waiting jobs he was doing to support himself, about anything and everything. 'He stayed with us occasionally in London,' says Harry. 'He never stayed for long periods; he would come and go. He talked incessantly but because he talked so much you couldn't keep up. You didn't really listen after a while, you would let most of it wash over you. He was very loud – just like a chat show host I suppose. He really hasn't changed, he was always quite extravagant.'

Like many of those who gravitate towards a career in show business, Graham was needy for attention. He was even conceited enough to assume that people would be interested in reading his diary. And, as it turned out, he was right. 'I know that Julie read his diary when he was staying with us,' says Harry. 'She told me she had read it and that Graham had written that he thought I was reading it! There were little notes in it for the people he assumed were reading it. He was saying hello to people. I wasn't surprised that he became famous. He certainly wanted attention.'

Not long after he started at Central, Graham and his diary left the squat and Julie and Harry didn't see him again for a couple of years. 'Graham just dropped out of our circle when he got back to London really,' says Julie. 'He was just doing his own thing.' But about the same time that he was losing touch with some friends, Graham renewed an old acquaintance. He received a letter from his former teacher Niall MacMonagle. 'One day when I was still living in Bandon, I met Graham's mother,' says Niall. 'I asked her how he was getting on and she gave me his address. I dropped him a note and we've kept in touch ever since.' Graham was delighted to hear from his mentor. 'When Niall and I got back in touch it was a badge of approval for me,' he said. 'He would send me little notes, always with a copy of a poem or a short story.'

While he was at drama school, Graham forged a friendship with one of the dinner ladies who worked in the canteen. Perhaps missing his mother back home in Ireland, Graham took to the older woman and the two became close pals. Her name was Betty Hoskins and she subsequently became famous to millions of Graham's fans as the cheery, long-suffering stooge on his show. No matter what humiliations Graham heaped upon her head, Betty never lost her indulgent granny grin. She appeared happy to be the butt of his jokes, and to dress up as Ozzy Osbourne or an aged hooker. For his part, and despite the jokes at her expense, Graham clearly felt a great deal of affection for Betty and made sure that she shared in his success.

With his family at home in Ireland, Graham needed all the friends he could get when a violent mugging almost cost him his life. In 1989, when he was in his final year at drama school, he was attacked as he walked home through Queen's Park, a district of north-west London. He was stabbed in the chest with a Stanley knife and left for dead.

'I had just about reached home when these two guys attacked me, beating me over the head with something heavy,' he later recalled. 'They didn't get much from me. There wasn't enough in my wallet to even buy a bus pass.' It all happened so fast that as his attackers ran off, Graham didn't realize how seriously they had hurt him. 'I could see that my hand had been cut but I didn't know I had been stabbed until I tried to get up off the ground,' he said. 'When I got up I had this funny "peeling" feeling. My t-shirt was drenched with blood and there was a hole in me.'

He managed to stagger to the nearby house of an elderly couple and while the man called the police his wife tried to comfort Graham. 'I lay bleeding on the doorstep and a little old lady came out and held my hand,' he said. 'I was very frightened when I was fighting it but then when I started passing in and out of consciousness that was quite a nice feeling really. You're not in pain, just very tired, and it is like your life force is draining away. You fight for a bit, then you don't bother. Once when I was conscious I could hear a policeman saying, "We'd better wait for the ambulance because there will be hell to pay if he croaks in the back of our van." And I thought, "Oh, this looks really serious if they think I'm going to die in the back of their van."'

Graham was rushed to hospital and stayed there for two weeks. He had lost half the blood in his body and suffered a collapsed lung. 'The morning after I was admitted the nurse said, "Do you want us to phone your parents?"' he recalled. 'I asked "Why, am I going to die?" She paused before she answered and I thought, "Oh, this IS really serious!"' In the event, Graham chose not to let his family know that he was in hospital. Sensitive to the panic and worry the news would cause at home, he decided not to tell them. 'It was far better to say, "Hi, I was stabbed but I've survived,"' he reasoned.

'None of us knew that Graham had been stabbed,' says his brother-in-law Noel. 'My recollection is that Graham rang up his parents and said "I'm coming home". He didn't give them any indication that anything had happened; as far as we were concerned he was just coming to visit. He went to their house first and then they all drove over to our farm. I was in the garden when he arrived with Rhoda and Billy and he told us what had happened. Everybody went berserk because he hadn't told us at the time. He had waited until he was better before he told anyone, but he always was overprotective of his parents.'

The drama college knew, of course, and his fellow students arrived in droves to visit him. For the would-be thespians, it was a real-life drama in the making. 'They were turning up by the busload and sitting on the edge of my bed crying,' he said. 'I could have been dead and the stabbing put life into perspective. I was in my final year at drama school and there were people running into the toilet and sobbing about their castings and things like that. But that experience gave me quite a level head and made me realize that certain things weren't that important. Obviously I wouldn't wish what happened to me on anyone, but there was a silver lining in that it did put everything into perspective. I am less afraid of things now. I don't place the same importance on them.'

When Graham left hospital his physical wounds were beginning to heal, but the emotional scars would take much longer to go away. It took him many months to recover and to begin with he suffered from recurring nightmares that left him a nervous wreck. 'It was very traumatic,' he admitted. 'When I left hospital, typically I didn't go for any help or therapy, so I walked around like a frightened rabbit. The big thing I learnt is that we don't want to die alone. I couldn't have given a shit about the old woman, but I did want her to hold my hand. It was really quite bad. I could have died there in the street.' Graham later tried to get in touch with the couple to thank them but the police refused to reveal their address.

Speaking about the event years later, he told in one interview how he had been attacked by 'two guys', and in another how he had been jumped by 'a gang'. But whatever their number, his assailants were never caught and Graham became just another crime statistic. One would think that a young drama student being stabbed and left for dead would have been reported in the local paper, but a glance through the pages of the local newspapers from that period reveals an endless list of muggings, stabbings and burglaries. Attacks against the person were so prevalent that in most cases the victims weren't even named.

Characteristically, Graham attempted to deal with what had happened to him with humour. 'He wrote and told me about being stabbed and even the way he wrote about that event was so hilarious,' says Niall MacMonagle. 'He wrote a very long letter describing what had happened. It was very serious but he was able to turn it into something funny. But that is Graham for you: he would never, ever indulge himself. I got the letter two weeks after it had happened. He had just come out of hospital.'

As well as the scars on his chest and hand, the stabbing may have left another legacy for Graham. It is possible that the Vitiligo that he suffers from could have been triggered by the trauma of the attack. The disease, in which the skin loses pigment, resulting in white patches, is something of a mystery to the medical profession. Doctors are not sure what causes it but know that it can be brought on by periods of physical or mental stress. While there is usually a hereditary component to Vitiligo, people who knew Graham when he was young do not remember him having the white patches on his head that are so visible today.

The condition affects around one per cent of the population and is non-contagious. Although the majority of sufferers are in good health and experience no symptoms other than the loss of pigment, Vitiligo can cause much anguish, especially among young people concerned about their looks. It can be particularly stressful when it affects the face or head, as in Graham's case. Going to the beach, or other situations involving prolonged exposure to the sun, are particularly difficult. The areas affected by the disease burn more easily and the contrast between tanned skin and the areas without pigment is more noticeable. As a result, sufferers are advised to keep out of the sun. Large areas of skin can be affected and there is no cure.

'I didn't notice that Graham had white patches on his head until he was in his twenties,' says Noel. 'Paula obviously hadn't noticed them before either because I remember her saying, "He's got white patches!" It was when he came over for a visit with his hair shaved back that we noticed.' Julie Forrester also does not recall Graham having the condition when he was younger. 'I don't remember it at school,' she says. 'I only remember seeing it on television.'

6 MOTHER THERESA MEETS
KAREN CARPENTER

Graham graduated from Central in June 1989, two months after his 26th birthday. He had finally achieved what he had always wanted: he had become an actor. There was only one problem: like so many others in his profession, he was an unemployed one.

After the cocoon of drama school, finding himself adrift in a fiercely competitive workplace came as an unpleasant shock. At each casting he went for there would be scores of other hopefuls, and that was if he managed to get to the audition stage at all. Rejected for dozens of jobs, Graham began to experience the harsh reality of entering a profession in which 70 per cent of people were out of work.

Matters were not helped by the fact that, despite having realized that he wasn't very good at serious roles, he continued to pursue them. On the few occasions that he did get lucky he found that he didn't enjoy it as much as he'd thought he would. 'I was crap,' he was to later admit. 'Happily, people realized this quite quickly and didn't employ me.'

His remark, made from the comfortable vantage point of one who by then had a successful television career, glosses over Graham's very real disappointments at this time. He had left drama school with high hopes of pursuing a glittering acting career, but in the event it was to be eight years before he would achieve any success at all. Eight long years spent waiting on tables and living in run-down council accommodation. Eight years of wondering if he would ever be 'discovered'. Graham had dreamt of treading the boards in the theatres of the West End, but for a long time the nearest he got to this was serving pre-theatre meals in a nearby restaurant. Not managing to find enough acting work to pay the bills, for many years his main source of income was the money he earned waiting on tables at the trendy Covent Garden French restaurant Melange.

At Melange, Graham's camp persona and extrovert nature were an instant hit with both the customers and staff. Unlike the people he had grown up with, his colleagues in the restaurant didn't know anything about his background and naturally assumed that he was gay. With his homosexuality now accepted as a given fact, it was as if a massive weight had been lifted from Graham's shoulders. He didn't have to pretend or explain any more; he could just get on with living his life. 'I didn't decide to be gay, it just happened,' he said. 'It was never a trauma, because every book you read when you are looking for the answers says, "everyone goes through their gay phase; don't worry." So I didn't.' But he admitted: 'Growing up in Bandon was a pretty isolating experience. Only two per cent of the population were Protestant, as we were, and even fewer were gay. In fact, I only knew I was different because I was Protestant. It was later, when I was

Top: Number 48, St Brigids Road, Clondalkin, Dublin: the house where Graham was born in 1963.
Above: Graham's family home in Bandon, County Cork, Ireland.
Inset: Graham as a schoolboy at Bandon Grammar School, County Cork.

Above: "Stardance", the San Francisco hippie commune where Graham lived for a year in the eighties.

Right: Obo, Graham's hippie lover.

Top: So You Think You're Funny? Graham on stage at The Gilded Balloon at The Edinburgh Fringe.
Above: Graham with his former boyfriend Scott Michaels.

Top: Graham with actress Jenny Agutter, promoting a charity campaign for the homeless.
Above: Trawling the web for Internet weirdos on *So Graham Norton*.

Graham with the bosom cushion that he presented to Dolly Parton on his show.

Top: Graham with Roger Moore (right) and Nigella Lawson (left) in a nativity play with a difference.
Above: Graham with Sir Elton John.

Top left: Graham wins Best Comedy Entertainer at the 2000 British Comedy Awards.
Top right: Do my ears look big in this? Graham cleans up at the 2001 Bafta awards.
Above: New York, November 2001: Graham's proudest moment. He wins an International Emmy for *So Graham Norton*. He is pictured with Jennifer Saunders (right) Joanna Lumley (left) and his series producer, Graham Stuart.

Left: Britain's unlikeliest double act? Graham with his reality TV partner Andrew Lloyd Webber.

Below: Are you seriously taking us out in those shorts? Graham with his rescue dogs Bailey and Madge.

living in San Francisco, that I realized, "Hang on, there's something else strange going on here." '

'I just kind of drifted out,' he explained. 'I always thought that it was a mistaken expression anyway – you can't just come out once, you have to do it over and over again, like you are constantly revealing any aspects of your life to people. I probably started describing myself as gay when everyone who joined the restaurant where I was working just assumed I was gay. I didn't say anything otherwise because I assumed I was as well.'

Accepted by his workmates for what he was, Graham finally found the courage to come out to his friends. 'One time he came back to the squat and said, "I'm gay, and I've had these experiences," ' recalls Julie Forrester. 'It was some time after America. We just said, "Oh yeah, Graham." He knew that we were already aware of it. It wasn't odd or anything, it was just like, "That's Graham and that's his niche." The last time I saw him was some time afterwards at a party in Bandon. He was out then and he arrived wearing a black leather jacket with studs on, kind of Marlon Brando-esque. But I never met any of his male partners. I got the impression that he never had serious ones.'

But the thought of announcing to his staid, middle aged parents that he was gay was something Graham couldn't imagine doing in a million years. 'Sex wasn't discussed in our house,' he said. 'I remember my sister, who was married for heaven's sake, announcing that she was pregnant and there was an embarrassed half pause, because that was the final proof that she had "done it".' In fact Graham would never pluck up the courage to tell his parents outright and when they did hear it from him it would cause a confrontation with his mother.

Graham loved living in London because of the city's tolerant attitude to different cultures and lifestyles. 'Tolerance is forced on people in London,' he explained. 'If you were a bigot here and rolled down the car window to shout "faggot" at every gay person you saw, it would take you all day to get to your desti-nation. People don't have time to hate us that much.'

In the first few years after he left drama school, Graham took whatever acting jobs he was offered if they gave him the oppor-tunity to perform in front of an audience. Even when there was to be no audience he sometimes took them anyway, once playing a dead body in a training video. 'He never said he was disillusioned,' says Niall MacMonagle, who received long letters from Graham at that time. 'For years and years he was just an ordinary jobbing actor. I have got letters from him when he did pantomime in the north of England and did these God awful stints just to make a few bob. But he never gave up. Even when times were pretty bad in the sense that he hadn't a bob, he had this extraordinary optimism to keep going.'

Graham and his former mentor had become good friends in the years since Graham had left Cork. He had visited the teacher and his academic wife in Dublin, and Niall had stayed with Graham on a few occasions when he was in London. None of the places Graham was renting was particularly salu-brious and Niall vividly remembers one place in particular, dubbed Cockroach Towers by Graham. 'He was living on the top floor of this really grotty, run down, high-rise flat some-where in east London,' he recalls. 'It was a building where, when we came home from a meal or being out, Graham would produce from his pocket a torch to guide us up the urine scented stairs. It was just grim, grim. But once you got inside Graham's door, he had made every effort to turn it into a really beautiful apartment.'

Graham lived in that tower block in Queensbridge Road, Hackney, for almost five years. He moved in during 1990 and did not leave until around 1995. The block has since been completely refurbished, but at the time Graham was living there he claims it was the most cockroach-infested block of flats in Europe. 'I was on the 18th floor and only found out afterwards that Sid Vicious lived on the 16th floor,' he said. 'It was horrible.' But as is his wont, he made light of his time there. 'One night, I went into the lift and there was a huge great Alsatian in there and it wouldn't come out,' he said in a newspaper interview. 'Because I lived on the 18th floor I couldn't really use the stairs, so in the end I got in the lift and the Alsatian just sat there staring – it was like being in a scene from that weird TV programme *Twin Peaks*. I had to stop the lift at every floor just in case the dog wanted to get out. Finally, we got to the 11th floor and he trotted off.'

He continued to apply for serious acting roles and was eventually offered a part in a production at the Liverpool Playhouse. His performance in that play was to prove to be a major turning point in his career; not because he was any good in it – he wasn't – and not because he was 'discovered' or anything like that. But what the experience did for Graham was to finally convince him that a career as a serious actor was not for him. 'In the play I had to get angry and kick over a chair,' he recalled. 'I dreaded that bit every night. I looked like an irate window dresser!'

Graham was later to be extremely candid about his short-comings as a thespian. 'Actually I am a failed actor,' he admitted in an interview. 'And I failed for the right reason because I wasn't very good. I can do hysteria but they've already made *The Towering Inferno*. Imagine the horror of me playing Oswald in Ibsen's *Ghosts*! So bad, so fantastically bad!'

He returned to London from Liverpool having resolved to concentrate on comedy. 'It was very clear I was getting nowhere with the whole acting thing,' he said. 'I just never worked, and when I did I didn't enjoy it. But I still wanted to perform, so I thought, "Well, I'm crap at being serious, but I can do comedy, so maybe that's what I should explore." That's when I thought comedy was the way to go.'

He was still working as a waiter to make ends meet and, unsurprisingly, enjoyed playing pranks on his customers. When he discovered that a restaurant he was working in was being closed down and he and his colleagues were about to be fired, he put a sign on the front door saying, 'Please use other entrance'. 'But there was no other door,' he admitted. 'It was hilarious watching people wandering about outside, pushing at walls, trying to get in.'

Graham also did bar work and one of the pubs he worked at was The Eagle, a popular pub on the Farringdon Road, just a few yards up from the offices of the *Guardian* newspaper. Graham quickly became well known among the journalists and other pub regulars for his camp rudeness to customers, 'No!' being his usual answer to almost any request. Bar work provided him with the perfect opportunity to show off. Wearing a tea towel, he would occasionally do impersonations of Mother Theresa of Calcutta. 'I was like Graham Norton off the telly 24 hours a day – very amusing, but you wouldn't want to be around him for long,' he has said of himself at that time.

Although he loved bar work to begin with, after a few years the novelty was beginning to wear thin. By his late twenties, he was still waiting tables, still serving behind bars, still waiting for his acting break. He no longer felt like cracking so many jokes. 'Behind a bar you are trapped, and like a caged animal you lash out,' he said in an interview. 'I had become the person I'd been terrified of becoming. No, I had become the person I didn't understand how anyone could become when I was 18, and there'd be some, God!, 27-year-old bitter queen working there. And you've just got to think, "Christ, where did he go wrong with his life?"' These harsh words, spoken in a rare moment when Graham wasn't following his usual practice of making a joke of everything, indicate just how desperate he felt at that time.

'No one deserves success like he does,' says Niall MacMonagle. 'Certainly Graham served a long apprenticeship. He was really just making a living, making ends meet.'

When Graham met a face from his past in 1991, he cut a somewhat dejected figure. Obo was on a visit to London from San Francisco and decided to look up his former lover to straighten things out between them. Although he had still not sufficiently recovered from his affair with Obo to entrust his heart to anyone else, Graham agreed to meet him. Seeing him for the first time in six years, Graham realized that he no longer felt so hurt. That old cliché of time being a healer had proved itself to be true and he was even able to forgive his ex-lover. While he didn't want to be a bit player in Obo's tangled love life he saw no reason why they couldn't be friends. 'He didn't seem to have any hard feelings any more about what had happened between us and we laughed and joked,' says Obo. But it had been a long time since the two had seen each other and Obo admits to being shocked at how low Graham appeared. 'We went out to dinner and a club and had a really nice time, but he didn't seem happy,' he says. 'He was working as a waiter again and he seemed sad.'

Graham was sufficiently down for Obo to consider that something really serious might be wrong with him. 'I wondered if he had Aids,' he admits. While Obo's fears were totally unfounded, it is possible to see why he would fear the worst. Coming from a city that had been so decimated by Aids, and knowing people who had been infected, it was under-standable that Obo would worry about the health of his gay friends. And while it had been nowhere near as badly affected as San Francisco, London's gay community had been hit by the Aids epidemic of the eighties and nineties. By 1994, there had been 6,612 cases of Aids reported in inner London alone, 80 per cent of which were gay men. Throughout the nineties there were 1,400 new cases of HIV infection among gay men in the UK each year, with London having the highest rates. Just as it had been when Graham was in San Francisco in 1984, it was an apprehensive time for the gay community.

Graham's reunion with Obo finally provided him with closure on their relationship. It had taken him almost six years to fully recover from the pain Obo had caused him and he was still determined to be picky about choosing to whom he would next give his heart. As Obo flew back to San Francisco and his life at the commune, Graham carried on serving meals and polishing glasses in London. But things were slowly about to change for

him. Recognizing his popularity with the punters, Mike Be..
who owned The Eagle and had become a good friend o.
Graham's, encouraged him to put on a show in a room above the
pub. Building on his tea towel impersonation of Mother Theresa,
Graham wrote a short one-man sketch, which he called *Mother
Theresa of Calcutta's Grand Farewell Tour*. In the highly irreverent
show, Graham portrayed the living saint as a mad Irish housewife. The press was invited – in the *Guardian* journalists' case
they didn't have far to go – and the show went down a storm.
Presenter Emma Freud loved it so much that she did a piece on
Graham on the Radio 4 arts programme, *Loose Ends*.

As word of his talents spread, Graham took his *Mother
Theresa* show to the 1991 Edinburgh Fringe Festival. The Fringe
had begun by accident in 1947 when eight theatre groups
turned up uninvited to the first Edinburgh International
Festival. Finding all the main venues full, they had put on their
shows at small venues away from the big public stages and the
Fringe was born. The following year, Robert Kemp of the
Evening News unknowingly coined the name that was later to
describe the largest and most famous festival in the world.
'Round the fringe of the official Festival drama there seems to
be a more private enterprise than before,' he wrote. 'I'm afraid
some of us are not going to be often at home during the
evenings.' The Fringe became a major showcase for new plays
– Tom Stoppard's *Rosencrantz and Guildenstern Are Dead* was
premiered there in 1966 – and quickly grew in size. By 1959,
there were already murmurs that it had become too big; there
were 19 groups in total. By the time Graham arrived in
Edinburgh, in 1991, there were around 600 groups performing
from 49 different countries.

Mother Theresa was a huge success for Graham at Edinburgh and over the next seven years he was to become a mainstay of the festival. Karen Koren, talent spotter of comedy hopefuls at the Fringe, remembers how he immediately stood out from the other wannabe performers. 'He was different and he took a lot of risks,' she says. 'Of the hundreds of acts that appear here, there is only a handful that are going to be future stars. I absolutely knew that Graham would be a star. I think it is his way of making people feel special when he talks to them – he looks you directly in the eye. The audience participation that he does on his television show is something he began here in Edinburgh.'

Performing at the Fringe, Graham appeared to have at last found his niche. 'The Festival is unique,' explains Koren. 'As Graham said himself, he couldn't really do the sort of stuff he was doing around the circuit in London. It was only at the Festival that he could do that kind of thing. It gave him the platform.'

Karen Koren was not the only one to recognize star quality when she saw it. Around the same time that he was making a name for himself at Edinburgh, Graham also came to the attention of London-based theatre producers Mark Goucher and David Johnson. The pair, whose company at that time was called G&J productions, instantly saw his talent and offered to promote him. 'David knew him first and had seen him do various stand-up routines in some of the gay clubs,' explains Mark Goucher. 'Then we went to see him doing *Mother Theresa of Calcutta* in some restaurant bar somewhere in the West End, I can't for the life of me remember where. I thought he was brilliant and we immediately wanted to work with him. I knew he would be successful. David and I both said that he would become one of this country's greatest talents; one of the great comic performers. We said this to Graham but he didn't believe us. He's very modest.'

No taboo was to be safe from Graham's merciless lampooning. In 1993, he followed *Mother Theresa of Calcutta's Farewell Tour* with an equally tasteless, equally funny show: *The Karen Carpenter Bar and Grill*. Set in a mythical restaurant owned by the anorexic singer, it featured Graham as Karen screaming at her brother and singing partner Richard. The bad taste jokes came thick and fast: 'There's Karen – no, that's a steamer.' He also did surreal impersonations of two gay icons: Shirley Temple and Imelda Marcos, with an aging Shirley Temple portrayed as still believing herself to be six years old and demanding to be allowed to sit on someone's knee and sing her song about soup.

It was all incredibly bizarre – and the spectators loved it. Graham told the audience he had visited the Carpenter home and been shown Karen's bedroom by her mother. 'She told me that Karen had collapsed on the stairs, but the police report said she had collapsed at the back of the wardrobe. Poor little Karen, they were looking for hours,' he quipped. Carpenter, whose anorexia was to lead to her death, was portrayed as a food-obsessed neurotic in curlers who was eventually transported into space to the tune of The Carpenters' hit record, 'Calling Occupants of Interplanetary Craft'.

The Karen Carpenter Bar and Grill also showcased at Edinburgh but for the first time Graham was professionally represented by Mark Goucher and David Johnson. 'I think he had done one or two festivals before us but when we took him to Edinburgh it was the first time he had been properly represented,' says Goucher. 'Before that he used to do it himself. We managed him and promoted his live work. We knew him as friends and it was a very happy arrangement.'

For his next Fringe show in 1994, Graham turned to one of the programmes he had so loved in his childhood – *Charlie's Angels*. All the years that he had spent glued to the television were now starting to pay dividends in the material they provided for his comedy routines. Graham's show was one of *the* successes of the festival that year. Billed as the story of 'three little angels and an Irish boy', it was a largely autobiographical account of his own life. 'The title brought the punters in but really it's about me, me, me!' he said unapologetically. Like many artists, Graham drew on his own experiences for his material. The confusion he had experienced over his sexuality, his flit to America, his time in the hippie commune – even Obo's promiscuous love life – all were featured in the act.

Performing in a small room at Edinburgh's Pleasance Theatre, Graham gave the audience his no holds barred account of a young Irishman's coming out and voyage of sexual discovery in San Francisco. He talked about how he had lived as an 'economic hippie' in a commune because he couldn't afford anything else. He had introduced his American vegetarian housemates to his version of salad, he said, and in return they had introduced him to multilateral relationships. He talked in colourful terms about losing his virginity and his encounters with 'rent boys, squat boys and one night stands'. Squat boys were apparently 'the same as rent boys, except you don't pay them'. The stars of the seventies series, on the other hand, were relegated to bit part players. Graham didn't even bother to portray the Angels; they were instead represented by a hair drier (Farrah Fawcett), a crash helmet (Jaclyn Smith) and a sensible jumper (Kate Smith).

Like his two previous shows, *Charlie's Angels Go To Hell* was judged a winner. 'Norton's concoction of iconoclasm, fun and off-beat self-analysis has fringe goers laughing all the way,' wrote the *Scotsman*'s critic Jan Brierley. 'His gently acerbic humour and finely timed analysis shone through sauna-like conditions in the Pleasance Attic, and an audience including two minors with either liberal or naïve parents.'

In November 1994, following his success at that summer's Fringe, Graham at last realized his dream of appearing in the West End. He was offered a 12-week run at the Arts Theatre in Newport Street, Covent Garden, with his own one-man show. He featured two of his Edinburgh creations, *Charlie's Angels Go To Hell* and *The Karen Carpenter Bar and Grill*, in a double bill.

The *Evening Standard*'s critic Andrew Martin likened Graham 'with his eye-rolling expressions of incredulity and rambling digressions', to 'an out of the closet Frankie Howerd.' But he warned that Norton's account in *Charlie's Angels Go To Hell* about losing his virginity was 'not one for the family'. That included Graham's own family. For many actors, getting their own show in the West End would be a moment of glory they would surely want their parents to share in. But for Graham, whose act left his gay status in no doubt, his family seeing him on stage was something he dreaded.

Little wonder that he was worried. As well as all the anecdotes about rent boys and shagging, in the show he told how since losing his virginity there had been 'a lot of pubic hair under the duvet'. 'By the way,' he asked the audience, 'Is there anyone in tonight that I haven't slept with?' On opening night he started to fret that his mother and father might turn up. He hadn't invited them, but might they choose to come and surprise him? What a potential disaster that would be! He realized just how scared he was of them seeing him perform his material. 'On the way to the theatre, I panicked,' he admitted at the time. '"What if they turn up?" I suddenly thought. They had never seen my comedy and I don't think I want them to. So I phoned Ireland to make sure they were safely at home. Then I knew I could go on with confidence. No way would I have wanted them to see me. I just knew they wouldn't enjoy it.'

While he had no qualms about using gay material in his act, Graham still couldn't bring himself to admit to his family that he was gay. 'I probably should have told them,' he said later on. 'But then – and this is probably very un-PC – I think a lot of coming out is selfish. You are not doing it for your parents; you're doing it for yourself. That's not necessarily a bad thing, but don't lie to yourself. Don't pretend that your parents are going to be grateful you've told them. They're not.'

While his parents may well have been shocked by some of the content of his West End show, the double bill was a big hit with audiences. '*Charlie's Angels* may go to hell, but Graham Norton will have a seat reserved in heaven if he keeps making people laugh like this,' wrote one impressed London reviewer. 'They are hardly pioneering in content, but his cheerily camp delivery, bitchy one liners and spot on characterizations make them much more than the set of kitsch references implied by their titles. The whole lot has such a feel good camaraderie that it is impossible not to like the guy.'

Mark Goucher and David Johnson produced Graham at the Arts Theatre and also staged another of his acts there, *Graham*

Norton And His Amazing Hostess Trolley. 'I can't remember if that one went to Edinburgh,' says Goucher. 'But we certainly did it at the Arts Theatre. Graham was performing in gay clubs and small comedy clubs and then he started doing his own stand-up show, which I don't really think we had names for, when we went to the Assembly Rooms at Edinburgh a few years later.'

Like most fledgling performers, Graham made his fair share of mistakes. On one occasion at Edinburgh he put an advert in the gay press for unsuspecting people who were 'looking for a good time, possibly with others watching' to ring in, little knowing that their calls would be broadcast live to a theatre full of punters in the city's Assembly Rooms. It was a cheap shot and he was quickly humbled. 'It was hideous,' he said. 'They were really nice, sad people who just wanted to have a wank. They became victims and we came out of it looking horrible. I did feel I was exploiting them a bit, but the bottom line was it wasn't very funny.'

But at least one critic thought otherwise. 'There's a devilish charm about Graham Norton,' they wrote after the Assembly Rooms gig. 'He comes on stage and gushes, so pleased to see us all. It sparks suspicion as to what pranks he is about to play... but the time comes to strike out. There's cruelty in his big joke, as he rings up some poor, unsuspecting fool that's answered his personal ad. This is no hoax and it's a perverse delight, making us squirm and chuckle in equal measure.' Although Graham was ashamed of his actions on that occasion, the idea would later be refined and incorporated into his television show with the famous 'Doggy Phone'.

As well as near-the-knuckle gay material, Graham's act also included a fair amount of Catholic baiting. So much so that many people believed him to be Catholic. 'I just pretend to be Catholic,' he told one misguided interviewer. 'If you want to do Catholic material you have to claim that you're Catholic. I guess all Irish have a bit of Catholic in them though.'

After plugging away for so long, by the mid-nineties Graham's talent was finally beginning to gain recognition. 'Graham did knock around for a good five or six years doing clubs and trying to break through,' says Mark Goucher. 'I think one of his biggest breaks was when David and I were producing a live version of *Just A Minute* with Nicholas Parsons at Edinburgh and we got Graham on to the show as a stand in.' *Just A Minute* is the long-running Radio 4 programme hosted by Parsons. Panellists, who include people like Paul Merton, Clement Freud and Stephen Fry, have to talk for a full minute on a given subject without 'hesitation, repetition or deviation'. Graham, for whom chatting away 19 to the dozen came as second nature, excelled at this. 'He was just great on the live performance,' says Goucher. 'And of course now he is one of the great regulars on the radio show.'

Although it would be a few years before Graham would be deemed famous enough to appear on the radio programme, Nicholas Parsons remembers being impressed by his engaging personality at the Edinburgh gig. 'We were staging a live version of the show in a tent on the top of Carlton Hill,' he explains. 'Tony Slattery was the regular because he was a very well-known name, and the rest of the contestants were stars from the Fringe. Graham was engaged as the permanent stand by. He had done a bit of stand-up comedy but he was comparatively unknown.

'We performed every morning and Graham was a tower of strength because he knew the game and he was always available if one of the others didn't turn up. Sometimes people couldn't make it, or they couldn't find the place, and into the breach stepped Graham. It was often a case of, "Graham you're on again," and he appeared frequently throughout that two-week run. I got to know him very well and I thought he was the most delightful, engaging person and so easy and comfortable to be with. People may not have come up to see Graham Norton, but they certainly enjoyed it when they did see him.'

Over the course of the fortnight, Parsons watched Graham become an expert at the game. 'He got better and better at *Just A Minute* and at the same time he improved his skills as a sponta-neous ad-lib comedian,' he explains. 'He was so reliable and at times very amusing, but he was still finding his professional identity at that time. Later on, he started guesting on other shows and really honed his skills and developed his persona. I don't cast for *Just A Minute*, but several years later when Graham was getting quite well known the producer said she was thinking of asking him to do the show. I said it was a very good idea because when he did it at Edinburgh he was excellent.

'By that time he had found his professional confidence and developed a comic persona which was working very well. He came on the show and he was absolutely excellent and they immediately asked him back. He has the gift of language like all Irish people do. There are very few Irish people who don't have a natural gift of language. It's second nature to them. They have a feeling for language and they are great talkers. If you go to Ireland, people come out with the most beautiful phrases and language. That is part of Graham's heritage. It's in him – he loves chatting.'

By 1995, Graham was also appearing on *Loose Ends*, the Radio 4 arts magazine programme hosted by theatre producer Ned Sherrin. The show, which at that time went out on Saturday mornings, is a humorous look back at the week's news and features celebrity guests from the art and film worlds. Graham enjoyed the immediacy of radio. 'On radio you can have an idea and get it on the airwaves in minutes,' he explained. 'Television is much slower.'

As well as being promoted by G&J Productions, Graham was on the books of Jon Keyes, an agent whose company Paramount International brought American comedians to the UK. It was Keyes who got Graham his first professional appearance as a stand-up. Although he had performed in several clubs and bars in London, Graham has stated that his first professional gig was at The Comedy Box in Bristol. Steve Lount, an independent promoter who ran the club, had originally booked another comedian for the night and wasn't too impressed when he was offered Graham Norton instead.

Lount's original choice had been Scott Capurro, an openly gay American comedian who was gaining a big profile on the UK comedy circuit. Like Graham, Capurro had started out at the Edinburgh Fringe. 'I had originally booked Scott Capurro because whenever we put him on he was a guaranteed sell-out,' Lount explains. 'When he pulled the gig we thought we would either have to cancel the show or put another act on. But his agent, Jon Keyes said, "We've got this other act called Graham Norton who's also quite openly gay and very, very camp." I said, "Yes, but what has he ever done? I've never heard of him before." Bearing in mind that this was a headline act; it wasn't a support act or an open spot. A headlining slot is a 40-minute set. But Keyes said, "Oh yeah, he can definitely headline", and I fell for it hook, line and sinker.'

And so it was Graham Norton, not Scott Capurro, who appeared at The Comedy Box on April 19, 1995. The Comedy Box is now housed at another location but at that time it was situated above The Bristol Flyer pub. It was a small room, which could take a maximum of 120 people. There were no frills; it was just a typical pub function room with red curtains and red wallpaper and wobbly chairs. 'It wasn't very well ventilated and it was a bit poky,' Lount admits. 'People had to squeeze in, but it was incredibly atmospheric.' The venue had the minimum facilities to run a comedy night: a PA system, lighting system and a small stage. Graham performed that night in front of just 83 people, all of whom had paid £5 to see him. 'When people heard that Scott Capurro wasn't coming the numbers had started to drop off,' explains Lount.

'Graham only got the gig on the strength of a white lie. He had never done any stand-up before. He had done theatre work and I think he'd appeared on various Radio 4 shows. But he went on and basically he got away with it – or we got away with it. I don't think we had any real complaints but it certainly wasn't a storming set.'

Graham has said that he ended up doing stand-up because 'I still wanted to show off, and that was an easy avenue to take.' But what he had been doing in his Edinburgh revues was essentially acting. *The Karen Carpenter Bar and Grill* and *Charlie's Angels Go To Hell* were really one-man plays, whereas traditional stand-up was another thing entirely. 'He was telling anecdotes but he's not really a stand-up comedian,' says Lount. 'He's really more of a presenter or a storyteller. Whereas Scott Capurro was very rude, very crude, very political, very brutal, Graham was very fluffy and was basically just chatting to the audience.

'He wasn't nervous. He may have been inside but he didn't come across as nervous at all. Put it this way, I didn't have a clue that he'd never done stand-up before and even then I didn't know it was his first professional booking until many years later. But I did think he was weak. Weak, but very charismatic. He carried the set on his personality, not his material. I may have had words with Jon Keyes the next day.'

Lount managed to negotiate a discount from Keyes for having to accept a replacement act. 'The fee for Scott Capurro would have been £140 but I managed to negotiate £20 off because it was Graham Norton,' he says. 'When Graham had finished we had a chat. He was a really nice guy. Basically he was as he is now, although obviously he is more confident now. I was impressed with his style and I said to him, "I bet you'll have your own Channel 4 series within a few years." So when he got *So Graham Norton* I couldn't believe it! He rose so quickly; he really wasn't known as a stand up comedian but because he was so charismatic you could see where he was going in terms of his career. Any producer seeing him would go, "Yes, he'd be right for our show."

'But as a stand-up comedian I would say he was hopeless. He wasn't gearing his stuff for punch lines; he was basically just being a funny person on stage. He wasn't doing stand-up comedy, he was doing anecdotal, storytelling-type stuff. If I saw Graham now, face to face, I would say to him, "You were shit that night." Maybe I wouldn't use the word shit, but he was rubbish. I'm not saying it just to be malicious; as a professional promoter I didn't think he was very good at the time.'

Steve Lount was in the habit of recording every act that

appeared at the Comedy Box, and listening to a tape of Graham's routine that night it is easy to see why he failed to impress. The most striking thing about his act is the amount of long pauses that occurred. And in between the pauses Graham spoke extremely slowly, perhaps in a bid to fill the 40-minute slot. He started off by picking on someone in the audience and ridiculing their hair, and then moved on to the subject of children. Children, he said, were like farts – in that people loathed other people's but quite liked their own. This remark drew some feeble titters from the audience but an extremely tasteless joke about personal hygiene was met with a stony silence.

Graham then began a series of self-deprecating remarks, and it was with this that he was at his funniest. He described how, as a result of the ageing process, rebel hair had begun sprouting all over his body. 'Every time I shave I have to shave higher and higher,' he complained. 'If I stopped shaving now my head would grow into some kind of giant fur ball like the cat sicked up. And I've got these weird patches of hair on my back – two of them – it looks like the devil's hoof prints. I could have shoulder topiary.' Hairiness was a theme he warmed to. Talking about a one night stand he purported to have had with a particularly hirsute man, he confided: 'The problem with people like that is that you can't just leave them – you've got to untangle yourself.' He also confessed another problem to the audience: he had breasts. 'When I am on the beach in Ireland, middle-aged women shout "hussy" and tell me to put my top back on,' he said. Perhaps this was the reason he was single, he mused. 'Breasts and hairy shoulders – not a winning combination.'

His skit on *Charlie's Angels* failed to get any response whatsoever, but he had more success talking about his personal predicaments. Explaining how he had discovered his sexuality in San Francisco, he gave the audience the benefit of his experience. 'Here's a tip,' he offered. 'If any of you are sexually confused, San Francisco is not a great place to go because there is too much choice there.'

Despite his first impressions of Graham's act, Steve Lount booked him on a second occasion that year. But that too was only by default. 'The second time was a reluctant booking,' he says. 'I didn't book Graham Norton because I wanted him or because I thought he was any good. But we were doing a post Edinburgh show and he was supporting another act which I'd already booked, a circuit comedian called Dave Thompson.' On that occasion, Graham and Thompson, whose alter ego was the *Teletubbies'* creation Tinkie Winkie, managed to make the tiny Comedy Box venue appear positively cavernous. 'There were only about 20 people in the room that night and it wasn't a great success,' says Lount. ' But it was an interesting combination. People didn't know Graham Norton then and they didn't have the same respect they would now.'

But Graham's career was now beginning to take off. In 1995, he landed a small role in the Channel 4 comedy series *Father Ted*. Created by Irish writers Graham Linehan and Arthur Mathews, the show starred Irish comedian Dermot Morgan as the lovable but disaster-prone priest. It was first broadcast in the UK on April 21, 1995, and was an instant success. Set on the fictional Craggy Island, the series centred around the comic mishaps of a group of eccentric priests. Ted's entourage included his dimwit sidekick Dougal, alias stand up comedian Ardal O'Hanlon; the permanently drunk Father Jack, played by Frank Kelly ; and their twittering housekeeper Mrs Doyle, played by Pauline McLynn. Highly irreverent and searingly funny, *Father Ted* became Channel 4's most successful series ever and went on to become a cult classic.

Graham joined the show in its second series. His character was Father Noel Furlong, a hyperactive, happy-clappy priest who cropped up to annoy the hell out of poor Ted. In the appropriately-titled episode 'Hell', Noel managed to wreck Ted and Dougal's peaceful holiday in a friend's caravan by turning up uninvited with a bunch of friends and holding an all night party. And he tormented them further in 'Flight Into Terror', in which Ted and Dougal are returning from a pilgrimage to the Shrine of Kinlettle. Ted, who has a phobia of flying, is sent into a panic when the hapless Dougal accidentally empties the plane's fuel tanks.

The role of Father Noel was ideal for Graham and he was perfect in it. Having described how he could 'do hysteria', he now had a perfect outlet for his talents. In 'The Mainland', an episode in series three, he gave a brilliantly nerve-shredding rendition of the Queen classic 'Bohemian Rhapsody'. Lost in a cave with Ted and Dougal, who had fled down the wrong path in their haste to escape from Victor Meldrew, Father Noel decided to pass the time with a bit of impromptu karaoke. When he had finished his dreadful caterwauling, he suggested to his dumbstruck audience that they should have a screeching competition; an unfortunate idea which mercifully brought about a rockfall on top of his irritating head. However, this was not before he had managed to wind Ted and Dougal into a state of terror by talking about the film *Alive*, in which people were stranded on a mountainside for months after a plane crash and were forced to eat the dead bodies of their fellow passengers in order to survive.

Graham has described the character of Noel as, 'certainly annoying – a bit like me really,' and told how some of the production team thought he had created a monster. 'In dress rehearsals executives from Channel 4 would say, "You've made him a little frightening," but it was really me just messing,' he said. Father Ted was such a hit with viewers that Graham soon began to be recognized by Craggy Island fans. 'The series is so huge I get people banging on restaurant windows when they see me inside,' he said. 'There was even a website called Tedspotting which people wrote to when they saw a Father Ted actor in the street. I was spotted in Bethnal Green Tesco's in east London buying toilet paper! I like to think I was buying other things as well, but it's still freaky deaky.'

Father Ted was voted Best Sitcom for two years running at the British Comedy Awards and also won a Bafta. But in February 1998, the programme came to a tragic and abrupt end when Dermot Morgan died of a heart attack. The father of three collapsed at his home in Richmond, Surrey, three weeks before the third series was due to be screened. His death was totally unexpected and deeply shocked the showbusiness industry. His partner Fiona said that she wanted the third series to go ahead as planned on March 6 as a tribute to him. For all those watching the final episodes there was a special poignancy to the show. Like the rest of Dermot's co-stars, Graham was devastated by his death. 'The funny thing is, I miss Father Ted every day,' he said in 1999. 'Not a day passes that I don't think of the late Dermot Morgan. He was one of the finest comedians ever to come out of Ireland.'

Only 25 episodes of Father Ted were ever made and Graham appeared in just three of them. But thanks to the show's cult success – and its constant repeats on Channel 4 and its satellite brother E4 – he will be forever associated with it.

As well as dipping his toe into television and appearing on radio, Graham continued to perform at the Fringe. His Edinburgh contemporaries in the nineties included many now famous names. When he first started going to the festival in 1991 people like Frank Skinner, Jack Dee, Eddie Izzard and Lily Savage were getting a lot of attention. When they moved on to bigger things, Graham appeared alongside entertainers such as Steve Coogan, John Thomson, Jo Brand, Mark Thomas and Lee Evans. More recent contemporaries of his would have been Alan Davies, Harry Hill, Jenny Eclair, Dylan Moran and Bill Bailey.

Arguably the highlight of the festival was being nominated for a much coveted Perrier Award, which carried as its prize a large cheque and a West End appearance. Previous winners had included Frank Skinner, Steve Coogan and Lee Evans and in 1997 – the festival's 50th anniversary – Graham was nominated. In his act that year Graham introduced the 'Kitty Phone', a kitten-shaped telephone for which you could obtain a certificate of adoption. This would be followed a few years later by the Doggy Phone when Graham got his own television series. Although he did not win the Perrier Award – he was beaten by *The League of Gentlemen* – the nomination alone was enough to kick-start Graham's career in showbusiness.

The next few years were to be some of the most fruitful of his life; both professionally and personally.

7 A DEAD SERIOUS LOVE

While Graham talked a lot in his act about how much sex he was having, at other times he made out that his love life was a disaster and that he was a hopeless prospect as a boyfriend. 'I indulge in serial monogamy,' he confided during a stand-up gig. 'That's when you go out with one other person and they dump you.' Another favourite line was, 'I'm single and it's my choice. It's my second choice.' He also gave his definition of multilateral relationships of the type that Obo had introduced him to in San Francisco. 'A multilateral relationship is one where one person goes out with more than one other person, whereas their partner gets shat on from a great height,' he commented dryly.

Sex, where to get it and how to get it, was something that greatly preoccupied Graham when he first came out. He even claims to have contemplated a career as a male prostitute. 'It was, weirdly, a way to have sex,' he said. 'I thought, "Ooh, I'll try this gay sex lark, but how?" I had no idea. So I thought, "If I become a rent boy, then I'll have sex with people."' Joking though he was when he made that remark, in all probability

Graham was like everybody else, in that he hoped to find 'the one' but was having fun looking. Like most people, he wanted to have someone special in his life – a 'significant other' to come home to every night – but this was something that had so far eluded him.

But in 1995 all that changed when Graham fell in love. As is often the case, he didn't see it coming and couldn't do anything about it when it happened. He was introduced to Scott Michaels, a 33-year-old American, by mutual friends one weekend in November. At the time, Graham hadn't been in a relationship for nine years. It had taken him a long time to get over Obo and he had resolved to be cautious about giving his heart. 'It was five years of recovery, and the rest being very picky,' he explained. 'And I'm quite self-reliant, so I just did without.' But Scott was only staying in London for the weekend and therefore didn't represent anything more than the prospect of a quick fling. 'I thought, "Well, he's going, I'll just throw myself into this for a long weekend, and that will be the end of it,"' said Graham. 'And of course it wasn't. My defences were down. I thought I was foolproof. Absolutely safe.'

In fact Graham had just met the love of his life. Scott Michaels would become the big romance of his life so far and the American's vacation in London would become a permanent move.

Michaels was actually holidaying in France but had gone to London for the weekend. He told Graham that he had a fort-night of his holiday left and would then be returning to the States. Scott had been born in Detroit but at the time he met Graham he was living in Los Angeles where he earned a living running tourist tours in Hollywood. As well as being physically attracted to one another, the couple discovered that they shared a wacky sense of humour and a love of celebrity trivia. Graham, who had spent his childhood glued to the television set and could tell you everything you wanted to know about the rich and famous, now met someone who knew just as many weird and wonderful snippets about them as he did.

Realizing that he had met someone who had the potential to become special to him, at the end of his weekend in London Scott invited Graham to go with him to Paris. Graham initially turned him down and waved him off, assuming that he would probably never see him again. But as he thought about what a great time they had had together he decided that he very much did want to see Scott again. Deciding 'what the hell', Graham called Eurostar and bought a ticket to Paris. If his change of heart had surprised himself, his new boyfriend was equally astonished when Graham called him to say he was catching the train. A delighted Scott offered to meet him at the Eurostar terminal at the Gard du Nord, but Graham suggested they meet in a bar that they both knew instead.

This plan was to go seriously wrong, however, and the fact that they ever linked up at all is thanks to a sequence of events that wouldn't have been out of place in the Hollywood film *Serendipity*. In the movie, which starred John Cusack and Kate Beckinsale as star-crossed lovers, a couple meet accidentally and are immediately attracted to one another. But the woman refuses to arrange to see the guy again; saying that if they are supposed to be together, they will somehow meet again. They do, of course, and presumably live happily ever after. And just like in the film, fate stepped in to bring Graham and Scott together in Paris.

Graham's train was horribly delayed and he had no telephone number for Scott in Paris. And, just as had happened when Graham couldn't find the boutique he was working in when he had last been in Paris, his memory let him down again. Running late and feeling stressed, his mind went blank and he forgot the name of the bar where he was supposed to be meeting Scott. Worse, he couldn't even remember the address of it. 'I got to Paris three hours late,' Graham later recalled. 'Rush hour. Traffic chaos. Get on the tube-y thing. Then I'm walking through these little streets, trying to find this bar.'

Scott, meanwhile, had left the bar, understandably assuming that he had been stood up and that Graham had changed his mind again. But then fate stepped in. 'I'm walking through these little streets, trying to find this bar, and I bumped into him in the street,' Graham revealed in wonderment. 'He'd abandoned the bar and he didn't know what to do, and we bumped into each other. It was one of those things. Really kind of cute. So it was immediately romantic.'

In Paris, the two continued the great time they had had with each other in London. Graham took Scott around his old haunts where he had stayed as a student, and to the Pompidou Centre where he had earned money mimicking the tourists. The days went by all too quickly and at the end of their time together Graham left to return to London and Scott prepared to fly back to Los Angeles. Despite the fun they had had, Graham couldn't see himself having a relationship with Scott. For how could they possibly make a go of it living on separate sides of the Atlantic? 'I was thinking, "Oh well, that was all very nice, but it can't work out,"' he admitted. Scott felt the same way. 'It was a terrific beginning to the relationship, although neither of us even entertained that idea out loud,' Scott says. 'We accepted that it was a holiday affair and we said goodbye.'

But within minutes of saying farewell to Scott, Graham knew that he didn't want it to be over. Maybe they could make a go of it, he thought, after all they wouldn't be the first couple to have a transatlantic relationship. All that meeting at airports and emotional farewells could even be romantic, and when they weren't together they would both be free to spend their time how they liked. Somewhere outside Paris he found himself looking at a newspaper to see what the London to Los Angeles fares were, and as soon as Scott got back to LA he was on the phone to Graham in London. 'After that, a single day would not pass without us speaking,' Scott says. And that was it. Graham was part of a couple at last.

Graham at that time had yet to break into television and had done only a little radio work. But although neither of them was earning much money, they managed to visit each other almost every month. In Los Angeles, Scott had a bizarre, 'only in America' job. Although he was a writer, his main employment was taking tourists around the death sites of the rich and famous. The holidaying ghouls would pay their dollars and be driven by Scott in an air-conditioned hearse to the various locations where unfortunate celebrities like Janis Joplin, Marilyn Monroe and River Phoenix had been murdered, overdosed on drugs, or suffered some altogether less traumatic death.

After a year of commuting, Graham managed to persuade Scott to come and live with him in England. Graham had by now left Cockroach Towers and was living in a rented flat in Shoreditch, east London. Scott originally arrived on a six-month visa and the couple had to then embark on a long battle with bureaucracy for him to be allowed to stay permanently. 'It was a time when there wasn't a proper acknowledgment of same sex relationships,' explains Scott, talking fully for the first time about his relationship with Graham. 'You had to prove that you had been together for a minimum of four years, and you had to have lived together for two years. But then the government changed it so that you only had to be together for two years. Graham and I were at the forefront of that whole issue. That's why when people started slagging off the Labour government I pointed out that if it wasn't for Tony Blair I wouldn't have been there.'

Graham and Scott were one of the first gay partnerships to be recognized as a couple by immigration authorities. Like Scott, Graham was hugely grateful. 'I never believed I would see a British government prepared to do anything for the gay community, so at least New Labour can take credit for one thing – making two blokes very happy,' he said. 'Gay people in particular bitch about the Labour government, complaining that social reform isn't moving ahead as fast as it should and so on. And yet it was Labour who introduced the legislation that allowed Scott to stay on after his initial six month visa ran out. I was really impressed by that.'

Soon after Scott's arrival in the UK, the couple left Shoreditch and set up home nearby in a rented house in the appropriately titled Equity Square, where they settled into domestic bliss. Graham had never completely given up on his ambition of becoming a journalist and got the opportunity to write when he was given his own monthly column in the gay newspaper the *Pink Paper*. In the column, which was called 'High Jinx', Graham would often give little insights into his life with Scott, whom he usually referred to as 'the boyfriend'.

Writing about how he had bought a car, even though he

couldn't drive, he assured his readers that it was all right because 'the boyfriend' could. He told how he had had visions of him and Scott cruising around London with the car stereo blaring, and by day two they were cruising all right – 'but towards Lakeside shopping centre to buy sheets in Debenhams.' Describing their preparations for Christmas, he said: 'The C-word creeps closer and closer, and like some sort of electric squirrel the boyfriend has been hoarding lights for weeks now.' They apparently had the 'gay-tasteful' variety, in garlands of simple white bulbs, and had enterprisingly decorated the tree with spray painted sun-dried tomatoes and chillies.

Readers were kept informed about many aspects of Graham and Scott's life, from a little row they'd had – 'a casual "Are you getting changed before we go out?" and suddenly I'm a small patch of evil on the sofa' – to the food that they ate. For example on the topic of potatoes, Graham's very favourite food – 'They just genuinely make me happy' – he divulged that he used to like them mashed with stilton and broccoli but that Scott didn't like it that way, so he would make it with milk and butter instead. Mash and omelettes – and of course Irish stew – were just about the only dishes Graham had ever learned to make. Describing himself as 'the ready meal king', he admitted that he wasn't keen on cooking. Mostly he and Scott would go out to restaurants, usually for lunch because Graham worked a lot of evenings. If they were eating in, it would generally be an offering from those well-known chefs Tesco, Sainsbury and Marks & Spencer.

Graham was so happy that he could not help but be effusive about his love. 'He's very funny. He's big, about 6ft 2ins, and he's just kind of a lovely person,' he told the *Mirror* touchingly.

And in an interview with the *Sunday Mirror*, his contentment at being in a couple was obvious. 'I would love to reveal that I lead a life of wild debauchery, that it is a non stop round of Caligula-style orgies and wine glugging,' he said. 'But I don't, and it isn't. Last evening we watched a little TV, drank our cocoa, had an early night. And when I was switching off the set I thought what a great night of telly it had been.'

For his part, Scott was happy to be written about. 'I didn't mind it because during that time it was a sort of thrill for me,' he admits. 'I was feeling proud. I never wanted to be like David Furnish (Sir Elton John's boyfriend who appears to be always by his side) but I did not mind being an acknowledged part of Graham's life. I meant a lot to him and vice versa. I looked after him – I definitely went into housewife mode. I enjoyed it because it was something I could do to properly contribute. I'd drive him to his comedy gigs and we liked travelling together so when he did travel pieces for different travel shows I would go with him. We'd go away for weekends and stuff like that. It was really sort of mundane but we'd have a lot of fun.'

It is an indication of how contented Graham was with Scott that he should be so upset when a newspaper article failed to mention his partner. A small piece on the television page of the *Daily Mail*'s *Weekend* magazine featured several snippets of information about him, but neglected to mention Scott. Flicking through the other pages, Graham was annoyed to notice that everyone but him had 'significant other' in their fact file. Even if they were single and had split up with someone a year ago the information was there. 'Only yours truly existed in an emotional bubble,' he complained in his *Pink Paper* diary. He argued that the paper must have been aware of Scott because he had talked about him in an interview, so he concluded that not mentioning him must have been an editorial decision. If it had been, it was one which Graham was at pains to understand. 'Why would it be so offensive to the readers of the *Mail* to find out that a poof was in a relationship?' he asked. Admitting that he really didn't know why it should have bothered him so much, he branded it 'insidious censorship', pointing out that the very term 'significant other' had been invented by the politically correct lobby so as not to suggest gender or sexuality.

Graham also revealed how Scott had taught him to show his anger. Being an American, Scott was used to getting good service and wasn't afraid to have a go at someone if things weren't right. 'When we moved in together the shower was broken and he said, "Get on the phone, shout at them!"' said Graham. 'I was going, "No Scott, you don't understand, here in Britain if you shout at people then they hate you and they'll never come and fix the shower." So after about four days of this, with no one coming to fix our shower, I did lose my temper on the phone and just unleashed this stream of vitriol, and of course within seconds someone came round.'

The couple even talked about having a marriage ceremony, but only jokingly. 'We talked about it laughingly,' says Scott. 'But we never made it official. It was something that neither of us ever really was interested in.'

But there was one particular bone of contention between them. Scott was very keen for Graham to tell his mother and father the truth about his sexuality, assuring him that if he came out to his parents it would change his life. But Graham, fearing that it might not change his life for the better, was equally adamant that he didn't want to. 'He did avoid it,' says Scott. 'I had come out to my parents years ago but Graham didn't want to. I don't think anybody *really* wants to, especially in places like Britain and Ireland where people don't want to talk about things that make them uncomfortable. He knew that it was inevitable that it would become public knowledge, but he never really went out and told his parents.'

Sensitive to his mum and dad's feelings, and reluctant to face the potential ordeal of broaching such a delicate subject with them, Graham chose the path of least resistance. He claimed in an early interview that his parents knew anyway. 'They would be stupid if they didn't,' he said. 'My mother will ring me and say, "Oh, I saw you on *The Stand Up Show*," in which I did ten minutes of wanting to stick it up some man in the audience. So either she thinks it's an act, which would be my poor mother clinging to the last vestiges of hope, or she knows, but we just don't discuss it.'

The Walker family, it seemed, was not big on heart-to-hearts. 'We don't talk about things,' Graham said. 'I suppose every family is dysfunctional – "it's not working, so I'm off." That's the way all families function. My sister is a farmer's wife, but we don't really talk about what each other does. I've no idea what she does – she could be a lesbian stand-up comedian for all I know.'

After a visit home to Ireland to meet Billy and Rhoda Walker, Graham felt vindicated when Scott appeared to have come around to his way of thinking. 'Having met my parents he turned to me and said, "No, you shouldn't tell them,"' said Graham.

But despite his reticence on the subject, Graham's family had started to realize where his preferences lay. 'We just assumed when, after four or five years and Graham never brought a girl-friend home, that maybe he was homosexual,' says his brother-in-law Noel. 'But we weren't sitting around discussing it. It certainly wasn't like that. I suppose it started to dawn on us after Elizabeth had gone and there had been no one else. I think we began to realize that maybe Elizabeth was the exception rather than the norm. I remember his mother saying to Paula, "Do you think he's a homosexual?" and Paula thinking that it was quite a possibility.

'But he didn't actually tell us. He dropped a lot of hints and we came to that conclusion; particularly Paula and his mother came to that conclusion. And then he said something – it may have been on a television show he appeared in – that made it clear that he was homosexual. But certainly hints had been dropped and a conclusion had been reached. I suppose in a way that if you thought about managing it, then that would be a pretty good way to do it. I think he was always concerned for his mother and father.'

The TV programme in question was a gay night that Graham hosted for Channel 4 in May 1998. By this time, Graham had been living with Scott Michaels for 18 months but he had still not told his mum and dad that they were a couple. And despite the fact that he believed his parents already knew he was gay, the manner in which they finally found out was to cause angry words between him and his mother. A flippant comment he made at the beginning of the show about 'being Irish and gay' was the unsubtle way in which Graham unwittingly broke the news about himself to his parents. And despite what his brother-in-law thought about it being a good way to manage things, Rhoda Walker did not agree. She was furious with

Graham for broadcasting the news to millions of people and she didn't shy away from taking him to task over it.

The remark led to Graham having the first conversation he had ever had with his mother about his sexuality. He reported it in his *Pink Paper* diary and it was obvious that he felt both hurt and annoyed by the way the conversation had gone. His mother's basic point, he said, was that he shouldn't be telling the whole world that he was gay before he had told his family. She told him that she had known for some time but hadn't wanted to upset his father by telling him. But asking if his father was upset, his mother admitted to Graham that, as it turned out, his father had also known. 'The bizarre implications of our twisted family holding on to all this knowledge, but never sharing it, unravelled as we spoke, ending with the phrase that I think everyone who comes out gets from their mother: "Well, it's your choice, but I can't help thinking that it's a very lonely life,"' Graham wrote.

With that damning remark from his mother, Graham must have felt justified in his initial decision not to come out to his parents. For who wants to be told the death knell news that they are destined to be lonely? Graham was sufficiently upset at his mother's comment to make a spiteful dig at her own marriage. 'I did the phone equivalent of just smiling and nodding, when I really wanted to say that it wasn't a choice and how much more lonely could it be than living in a bungalow in the middle of nowhere with a man you don't speak to,' he wrote.

He even claimed that his mother had specifically told him NOT to tell her or his father that he was gay. However, Scott Michaels casts doubt on this. 'I don't think that's true,' he says. 'Whenever the subject came up, the subject was changed, but she never came right out and said, "Don't say anything." She may have insinuated that she didn't want to go down that conversational route. Graham wasn't too upset about her comments because we were together then. Most people say that about gay people in general – that you're going to end up alone – but it's not necessarily the case. You're never really alone because you always have friends, and gay relationships are hard to come by anyway.

'I think it was one of those things, like in any family, where it was pretty much well known but never ever discussed. It wasn't talked about before and that was the route that Graham chose to take. But it didn't really make any difference between him and his mother. They had a conversation and all was fine afterwards.'

After the air had been cleared, things went on much as they had before. 'I think his mother was just wonderfully supportive of him all the way,' says Graham's friend Niall MacMonagle. Billy Walker would quite sweetly refer to Scott as Graham's 'little friend' and he and Rhoda were sufficiently comfortable with the situation to visit Scott and Graham at their home in London. This too was shared with the readers of the *Pink Paper*. 'Aagh! My parents are coming to stay,' he wrote in his diary in August 1998. 'My mother will be putting on her white gloves in preparation for her spot checks, while my father is starting to worry about what time they should leave so they don't miss the plane home.'

What to do with them for five days was the main considera-tion. 'While London may have some of the best restaurants in the world, which ones serve everything with potato?' he said, rather condescendingly. 'I want them to have a nice time and yet I can't help thinking that every activity outside wandering around John Lewis's furnishing fabrics department may just be something they endure.' And in a later interview he mentioned another visit. 'My mother has been staying with us for four days and we had the same conversation we've had every morning,' he said. 'We discussed the heated over-blanket that I purchased specially for her visit, that doesn't work.'

'It was never awkward when his parents came to stay,' says Scott. 'His parents were terrific and I was really fond of them.' Graham also took Scott to meet the rest of his family in Bandon, where they stayed with Rhoda and Billy. 'After Elizabeth, the next person Graham brought home was Scott,' says Noel. 'They came over a number of times and the family liked Scott. Sitting around the table at dinner, he would be very friendly and chatty. He looked like quite a manly person because he was quite tall and quite bulky. I think he provided a manly element in Graham's life, in that he did the driving and he drove a Jeep.'

But one thing in particular about Graham's partner was a source of mystery for his family. 'I distinctly remember that we were all trying to find out what Scott did for a living,' says Noel. 'It was very difficult to find out exactly what he did. There were many times that we asked, but we never knew. There were a lot of things that he was going to do, or trying to do, but we never found out what he actually did. And that's largely because he didn't tell us. I wouldn't say he was living off Graham but he was at a stage in his life when he didn't have a job.'

As a condition of his residency, Scott was not allowed to work for 18 months when he came to Britain. But despite the probing, all that Graham's sister and her husband could establish about his line of work was that it had something to do with death. 'It seemed that he was very much into graves,' explains Noel. 'He was fascinated by them. He wasn't weird, but he did have a thing about graves and cemeteries.'

In fact Scott Michaels had a lifelong obsession with fame and his hobby was hunting down the graves of the rich and famous. He knew virtually all there was to know about how and where various celebrities had died and the tour he used to run in Los Angeles had featured the death sites of around 80 people. 'It has definitely always been an interest of mine,' he explains. 'I first acknowledged it around 1985, when I lived in Chicago. I started going to cemeteries a whole lot and researching them. I fell in love with it and decided to turn it into a career.'

Some people might have been put off by the morbid nature of his preoccupation, but not Graham. 'Graham didn't think it was peculiar, he really liked it,' says Scott. 'When we first hooked up it was sort of a relief because neither one of us had to be the dull partner.'

Prevented from working and with time on his hands, Michaels decided to set up a website devoted to the subject. Called findadeath.com, it featured the final moments of dozens of famous names, telling in irreverent detail exactly how, when and where they had met their maker. He provided a wealth of fascinating trivia about each corpse, including nuggets of information such as the last meal they had eaten before they died.

'Worrying' is how one critic described Michael's obsession, but other visitors to the website were more outspoken. He posted some of the more disparaging emails he had been sent on to his website, including one which purported to be from Mick Jagger's daughter Elizabeth. Signing herself Libby Jagger, the model daughter of Mick and Jerry Hall had apparently sent in the following diatribe: 'You are absolute scum, the only factor which stops me feeling angry is pity, you are NOTHING, and you always will be. I hope you rot in hell motherfucker.' As Elizabeth was a friend of Fifi Geldof, daughter of the late Paula Yates, Michaels assumed her fury was a response to him including Yates's death on the site.

Elizabeth Jagger was not the only person to think poorly of Scott's project. George Richey, husband of the dead country and western singer Tammy Wynette, had apparently written: 'I would love to have a man to man talk with you in person, that is, assuming you call yourself a MAN!! I don't view you as a man!!' Michaels remained unfazed by the insults. 'George Richey is just a jerk,' he wrote in retaliation. 'He claims that I had a lot of information that was wrong on the site,' he says. 'The correspondence was pretty nasty but with every single item he said was wrong, I was able to go back and say it was right. I pride myself on the research.'

As Graham became more well known, he was able to plug his boyfriend's enterprise in newspaper interviews. Asked what websites he particularly liked, he always mentioned find-adeath.com. 'The pictures are fantastic and the stories are funnily written,' he praised in the *Guardian*. 'It's the sort of thing that's perfect for the web.'

With his sexuality in the open and with things smoothed over with his parents, Graham breathed a sigh of relief. It wouldn't be until some years later that he would realize just how difficult his very public homosexuality had been at times for his parents. 'There is one thing I feel badly about – that I didn't give my mum and dad a choice,' he said. 'By that, I mean that other parents of gay children can choose who they tell; they will keep it a secret from that nosy cow down at the filling station because she'll just spread tittle tattle. But because I was well known, every nosy cow knew anyway. My parents had no control over what was said. Sometimes I've felt a bit guilty because in cosmopolitan London it's easy to forget that if you're living in a small, closed off community such as Cork, the fact that you have a gay son on TV is a bit, well, in your face really. I am certainly aware of that.'

And as far as embarrassing his family on television was concerned, Graham admits that he could hardly have got off to a worse start. His first regular television job was in 1996 on the risqué late night Channel 4 sex quiz, *Carnal Knowledge*. Devised by the actress Maria McErlane, who had appeared in various TV shows including *Eurotrash*, *Hale and Pace*, *Jo Brand Through the Cakehole* and *The Fast Show*, it was hosted by her and Graham. *Carnal Knowledge* appeared on Channel 4 and Sky in 1996 and 1997 but was not considered to be a good programme. Asked what he thought was the defining moment of the show, Graham himself could only say, 'That 99 per cent of the straight couples said the doggy position was best.' But then again, he admitted, 'maybe it was just easy to draw.'

Mr and Mrs Walker, at home in their bungalow in Bandon, did not tune in. 'My mum can get [British TV] in Ireland, but she didn't watch that, oh no,' said Graham. 'She'd only to see the title, never mind that it was on at 20 to one at night, to tell herself, "That's not for me."' But Julie Forrester remembers switching on her television late one night and spotting her old school pal on the screen. 'I saw Graham on *Carnal Knowledge*, which was an awful programme,' she said. 'I was cringing away but I was thinking, "This is Graham, there's no pretence there."

That's what Graham is like. He doesn't have a secret side, not that I ever saw. Maybe it's a very secret side, but Graham is all out really. He's very much "what you see is what you get."'

At the same time as hosting *Carnal Knowledge*, Graham was appearing in the highly acclaimed *Father Ted*. The irony of this dichotomy was not lost on him. 'It was weird to be on the coolest show and the least cool one at the same time,' he admitted. He was doing other television and radio work, including making several appearances on the BBC2 music panel game, *Never Mind the Buzzcocks*, and was continuing to do his live shows. In his stand-up routines, Graham revelled in taking the mickey out of straight men. It was his opinion that the main difference between a straight man and a bisexual man 'is about four and a half pints of lager'. 'Straight men just can't imagine the bliss of being in a relationship with someone who finds farting as funny as they do,' he said.

It wasn't just straight men that he mocked. He was equally adept at sending himself up on the grounds of being both Irish – 'the final round of *Irish Gladiators* is called The Emigrator; the winner is the first person to end up in a pool of piss in the Kilburn High Road' – and gay – 'before I went out I cleaned the kitchen; because I'm gay, it's the law.'

His comments did cause him some problems in 1997 with the right-wing fascist group Combat 18. 'I got death threats from them and a show I was working in had to be stopped after a bomb scare,' he recalled. But his partner Scott Michaels doesn't remember it being quite so dramatic. 'It was so not a big deal,' says Scott. 'It was one night in Norwich or Leicester or some-where, and it was a gay night, it wasn't him in particular. They said something about there being a bomb in the theatre and everyone had to leave the theatre. It was one night; it was never a long-term thing. Graham has never been singled out.'

While Scott ran around after Graham and did his best to busy himself with his website, Graham's career was shifting up a gear. In March 1997, he was offered the opportunity to host a quiz show on the newly launched television station Channel 5. *Bring Me The Head of Light Entertainment* was a comedy panel game show devised by the stand-up comedian Lee Hurst and written by Iain Pattinson, a script writer for the Radio 4 institution *I'm Sorry I Haven't A Clue*. Two teams of comedians, captained by Lee Hurst and Fred Macauley, 'engaged in a battle for laughs', egged on by Graham. The rather long title of the show was often shortened to *BMTHOLE* by those who worked on it, but the abbreviation was clearly too good to resist and according to internet website The UK Gameshow Page, the production team preferred to call it *'BUMHOLE'*.

This was in no way a reflection on the show, however, which was actually considered to be rather good. It was sufficiently successful for Channel 5 to commission three further series and it also scooped a top award. In the second series, which began in January 1998, Hurst and Macauley were replaced by Paul Thorne and stand-up comic Dominic Holland. They stayed on for a third series in February 1999, but that was to be Graham's last series. By then he was too busy with his own show, *So Graham Norton*, to continue with *Bring Me The Head of Light Entertainment*. But he went out at the top, with *BMTHOLE* winning a prestigious award at the Montreux Festival for best gameshow.

'Graham knew what his brief was on that show and he delivered superbly,' says a senior executive on the programme. 'When we won the Montreux Bronze I think Channel 5 felt that it was an indication of the strength of the show. But I don't think it was. I think it was a reflection on the skills that Graham brought to it. And I think that is probably why it only managed one further series after he left. It wasn't re-commissioned after that. It was Graham who won really – it was a reflection on him rather than the show.'

After his nomination for the Perrier Award at Edinburgh in 1997, Graham was asked to stand in for Jack Docherty on his late-night Channel 5 chat show. Docherty, who was born in Edinburgh the year before Graham, had built a reputation for himself with TV shows like *Edinburgh Nights* – which Graham also appeared in – and *The Creatives* before getting his own nightly chat show on Channel 5. While Docherty was on holiday, Graham took the chair to present the *Not The Jack Docherty Show*. Graham had always loved chat shows. As a small boy he used avidly to watch Gay Byrne's *The Late, Late Show*, dreaming that one day he would be the guest – 'the one people were excited to see'. Standing in for Docherty, it was obvious that Graham had found his niche. 'It was very odd because it was like, this is the dream job and someone else has already got it,' he said at the time.

But his time was about to come. Stepping into Docherty's shoes was to be the break that would turn Graham from struggling wannabe to successful television host. In December 1997, just five weeks after his stint, he was voted Best Newcomer at the British Comedy Awards. It was an award that Docherty himself had expected to win but on the night it was Graham who was the panel's choice. They were impressed both by his performances in *Father Ted* and by his stint presenting Docherty's show.

Docherty was reported to be 'dumbstruck' when he lost out on the prestigious award. He had apparently been sufficiently confident of winning to have penned an acceptance speech. Rather embarrassingly for Graham, they were sitting at the same table and he later said that Channel 5 had put him and Docherty in a 'very awkward' position by nominating them both. The next day's newspapers reported an 'insider' revealing Docherty's devastation. 'Jack was gutted,' they said. 'Before the ceremony, Jonathan Ross told Jack he was sure he would win it. Jack thought it was in the bag and he even wrote a thank you speech. It came as an absolute bombshell when Graham won it. And it was a bit hard when the person that beats you is your stand in.' Ironically, one of the people who had helped launch Docherty's show was Graham Stuart, a television producer who would later go on to become executive producer on Graham's show, *So Graham Norton*.

Graham was presented with his comedy award by the actress Kathy Burke. 'Oh, it's an Irish homosexual,' she exclaimed upon opening the envelope. 'You are all right about that, aren't you?' she asked him, somewhat belatedly, once they were backstage.

A clearly ecstatic Graham wrote about his triumph in his *Pink Paper* column. 'The Comedy Awards themselves are a fantastically long, dull affair, but here's a tip if you are ever asked to attend: winning one really cheers the evening up,' he wrote. 'Having never won anything before, I was unprepared for just how happy it makes you.' He admitted that while he had managed to thank a radio producer that he had worked with five years ago, he had failed to mention anybody from Channel 5 or *The Jack Docherty Show*. 'Happily, they forgave me – either that, or they got as drunk as me and don't remember,' he said.

At that stage in his career, Graham was accepting virtually every job that he was offered. In one week alone, in January 1998, he interviewed Rod Hull on the Radio 4 show *Loose Ends*, appeared as a panellist on *Just A Minute*, and returned as the presenter of *Bring Me The Head of Light Entertainment*. He said he was trying to be careful because, at the age of 34 he wanted to be 'in it for the long haul', but admitted that he was loathe to turn things down in case he missed out on a shot at stardom. 'I'm not in a hit and that's the trouble,' he said. 'When you're being offered new shows or pilots you think maybe that'll be the hit, so it's very hard to say no. And if you haven't worked, and remember eating a can of beans, it's hard to turn things down.'

All that was about to change, however. In terms of breaks, winning the British Comedy Award was 'the one' for Graham. Channel 4 came a-knocking at his door with an offer he couldn't refuse. He was about to get his very own show.

8 SO GRAHAM NORTON

The decision to give Graham his own show was taken by Michael Jackson, the then chief executive of Channel 4. Jackson had started his career at Channel 4 and enjoyed a rapid rise through the BBC before returning to the station to take the top job. He considered Graham's talents to be a perfect draw for the channel's young and upmarket audience profile, and *So Graham Norton*, along with *Ali G* and *Big Brother*, would later come to be seen as keynotes of the Jackson era.

Graham was understandably ecstatic to have his own series. At the age of 35, and a full nine years after leaving drama school, he had finally made it. The fact that his programme was to go out on that coolest of stations, Channel 4, was the icing on the cake. But experience had taught him that nothing was ever that easy and no sooner had the initial euphoria begun to wear off than the doubt began to set in. What if nobody tuned in? What if it was a complete disaster and everyone hated it? After trying so hard for so long, Graham knew that he couldn't stand the prospect of having to start all over again if the programme bombed.

'In general I'm looking forward to it, it's what I want to do, but sometimes I think, "Oh sweet Jesus, it's going to be an abortion,"' he admitted in an interview. 'If for whatever reason it bombs really badly, my career will go back a few notches, and it can take a long time to come back from a big disaster. We're aiming for middling.' The pressure was on and Graham was clearly feeling the heat. 'The good thing is, I've already done a lot of things that nobody thought could possibly work,' he added, seemingly as keen to convince himself as anyone else. 'I could be proved horribly wrong, but that's where Edinburgh's useful. I can say, "Look, I did this every night for a month and it only bombed once." '

To begin with, Graham wasn't even sure if he wanted the show to be named after him. 'It felt unlucky, very "look at me," ' he explained. But Channel 4 was adamant. It was Graham Norton they were 'buying'; he was the star and it was his name that would hopefully pull in the viewers. There was no sense in leaving his name out of the title. Graham graciously admitted defeat and must secretly have been thrilled to see his name in lights. The show's title, *So Graham Norton*, was chosen in honour of his habit of enthusiastically prefixing 'Sooo' in front of practically everything he said.

It was Graham's show and he wanted to have full control over it. But with power comes responsibility, and this was a sobering thought that had not escaped him. 'If you're a guest on someone's show, it's never your fault if it's a pile of cack,' he said. 'I wanted to have complete ownership, for the mistakes to be my own, but now it's down to me it could be very damaging, and that has dawned on me.' Having his name in the title was definitely an added source of pressure. 'I've been built up so I can spectacularly fail with this,' he worried. 'People might see me as a special-needs pupil – "He was rubbish, but my God he was trying." It's God's joke, "Let him think he's successful, give him his own show, and then watch him die on his arse."' Graham was clearly a jittery bundle of nerves. 'The higher your profile becomes, the more aware you are that people out there might hate you,' he continued. 'That's a new experience for me because up till now I have just pottered along doing late night shows and Edinburgh and haven't had much attention. Suddenly I've realized it is not all sunshine and light.'

So Graham Norton was scheduled to begin a seven-week run in July 1998. It would be, Graham explained, 'More Barrymore than Parkinson. It's a mixture of guests and interviews – essentially like a thousand other shows, except with me presenting it,' he said. The series was made by United Film and Television, the production company behind *Bring Me The Head of Light Entertainment*, and the senior executives chosen for the show had between them worked on some of Channel 4's most popular comedy shows. The director Steve Smith had previously worked on *Clive Anderson Talks Back* and would go on to direct *Da Ali G Show*. The producer was Jon Magnusson, who had produced Griff Rhys Jones and Mel Smith's television series, *Alas Smith & Jones*. And the executive producer of the series was Graham Stuart, who had helped launch *The Jack Docherty Show* on Channel 5.

But despite the experienced back-up, Graham suffered bouts of insomnia during the planning stage of the first series. 'I used to wake in the night, having a panic attack,' he later admitted. 'I was shallow breathing and gasping for air, it was awful. I thought, "God, is this going to be the future?" So I gave myself a good talking to and convinced myself to care less, and it worked.'

When the series went into pre-production, Graham and the team set about deciding their 'most wanted' list. Graham Stuart had been a big fan of chat shows since he was a small boy growing up in Dundee. He believed that the secret to attracting celebrities was to make friends with their agents and representatives first, and says that this was how they succeeded in getting so many big names on the show from day one. 'What people don't realize is that it's about the way you pitch it,' he said. 'When we started *So Graham Norton* it was an unknown show but we had A-list guests in series one. We have developed a system which means we will always get big guests.'

On the subject of his own personal wish list, Graham didn't hesitate to name Dolly Parton and Cher; arguably the biggest gay icons of recent times. 'They are my favourites,' he gushed. 'Dolly is just amazing. She oozes love. And Cher is just Cher. She's much more genuine than Madonna.' Asked what he would ask them, he replied, 'Nothing. I'd just like to meet them.'

This was a very telling remark, in that it summed up, in a nutshell, Graham's whole attitude to celebrities. He had grown up idolising them for their glamour and fame and, like the ardent fan that he was, he would be satisfied merely to see them in the flesh and bask in the aura of their presence. Why should he want to ask them anything? He had an encyclopedic knowledge of celebrity trivia and arguably knew everything there was to know about his guests already. Besides, he might ask a question that inadvertently caused offence, and that would never, ever do. 'We tend to get people we just want to meet,' he said. 'And why they come on is kind of a mystery because the people we want are famous enough and rich enough so we don't have much to offer, except hopefully they'll have a laugh.'

So Graham Norton began on Friday July 3, 1998. It had been recorded the previous day in front of an audience and went out in the 10.30pm slot that generally followed the hit US comedy series *Frasier*. It was the slot often occupied by *Eurotrash* and it was no coincidence that Graham's show should be allocated this time. Both shows were aimed at the post pub 'lad' crowd, and both shows had a tongue in cheek fixation on sex and debauchery. *Eurotrash*, which began in 1993 and was hosted by the Frenchman Antoine De Caulnes, featured weekly doses of naked people, bizarre fetishes and strange behaviour from all over the continent. Among the huge array of kinky Europeans featured on the show during its 15 series to date were the Furries – people who dressed up as furry animals; Italian porn stars; and an unfortunate man who thought he was a penguin.

Other 'entertainment' was provided by Scandinavian burping contests, panty-sniffing Hungarians, and various ropy musical acts. Much of the humour was derived by dubbing absurdly inappropriate British regional accents over the voices of the various outlandish interviewees. Rubber-clad Germans would thus end up sounding like cagey Scousers. Graham had appeared on *Eurotrash* himself, reporting on a gay German soap opera. And he got on so well with the soap actors that he was invited back and made a cameo appearance in the programme on German television.

Like *Eurotrash*, *So Graham Norton* was all about sex. Graham made no apology for this. 'Sex interests me and makes me laugh,' he said. 'I think people like to talk about their own sex life and other people's, or just sex in general. It doesn't matter whether you're at a dinner party or having a laugh with your mates down the pub, you always end up talking about it.'

But whereas *Eurotrash* would have difficulty attracting genuine stars on to the decidedly lowbrow show, celebrities were to be a major ingredient in *So Graham Norton*. And as Graham Stuart had predicted, they appeared to have no problem attracting premier league names. One of the first to appear was Joan Collins, one of Graham's favourite childhood idols. Looking incredibly relaxed and sipping occasionally from a glass of white wine, La Collins was clearly enjoying herself. She didn't even lose her cool when she found herself speaking on the telephone to a man with a fetish for gloves. 'Keith' from New York was what Graham rather generously described as 'a lonely guy'. He loved gloves, particularly the ones that Joan wore on Dynasty, and apparently liked to put them down his pants. He had been found, naturally, on the internet and the hapless weirdo was literally overcome to find himself speaking to Joan herself.

Once Miss Collins had been on the show, word spread around her chums and soon they were all only too happy to appear. 'When we started the show, it was like, "God, who the hell will we get?"' said Graham. 'But then Joan Collins was a real breakthrough for us because after she appeared on the show we got Roger Moore and then people were thinking, "Well, it can't be that bad."'

When Roger Moore came on, dressed in what else but a black dinner suit, he put on an Irish accent and announced himself to the audience. 'The name's Norton... Graham Norton,' he said. And in a clever bit of camera trickery, he ripped his face off and – lo and behold! – it was Graham.

In the opening title sequence of his first series, Graham was seen taking a pig for a walk before ending up in a phone box surrounded by the calling cards of prostitutes. Spending a day with two piglets in order to film the opening credits, Graham discovered that the old maxim of never working with children or animals still held true. He shared his experiences with the readers of his *Pink Paper* diary. 'They were like the children of Satan and just screamed all day, unwilling to do anything their handler asked them,' he wrote. 'Mind you, I'm not sure how expert he was. At one stage, he confidently told us that he could get one of the piglets to look like it was drinking a milkshake. This seemed unlikely since he couldn't get the little runts to walk, which I would have thought came a tad more naturally. I walked away from the experience happy in the knowledge that I would never meet another pig.'

However, he was to meet a member of the porcine family sooner than he realized. Appearing on the *This Morning* show with Richard Madeley and Judy Finnigan, he was dismayed to see that his fellow guests were none other than the celebrated escapee piggies, The Tamworth Two. 'My life turned around to mock me,' he noted sagely.

The pilot of *So Graham Norton* included a hilarious call to a German sex line worker named Bella whose steamy efforts to arouse Graham via a translator inevitably met with failure. In his early shows Graham managed to persuade his famous guests to do and say the most unlikely things. He got Mo Mowlam to preside over a doggy wedding, Ursula Andress to tell him what Marlon Brando wanted to do to her, and elicited from Judith Chalmers the rather startling admission that she doesn't wear pants. *Blue Peter* legend Valerie Singleton shocked the audience

– most of whom were at the age to have grown up watching her on *Blue Peter* – by demonstrating how to roll a napkin into the shape of a penis; and wine expert Jilly Goolden chatted with supermodel Naomi Campbell about a dubious-sounding drink called Caribbean Love Juice which was supposed to be an aphrodisiac and was 'white and sort of globby'.

Famous gay icons were well represented, with Ivana Trump, Joan Collins, Grace Jones and Julie Goodyear all making an appearance. The internet was also a staple part of the show, and Graham and his team of researchers trawled the web for hours to come up with the world's weirdest, oddest people. For some reason, most of these turned out to be American. Naomi Campbell found herself speaking to a woman calling herself Miss Muddy Two Shoes, who became turned on by splashing around in the mud; former Bond girl Ursula Andress was connected to a James Bond pervert; and American actress Carrie Fisher was delighted to discover a Mormon website dedicated to 'Masturbation Prevention'. Helpful tips from the site included pearls of wisdom like, 'Try to be alone as little as possible' and 'when going to bed, dress yourself in such a way so as to make any temptation to touch yourself impossible.' Graham treated the sixties model Twiggy to a webcam of an unfortunate elephant keeper whose head became lodged in the elephant's bottom; and weatherman Ian McCaskill found himself talking live to a woman on a sex line.

All laughed uproariously. Even when it looked as if Graham had gone too far, as in the case of Madame Pi-Pi, who urinated into a glass via a live webcam, Graham's guest, the Hollywood actor Roy Scheider, appeared to love it. It was all down to the cheeky chappie way in which Graham handled his show.

'Graham gets away with the most outrageous things,' says his friend, the veteran entertainer Nicholas Parsons. 'In fact I think he probably gets away with more than anybody has ever got away with on television. Some people will push back a barrier and the way they deliver it means it might be funny to some people but slightly offensive to others. But Graham does it with such a naughty impish cheekiness that even if they don't laugh, people accept it and are not offended. It's a skill; a natural gift which he has and exploits. He is like a naughty little schoolboy who is showing off in front of his parents or his teacher. And he does it in such a way that he's laughing at himself. He's saying, "Aren't I naughty? Aren't I wicked?" I once described him in an introduction on *Just A Minute* as the leprechaun of comedy. He has a wonderful impish charm which everybody responds to. It reaches across all class and social barriers, and age barriers.'

But mistakes were made. Lee Majors, the former Six Billion Dollar Man, was clearly nonplussed by an item about a guy who liked to suck people's soiled pants clean. 'But it was stupid of us because Lee is a man of a certain age and he doesn't want to hear about people sucking pants,' said Graham, showing wisdom after the event. And the incident with Miss Muddy Two Shoes culminated in that last taboo of swearing – the c-word – being used on television. No sooner than it was out of the mucky woman's lips, than Graham cut the phone connection. Looking genuinely shocked, he immediately turned to his elderly stooge in the audience and said, 'Sorry Betty!' Naomi Campbell just looked blank and a bit confused.

With the weekly screening of *So Graham Norton*, Betty Hoskins, Graham's former dinner lady from the Central School of Speech and Drama, quickly became a star in her own right. One fan even devised a game called Betty's Drinking Game. For viewers wishing to take part at home, the rules were thus: You could have one drink for every time that Betty was mentioned on the show, and two drinks if you actually saw her. In some episodes you could become drunk quite quickly. In one programme Betty featured in a *Stars In Your Eyes* sketch in which she was transformed, quite literally, into Joan Collins. And who could forget the endless mirth obtained from the ongoing story of Betty's Vibrating Tongue? A grotesque vibrating tongue – 'for ladies' – was handed round and much admired by a succession of Graham's guests before being given to Mo Mowlam to keep.

But sometimes Graham foxed his guests by keeping things relatively clean. Actress Julie Goodyear, alias Britain's most famous barmaid, *Coronation Street*'s Bet Lynch, looked disappointed to be told that she wouldn't be speaking to a weirdo. It seemed that Goodyear had been gleefully anticipating chatting with an internet oddball. 'Let's ring up a pervert!' she exclaimed within minutes of arriving on the show.

Perhaps one of the most interesting aspects about *So Graham Norton* was that unlike most chat shows, the guests did not have anything to plug, promote or sell. They really were, as Graham said, just along for the ride.

Although the double – or single – entendre ruled, irony was on display, even if it was unintentional. In one instance the pneumatically enlarged glamour model Jordan was asked by Graham exactly how she would be entertaining the British troops in Bosnia, and solemnly replied, 'I will entertain them with my personality.' But Jordan proved that she is sharper than she looks by telling Graham she was sure that he could probably entertain the soldiers better than she could. And television vet Trude Mostue pondered aloud on why men like to talk about the anal and testicular area, and then went on admit that she had a 'little collection of testicles, from camels and squirrels'.

From the beginning, *So Graham Norton* divided the critics. Some thought the show marked a new low in television standards, others hailed it as a brave pioneer of a bold new kind of comedy. The *Sunday Times* declared Graham an 'Enemy of the People', criticising him for trying 'to pass off schoolboy smut as post-modern irony'. Others thought that he represented a new deal in gay performers – a man who could drag TV out of its coy, camp past and into a new era of frankness and equality. Graham, however, had no time for such pseudery. 'You just get on and do what you do,' he said. 'I didn't know we were trying to pass it off as post-modern irony, I thought we were just kind of going, "This is funny. It shouldn't be, but it is." I've certainly never said, "Welcome to my festival of post-modern irony." '

As Graham was at pains to point out, his wasn't a chat show at all. 'Because they sit on chairs there's a temptation to see it as a chat show, but it's not in fairness,' he said. 'We are aware of its failings on that front. I don't really talk to the guests at all. I just talk at them and hold up some stupid pictures of things they wish they hadn't done. The guests generally seem to enjoy it, I'm glad to say.'

He tried to be philosophical about the potential to fail. 'If it all goes wrong, I'm very good at waiting on tables,' he said. 'I did it for eight years and was fantastically rude to people. I wasn't happy in my work and sometimes I feel I took it out on the customers. I bet people watching Channel 4 now will say, "Isn't that the bastard waiter who ruined our Valentine's night?" They will phone Channel 4 duty office and say, "Where's our coffee? We've been waiting two years for it." '

Being mean to his guests wasn't Graham's style. 'I want guests to have a nice time and enjoy it so they come back again,' he said, showing that he was in it for the long run. 'I don't want anyone to be a victim. Maybe a stooge, but not a victim.' Stooge, then, would be the word to describe Miles O'Keeffe, the American actor who found himself the subject of Graham's unwavering attention throughout an entire series of *So Graham Norton*. But what started out as a wicked mickey take, actually turned into something rather sweet.

It began when Graham managed to get hold of the actor's home telephone number and kept ringing him up from the show. O'Keeffe had appeared as Tarzan in the film *Greystoke* with Bo Derek but, it transpired, had been in very little since. Graham persisted in ringing him up, essentially just to get a rise out of him. 'He likes the attention,' he told his viewers. Actually O'Keeffe did seem to like the attention and to give him his due, he took it all in good part. Graham put him on to his co-star Bo Derek when she appeared on the show, although it was obvious they had not spoken since making the film. And he even telephoned O'Keeffe's mother in Memphis and connected her to the *Jaws* actor Roy Scheider for a chat.

Graham appeared to be obsessed with O'Keeffe's career, or lack thereof, and eventually took it upon himself to ring up the man's agent in America. 'We've been stalking him,' he admitted unashamedly, before proceeding to quiz the agent about what O'Keeffe was up to work-wise. Told that there were 'things in the pipeline' – agent speak for nothing at all – he asked what sort of things Miles had been up for but hadn't managed to get. When the agent laughed, Graham came down on him like a ton of bricks. 'Oh you can laugh!' he shouted into the telephone. 'It's Miles' career!' The unfortunate agent, clearly stunned, immediately stopped laughing and said, 'Well what do you want me to do?' 'Ring people now and get that man a job!' ordered Graham.

Whether it was by coincidence, or as a result of the dressing down Graham had given him, the agent appeared to have pulled his finger out for Miles. The touching postscript was shown to viewers in the last episode of the series when O'Keeffe appeared on the show via webcam. 'I am doing a movie job here in Beverly Hills,' he said proudly. 'Thank you for having me on your show, Graham.'

A rich seam of entertainment was provided by foreign telephone directories. People with 'funny' names, such as Mr Bollok and Ms Djerkov, were telephoned from the show and routinely humiliated. Further laughs were ensured when Graham called Frank Bollok up on his Kitty Phone and the unwitting man pronounced his name as 'Bow-lock'. Other improbably named individuals included Daniel Bumgardener, Jose Cuntin, Gary Wankoff and Barry Suckoff. But the case of poor Gary Wanker proved to be toe-curlingly embarrassing for the show. Chancing upon the name in a telephone directory, Graham called him up, hoping to have a bit of fun at Mr Wanker's expense. But to his frustration, all he ever got was the man's answer machine and so he left messages claiming to be an Irish Wanker who was planning a Wankers' convention. One can only imagine his mortification when a letter arrived from the man's friend, explaining that the reason he was never at home was because he was in hospital being treated for depression. 'He came home to find a string of messages from me,' said Graham. 'Oh dear.'

Graham's preoccupation with visiting internet sites on the show prompted the *Observer*'s Lynn Barber to describe him as 'a 21st century Larry Grayson with access to the Web.' And it was perhaps inevitable that comparisons would be made with Grayson. As the seventies star of the hugely popular BBC show *The Generation Game*, Larry Grayson was arguably Britain's most famous camp entertainer. He flirted madly with his male and female contestants of all ages and managed to inject sexual innuendo into even the most innocent or banal remark. This would be achieved with an arched eyebrow, a pursed lip or a knowing look. His jokes revolved around a host of characters, including Slack Alice; Self Raising Fred, The Baker; Once A Week Nora; and his imaginary friend, Everard.

With catchphrases like, 'What a gay day,' 'Shut that door!' and 'Seems like a nice boy,' Grayson was held in great affection by TV viewers and built a long career in showbusiness with his peculiarly English form of camp humour. He had started out by performing in working men's clubs, where his material was initially considered subversive. Like Graham, he was particularly popular with women and he claimed to have found much of the information for his act by sitting behind women on buses. He got his first big break in 1971 when Anglia television signed him for *The Saturday Variety Show*. He was given his own series *Shut That Door* the following year, but it was *The Generation Game* which really made him. At the peak of its popularity, the show was attracting a now unheard of 18 million viewers. Grayson retired in 1981 and died in January 1995, aged 71.

While he could only dream of having Grayson's viewing figures, Graham's show was a cult success. This led to comparisons with a host of other famously camp entertainers, including *Carry On* star Kenneth Williams, the chat show host Russell Harty, Frankie Howerd and modern day performers like Julian Clary and Dale Winton. 'Because Graham is quite camp and gay, you could say that he is like Kenneth Williams, but he's not at all,' argues Steve Lount, who hired Graham for his first professional stand-up gig. 'Kenneth Williams was a different kind of thing altogether. I think Graham is probably the modern Larry Grayson. That is the person he most resembles. Julian Clary is camp, but downbeat camp. He is more innuendo and double entendre, whereas Graham is pretty much single entendre and in your face. Graham is trying his best to look the part. He is a nice looking bloke, but you could almost argue that Julian Clary is glamorous. He certainly wears more provocative outfits.'

The *Glasgow Herald*'s Jennifer Cunningham went so far as to brand Graham television's equivalent of a eunuch. 'In a long tradition of Kenneth Williams, Larry Grayson and John Inman, he gets away with a sexual voyeurism which would otherwise be unacceptable by parading a sexless public persona,' she wrote. 'He is to a 21st century television audience what eunuchs were to the Roman empire.' But it was Russell Harty who was *The Times*' critic's choice as the entertainer whom Graham embodied the most. 'Like the late Russell Harty, Norton has the genuinely rare ability to make celebrity guests go one step beyond the bounds of propriety,' noted Clive Davis. 'Harty, though, usually saw his task as wheedling out small, but fascinating, nuggets of conversational or green room gossip. Norton is much more interested in persuading his celebrity guests to talk dirty, wave sex aids in the air or rummage through a stranger's ancient, soiled underwear... Times move on, and Norton has carte blanche to push the barriers of taste to the limits and beyond.'

However, Nicholas Parsons argues that Graham is actually unlike any of the people mentioned above. Parsons, who has been in showbusiness for more than half a century and has seen many performers come and go, believes that Graham is truly unique. 'One of the reasons that he has become such a success is because he has established a unique persona,' he says. 'You may see shades of Larry Grayson or Julian Clary, or this comedian or that, because we all have influences in our professional life, many of which can be quite unconscious. You are unconsciously affected by all kinds of performers without realising, because you learn by observation and develop your own style. But Graham has developed his own particular style and way of doing things. He is not a carbon copy of anybody and he doesn't try to ape anybody. Some people completely copy other performers and they have a measure of success. But if they haven't got something which is intrinsically their own persona, they fall apart quite soon.'

Parsons, who was invited on to the pilot programme of *So Graham Norton* and says he was 'very disappointed' to discover that he wasn't available, adds: 'Graham has found his own niche and that is why it has taken him a long time. He is as successful as he is because he is his own person. He has never reminded me of anybody. At no stage have I said, "Oh, there's shades of X,Y or Z there." He has always come across as Graham Norton and that is the best compliment that I can pay him.'

A *Sunday Telegraph* writer agreed that it was wrong to

compare Graham to entertainers like Grayson, Williams and Howerd, but for altogether less flattering reasons. 'The association is surely offensive to men whose skill lay in the subtle deployment of innuendo, and whose mission was always to entertain in the broadest possible sense,' they argued. 'Howerd would have thought there was more to humour than trawling the internet for twisted web sites or lowering a camera down a guest's underpants. Williams' idea of what was funny went beyond displaying holiday snaps of drunken girls urinating.' The journalist was clearly not a fan of Graham, whom they described as 'a television host whose hit show, like a huge, filth-lobbing mortar, tosses into the nation's living rooms the grossest comic possibilities of sex and the lavatory'.

Graham confessed that his TV persona was much like his own. 'I don't think I'm hugely unlike I am on television, it's sort of like me with the power boost on,' he said. 'It's a fighting persona, one I developed waiting tables and doing stand-up, where meekness will leave you dead in the water.' And he was certainly larger than life. Wearing a variety of brightly coloured outfits, he was given to suddenly leaping up from the stage and running into the audience to thrust a microphone in to the face of a desperate confessor. Many of the more outrageous elements of Graham's show came from the audience. People who looked perfectly normal and unassuming would stand up and confess on television to the most peculiar and embarrassing things. Graham said one of his favourites was the man who told how he could absorb a litre of water through his bottom. 'Now how did he discover that?' he pondered. Graham received all these gems with a bemused expression that suggested he had never heard such goings-on in all his life.

There were the inevitable suggestions that some people were simply making things up to get their 15 seconds of fame, but Graham didn't think so. 'I tend to think the people in our audience are nicer than that,' he said, trustingly. 'They don't just want to be on the telly, or I don't think that's their big driving thing. If they tell a story and we think "Oh, you've so made that up just to get on TV," then we'll cut them out.' But he admitted that the bizarre and outlandish things that his audience came out with often amazed him. 'Sometimes I am left in shock,' he said. 'Someone asked me if I would ever say such things about myself, and I would – but only in a private situation, out for a few drinks or chatting with friends, when I would know that what I said was not going to hurt my mother, or my partner, or whoever else was involved. But on nationwide TV for heaven's sake? Sometimes I stop them and ask, "Are you really sure you want to tell this story?" but on they go. I'm dead sure some will have had second thoughts afterwards.'

Some might say that the reason people volunteer themselves in this way is because, in a society where celebrity is everything, they are desperate for their own small crack at the limelight. If that is true, then Graham was somewhat missing the point. But he has a genuine interest in people and it is for this reason that people will confide things to him. 'For brief spells every member of the public can be interesting,' he has said. 'You wouldn't want to be trapped in a lift with them, but everyone has one extraordinary thing about them – like their husband has been living for years with the next door neighbour.'

Sometimes there was fallout from the show, as Graham explained in a newspaper interview. 'I recently bumped into a girl who had talked on the show about having sex in the toilets on the Eurostar,' he said. 'She said her father had been appalled. Another girl told a story about her father finding a dildo in her bed and she must have thought, "Well my parents don't watch this kind of show." Wrong! They do. There was a big sense of humour failure with that family. Apparently they didn't speak for six months as a result. Just as peace was on the cards and they were about to patch it up, Channel 4 repeated the show with her confession. And it's also in the video. It's never going away.'

Sometimes the audience even surprised one another. 'We had a mother who told a lurid tale about how she once had sex in a toilet and her daughter, who was sitting next to her, was horrified,' said Graham. 'It seems like madness to me. But perhaps it's something they put in the studio air conditioning.' Not all of the admissions from the audience were tawdry, however. Some just served to show how gullible people can be, such as the young woman whose mother had told her that her father was the actor Steve McQueen. She hadn't realized the lie until she was 15.

Graham also shared riveting, behind-the-scenes details about his life as a television host with the readers of his *Pink Paper* diary. These included juicy gossip about celebrities and their various demands. Grace Jones, for example, who was one of his first guests, had proved to be a somewhat difficult and elusive person. 'We've been putting her up in a hotel for nearly a week now,' Graham divulged. 'But every time myself and the researcher go to meet her she mysteriously fails to appear. At this stage I think my chances of catching a glimpse of the Beast of Bodmin wandering through the make-up department of Selfridges are slightly higher than the likelihood of seeing La Jones.'

It seemed that the singer had the *So Graham Norton* production team jumping through hoops, and Graham shared it all with his readers. 'She flew in on Sunday night and went to the hotel room we had booked for her,' he revealed. 'She declared it too small – not for herself, you understand, but for her clothes. Following her brief "brat attack" she moved to a different hotel. She walked into the suite and loved it so much she rang us to say so. She was bouncing on the bed and gushing about how perfect it was when the phone suddenly went dead. Then Miss Jones spoke. "I just heard a bus, I can't sleep here."' He ended the anecdote by concluding, 'Viva la Diva.'

However, all's well that ends well and Grace Jones did eventually appear on the programme. Wearing an odd spiky contraption on her head, she chatted on Graham's Teddy Bear Phone to a New York man who specialized in cleaning people's apartments in the nude. Discovering that he was speaking to Grace Jones herself, the man delightedly offered to clean her apartment for free if she would only send him a signed photograph of herself. And at the after-show party, Graham was treated to the slightly bizarre sight of Grace Jones chatting over a glass of wine with his mother, who was on a visit from Ireland. However, the couple didn't talk for long. 'Not because Grace had to go, but because my mother dumped her like a hot potato the second she caught a glimpse of Judith Chalmers across a crowded room,' Graham revealed in his diary. 'I have never suspected my mother of being a lesbian, but she loves – I mean loves – that woman. My father too was deeply smitten by the queen of beaches.'

Looking back at the early episodes of *So Graham Norton*, it is amazing to see how different Graham looked. Chubby would be the kindest way to describe his appearance at that time and even he considered that his face resembled mashed potato. He weighed in at a hefty 13 and a half stone, which for someone who is five foot ten inches tall was at least a stone overweight. And although the flamboyant clothes were in evidence, he had yet fully to hone his sparkly showbiz image. He looked an altogether paler imitation of the slick entertainer that he now is.

As a recognisably gay performer, Graham realized that, whether he liked it or not, he was now a potential role model for people. And just as had happened when he had seen Larry Grayson on the television as a young boy and recognized aspects of himself, so Graham now worried about the consequences. 'I remember thinking, "Oh God, does that mean I'm going to grow up to be like him?" which, I suppose, in lots of ways I have,' he recalled. 'But I'm fine about it. But the gay people I worry about watching the programme are the young ones who haven't got a clue and who are sitting in terrible towns and the only gay person they have access to is me,' he fretted. 'It must be a horrible spectre to think, "So I'm gay. Does that mean I have to grow up into that joke. Will I have to wear shiny suits and run up and down stairs a lot?" That's where I feel some responsibility.'

He received many letters from gay fans, some of which painted a depressing picture of their lives. 'There is a false sense of happiness in London because there's such a large gay population,' he explained. 'But up and down the land, because I get letters that are miserable, things haven't moved on very far.'

He acknowledged that in the anything-goes environment of the late nineties, his sexuality was not the no-no that it would have been 30 years before. Gay characters had appeared in soaps, although as he pointed out, 'They are always so dull, aren't they?' And revolutionary TV series like Channel 4's 1999 drama *Queer As Folk* had further pushed back the boundaries of acceptable television. 'If I had been born a generation earlier, I would never have had this level of success,' Graham said. 'I have a sex life and don't try to hide it. But I'm not a gay performer. I'm a camp performer.'

But at the same time, camp was a word that he professed to hate. 'It's a very bad word,' he has said. 'It's something that I wouldn't have chosen to be. It was much harder to acknowledge that I was camp than being gay. Admitting to yourself that you are gay is a piece of piss compared to realising that you are camp. I didn't know until university, when so many people told me that I cottoned on. There is an odd self-blindness about campness. Acknowledging that you're camp is much harder because every man wants to be able to pass for straight. It's what every gay man aspires to. We fancy men. That's the point.'

Martina O'Carroll, who had watched Graham make one of his first ever public appearances when he was in *Waiting for Godot* at Cork University, is pleased to see him so apparently at ease with himself on TV. 'I think Graham's confidence is probably better today because he doesn't care what people think about him anymore,' she says. 'He's not afraid to be camp or gay. He's quite proud of who he is and what he's achieved. But 20 years ago he might have been very nervous to be gay. It must have been very hard for him and I'm sure his development must have been compromised somewhat at the early stages of his career by the fact that he was nervous about being gay. And that's very sad.'

Regardless of who was appearing on his show, Graham always seemed to be able to trot out some obscure fact or anecdote about them. Like the viewers at home, his interviewee probably assumed that he, or more likely his researchers, had simply been doing their homework. But in fact in nine cases out of ten the information was already stored in Graham's brain. 'When he comes out with a film fact on his show it is because he has lived it; he actually knows it and he would have known it in 1975,' explains his brother-in-law Noel Giles. 'The people who appear on his show are his childhood heroes. They are people that he actually knows about and when he pulls things out of the drawer it could just as easily be something he had as a kid because they literally are people he has followed all his life. Even as a young fella of 11 or 12 he would talk about programmes as a factual conversation piece. He would say, "That person was in such and such." I wasn't particularly surprised when Graham became famous because I always felt there was potential. He always was different. He didn't just become interested in comedy at 25. He was writing his own material from the age of 11.'

For the most part, the famous faces had managed to live up to Graham's expectations. But without naming names, not all of them had. 'Meeting my personal icons is truly thrilling,' he said. 'Finding some are duller than a towel sandwich is not.'

By the time that the second series of *So Graham Norton* started on November 19, 1999, Graham was on the verge of mainstream recognition. Some critics questioned whether it was now time for him to ditch the camp persona. 'If Norton is to achieve true stardom and land a job hosting a prime-time show on ITV, then he needs to broaden his appeal by tripping off down that well-trodden path of gay presenters who bland out to gain a wider audience,' advised TV critic Jacques Peretti in the *Guardian*. Peretti pointed out that Larry Grayson had done just that in the seventies by toning down his live show to host *The Generation Game*.

'The reason Channel 4 seems intent on portraying Graham Norton just so is because Norton stands at the crossroads between this tradition of popular camp entertainment and "post gay" programming,' Peretti reckoned. 'Clearly there is still a huge mainstream image for an abiding notion of camp entertainment, yet at the same time a growing appetite for a franker, modern gay image, as illustrated by the success of *Queer As Folk*. If this is the case, then Norton… seems perfectly placed to fill that nouveau niche.' And he added: 'In 25 years, when Norton is hosting *It'll Be Alright On The Night 48*, he'll look back and wonder what that camp rubbish at the beginning of his career was really all about.'

But Graham reckoned that a lot of his appeal was down to the simple fact of his being Irish. 'Terry Wogan said the Irish thing made you classless,' he explained. 'It was one less thing between the audience and you. You came on and spoke and they weren't thinking, "He's posher than us or he's working class so he hates me." And I think there is also a huge amount of Irish guilt for making us eat all those diseased potatoes. They laugh out of guilt – "Oh dear, we starved his forefathers, we had better laugh." '

Graham revealed that his mother was not particularly shocked by his show. 'Occasionally, Mum will ask why I had to show certain things,' he said. 'After the show she'll call and say something like, "I did really enjoy the show, but there was no need for that business with the donkey." But then I'll cajole her into saying it was funny and she'll agree. I've seen her laughing at quite rude things, so I think secretly she does quite like it.' And according to former school friend Helen Dean, Rhoda has a good sense of humour herself. 'It's the humour of the young, so why should any of us think bad of it,' said Mrs Walker in a rare interview with the *Daily Mail*. 'It is different from what humour was when I was growing up, but you've got to admit, it is very funny. I watch every show and no one need take offence. I don't, even when I don't understand some of the words. We all need a good laugh.' But when Miss Muddy Two Shoes blurted out the dreaded c-word on the show, Rhoda Walker couldn't for the life of her work out what she had said. 'My mum rang up to say, "I don't know what that women said, I couldn't make it out even when I rewound it,"' Graham explained. 'She was desperate to be offended, but was let down by her hearing.'

Graham admitted that it was one of the proudest moments of his life when he invited his parents over to watch him record the show with Grace Jones. 'It was certainly one of my most liberating moments and my parents got to see for themselves what I do for a living,' he explained. 'It was fantastic. It was like I can finally do something – and stick at it.'

In May 1999, Graham also presided over another new show, *Unzipped*. It was a documentary-style series exploring the fame culture, covering football, television, politics, fashion, movies and royalty. 'I just love scandal and dirt,' he admitted. But even with the unsavoury people that he featured, like the girl who would sleep only with footballers, he resolutely failed to put the boot in and be nasty about them. This went for his *So Graham*

Norton audience too. 'My absolute downfall is when I've met the person, because by and large people are really nice,' he admitted.

'Unlike the daytime confessional shows we don't judge them, we celebrate them. These are very like the stories people tell on Kilroy or Trisha, but there they would be told, "I beg you to seek help." We, however, just cheer and say, "Hey! Good for you! You got blind drunk and fell over in a mountain of your own vomit, that's really fantastic, we're thrilled for you!" We don't judge mistakes, we celebrate them, and perhaps that's why people are happy to talk.'

With few exceptions, Graham was never less than deeply reverential towards his celebrity guests. 'I don't see the point in hurting people,' he says. 'On *So Graham Norton* only two guests have walked away unhappy.' But even then, he wouldn't say who they were. 'We only involve people as far as they want to be and I don't like watching guests squirm,' he said. 'I have to turn off some TV shows because I just can't watch. By and large people have walked away happy.' One noticeable exception was Raquel Welch. When she appeared on his show she was so frosty that he ended up calling her a 'grumpy bitch' and cutting her satellite link. She had advised Graham to 'aim for a higher level of taste'. 'She was just being so annoying and the audience turned against her,' he explained.

Although he was almost never rude to his guests, Graham wasn't afraid to have a bitch at other celebrities when the mood took him. Taking a swipe at the *EastEnders* actress-turned-singer, he said: 'Look at Martine McCutcheon. She gets up and sings, "This is My Moment" and you think, "Too right, love." ' He also had a pop at Geri Halliwell, who had just walked out on the Spice Girls to go solo. 'Am I the only person who is having sleepless nights worrying about the departure of Ginger Geri?' he asked his *Pink Paper* readers. 'Not only has she spent the last 12 months slowly growing to resemble Karl Malden, but she has just walked away from the only decent job she has ever had. Her CV is fairly eccentric to say the least. On one line she's got "Topless TV hostess in Turkey" and the next line is "Multi-million pound earning superstar with a wide range of birth certificates". At this late stage in the game her only realistic career option is to accept all those jobs that Cilla Black turns down.'

Graham even dared to criticize that most famous of all gay icons, the late Diana, Princess of Wales. Writing in the *Pink Paper* in 1998, a year after her death, he said: 'I'm struck by just how unremarkable she was. A mother of two who did some charity work – fabulous, but I doubt she ever broke a sweat.'

The side of himself that Graham revealed in his *Pink Paper* diary was somewhat at odds with his more public television persona. While Graham Norton the TV star was fluffy, funny and non-threatening, his monthly column displayed an altogether more outspoken, at times even angry individual. 'The age of consent fiasco, the General Synod's vote, Radio 5 cancelling *Out This Week*, suddenly everything isn't going our way,' he complained in September 1998. 'We are discriminated against. We are, and it's not a word to use lightly, oppressed.'

He could be sarcastic too. Writing about his experiences at Glastonbury – or Straight Pride as he called it – he claimed nothing could convey the full horror and dreariness of it all. But sitting in a plastic chair and holding a pint of lager, he suddenly had an idea. 'James Cameron shouldn't do a *Titanic* sequel,' he said. 'Instead he should do a companion film, *Glastonbury*. I know it doesn't sound like an obvious hit but I for one would pay good money to see Leonardo and Kate falling 50 feet into a latrine.' And appearing on Gay Byrne's *The Late, Late Show* in Ireland, he was amused to find himself on with the eccentric singer Sinead O'Connor who had just been ordained as a priest. 'It was a bit scary watching her,' he said. 'Oh, all right, it was fun watching someone having a breakdown on live television,' he added. But appearing on the *The Late, Late Show* had been one of his life's ambitions and meeting Byrne, his childhood idol, did not disappoint. 'I was a guest on one of his last ever shows and I thought if I'm still working in 37 years, I hope I'm still enjoying it as much as he is,' he said in awe.

With his star firmly in the ascent at Channel 4, Graham was the natural choice to host the station's *Staying In Party* to celebrate the coming out of American comedian Ellen de Generes in her own sitcom, *Ellen*. 'The actual evening was a nightmare,' he said. 'There were all these egos floating around the room anticipating becoming Ellen's best friend.' The evening's events were duly shared with Graham's readers in the *Pink Paper*. 'As the time drew near to meet Ellen, I was very excited but not really nervous,' he said. 'Our first encounter was over dinner and conversation was surprisingly easy. Then someone mentioned George Michael, and I made some lame joke about his only crime being the misuse of a Nicorette patch (apparently you are only supposed to apply them above the waist). "Oh, that's rubbish," Ellen replied. "I spoke to him just after it happened." Suddenly I realized I wasn't just talking to another famous person, I was talking to a really famous person.'

Graham was very proud of the concept behind the *Staying In* programme and said he hoped that the evening 'didn't alienate people or make too many gay teenagers want to commit suicide.' He knew from experience how inept the media's handling of homosexuality could at times be. 'When I watch gay programmes or documentaries I do cringe sometimes and think, "God, I don't want the neighbours to think I'm one of them,"' he said.

It was the often negative stereotyping of homosexuals that prompted Graham to have a pop at the singer George Michael in his *Pink Paper* column. Michael had just been arrested for performing a lewd act in a Los Angeles public toilet and the burning question that everyone wanted to know, claimed Graham, was would Elton John sing at his trial? Graham suggested a sensitive reworking of one of his old classics – as the singer had done at Princess Diana's funeral – and proposed 'I Guess That's Why They Call Them The Loos'. Graham could not understand what had possessed George Michael to do what he had. 'Why would someone with £50 million in the bank and a $4 million mansion just down the road be spending his after-noons with his drawers around his knees in a public toilet?' he pondered. On a more serious note, he was disappointed by the bad publicity that the singer had brought on the homosexual community. 'Yet again the world is forced to see gay men reduced to sex-obsessed dogs snuffling around in a twilight world,' Graham wrote. 'No matter that George has had seven top ten albums and 25 top ten singles – for ever more he'll just be a really famous wanker.'

Graham was involved in gay issues and always made a point of attending the annual Gay Pride rally in London. But he was sensitive to how certain topics might be construed by some sections of society, particularly delicate matters like the debate on the age of consent. Asked to speak on the subject at a Stonewall event attended by MPs from various parties, he admitted that he couldn't help but feel awkward. He explained his dilemma in his diary column. 'The equal age of consent is such a tricky issue, because no matter how fervently you support the concept of equality, if you speak in favour it can't help but sound like some wet-lipped, trouser-fumbling plea to be allowed 16 year olds,' he wrote.

Graham's career was going from strength to strength and after being poor for so long, he at last had a few quid in his pocket. As a result, he could afford to say goodbye to the various rented flats that he had called home since his arrival in London in 1985. To celebrate his success, in June 1999 he splashed out on a new pad for him and his partner Scott. The house, situated in a conserva-tion area of Bow, east London, formed part of an old building which had been converted. It boasted a sitting room with a 24ft high domed ceiling, wooden floors, three bedrooms and a walled garden, and cost Graham an estimated £400,000.

He could well afford it. By the end of the nineties, Graham had established himself as one of television's major players and between three million and four million viewers regularly tuned in to watch his show. In December 1999, he and his team were delighted when *So Graham Norton* was voted Best Comedy Talk Show at the British Comedy Awards. It beat off competition from Paul Merton's BBC2 show *Room 101*, and it was the second time in three years that Graham had won a gong at the prestigious event. But Graham would shortly have to make more shelf space available in his home, for there were more awards to come.

9 NORTON TRIUMPH

Graham topped off a successful 1999 by hosting Channel 4's millennium night celebrations, *FY2K*. As the station's brightest star he was the obvious choice to provide an amusing alternative to 'Auld Lang Syne' and he did not disappoint. As the midnight hour approached, Graham ensured that for Channel 4 viewers, at least, the moment that they entered the year 2000 would stay in their memories for many years to come.

Escorting a stunning blonde woman who was clad only in a skimpy red satin bikini and cape, Graham promised the studio audience and viewers watching at home that they were about to see something truly spectacular. On the strike of 12, he explained, the young lady (whose name was Helga) would trigger off a firework spectacular by shooting a ping pong ball at a target in the centre of the stage. Helga, it transpired, had a very special talent indeed: she would activate the fireworks by firing the ball from her vagina.

Looking like a very naughty schoolboy, Graham duly handed Helga a ping pong ball with his picture on. 'That's the first time my face has ever been there,' he couldn't resist quipping. As the beautiful Helga removed her panties and straddled a large mushroom-like seat, one can only imagine the view that the men sitting directly in front of her must have had. 'And you thought you had crap seats!' Graham teased the incredulous onlookers. Viewers were spared Helga's blushes but there was no mistaking the tiny object that whizzed out from beneath her cape and struck its target, bang on cue. Beat that, Andy Stewart.

'We gave the viewers a quality sex act,' Graham said proudly. 'It was such a great trick. I must say, there are very few moments in your life that you're very proud of, and the ping pong ball is one of them. It is television history.'

The second series of *So Graham Norton* was running on Channel 4 and was proving to be a ratings winner, attracting three million viewers a week. It had become a cult success and, because the audience played such an important role in the show, it was hugely over-subscribed every week. People were literally queuing up for the chance to make their confessions on TV. When he hosted the millennium night celebrations, Graham had just returned from a visit to America to discuss his career prospects Stateside. Executives at Paramount TV, the television arm of the giant Hollywood studio, had been sufficiently impressed by tapes of *So Graham Norton* to fly him to Los Angeles for talks. It was rumoured that an American version of the show could be in the pipeline and the big question was whether it would be with or without Graham.

Professionally, Graham's life was great, but privately he was under a great deal of strain. His father's health was not good and this was causing Graham and his sister and mother an enormous amount of worry. Billy Walker had not been well for some time but it had taken many months to get to the bottom of what exactly was wrong with him. 'Clearly there was a deterioration over a period of time, and we were all wondering, "Why is this happening, what is wrong with him?" ' said a family friend. Finally, in 1997 Billy was found to be suffering from Parkinson's Disease, an illness characterized by rigidity and shaking of the muscles. After being in the dark for so long, it was small comfort for his family at least to know what was wrong with him. 'When Parkinson's was diagnosed things suddenly slipped into place,' said the friend. 'When we thought about incidents that had happened over the previous months we could say, "Oh, that accounts for that." '

Graham was devoted to his dad and made regular trips home to Bandon to visit him and his mother. At one point he went every weekend for six months. In 1999, although the 72-year-old Billy was by then quite poorly, he managed to make the journey to London to watch Graham's show being made. It was a proud moment for Graham and one that he would later come to treasure. 'He and mum were so pleased to see the glamour and scale of the job,' he said. 'In a sense the show has been liberating. I saw my parents laughing at dirty jokes for the first time. It was quite illuminating to see how my mum and dad could actually sit down and laugh at filth. Because, let's be honest, that's what we're dealing in. Mum used to blanche a bit and say it wasn't quite her cup of tea, but now she doesn't even do that. Naturally it was awkward at first, I'm always their little boy, no matter how I've grown up. But at least I think I can say I haven't been a disappointment to them – a puzzle sometimes, but not a disappointment. It sounds corny, but they just wanted me to be happy.'

Graham took much comfort in knowing that he had his parents' approval. He visited his dad as much as his busy schedule would allow, but it was painful for him and the rest of his family to see Billy deteriorating before their eyes. 'Shaking is the commonest symptom with Parkinson's and over a period of time you lose the use of your legs,' explained the family friend. 'But right up to the last few months, Billy was able to get around. He was only in a wheelchair at the very end.'

The end came in April 2000. Although Graham had known that his father was dying and had tried to prepare himself for the fateful day, nothing could prevent him from being completely devastated by his death. Having spent the majority of his 37 years skipping through life without a care in the world, he was now faced with the tragedy of losing a parent. For someone whose life revolved around the fantasy world of show business and having a good time, it was a cold hard shock. And although he had his partner Scott to lean on, as well as his mother and sister, Graham was unused to showing his emotions. 'When his dad died it was just horrible for Graham,' explains Scott Michaels. 'How does anyone cope with something like that? It was a point when he realized, "This is actually serious, this is actually life," and it was a diffi-cult time for him.'

It was a visibly subdued Graham who returned to Bandon for his father's funeral. When it was over he and his mother had a long talk. Graham had been told that he had been nominated for a Bafta, the prestigious award of the British Academy of Film and Television Arts. The ceremony was to take place in London the following week but in the circum-stances Graham did not want to go. It just wouldn't be right, he felt, to attend what was basically a glorified party when his father had just died. But in the event he had no choice: his mother told him that he had to go.

Rhoda Walker knew that it was what her husband would have wanted, and she gently explained to Graham that there was no way he would have expected him to miss out on such an important occasion in his career. And so it was that Graham, still not fully convinced that he was doing the right thing, duly attended the ceremony at the luxury Grosvenor House Hotel in Park Lane.

It was a big night for Graham. Simply to be nominated for a Bafta was considered an enormous accomplishment; actually to win one was confirmation that you had truly arrived on the A-list. When Graham's name was read out as winner of the Best Entertainment Performance he delightedly raced on stage to accept his award. Being presented with the Bafta was a bittersweet moment and he couldn't help thinking that he wished his father could have been there to see him. Holding his award in the air, he did the next best thing and dedicated the trophy to his dad. 'This is for Billy Walker,' he said simply, before stepping down.

Few people watching would have known who Billy Walker was, and Graham did not choose to enlighten them. It was a highly personal gesture at a very public moment, and one that he would have preferred not to have made at all. But, as he later revealed in a newspaper interview, he had felt compelled to mention his dad to quell the gossips in his home town. 'I knew I had to say something because I just imagined people in Bandon saying, "His father is not cold in his grave and there is his son poncing around getting awards," ' he said.

But Graham's brother-in-law Noel Giles cannot understand why he should say such a thing. 'There is something else going on there because that is not the way it would have been looked at,' he insists. 'It is just a ridiculous thing to say. Of course he had to accept his award, people understood that.' Perhaps Graham felt guilty to be attending an awards ceremony when his father had just died, and was simply being over defensive of his actions. 'I felt very conflicted at the time,' he admitted in a newspaper interview six months later. 'I didn't want to go. Dad had just died, but Mum told me I had to go. So I dedicated the award to Dad, to Mum, to the community of Bandon where I grew up. Until then I had never liked Bandon much. But it is good in death. People rallied around.'

Graham also explained the different emotions he had gone through after his dad's death. 'It was sad but it was also a relief,' he said. 'You never wish someone dead, but he had been so ill. He spent the last year in a nursing home and we felt bad we couldn't do more. I do think about him a lot, but at least I had time to come to terms with his death. If someone dies of a heart attack, they are ripped away from you. At least when Dad died there was no unfinished business. We had always been able to say that we loved one another. In a way, death was a release for him, and it would be selfish of us to wish him alive.' Graham had also found comfort in the fact that Billy had lived long enough to see his achievements. 'Dad was proud of my success, I know he was,' he said.

Graham admitted that it wasn't until his father had passed away that he fully understood what had made him tick. 'I begin to see now what he got out of his life, without feeling he had to be pressured or pushed into a vocation like today's generation are,' he said. 'I don't think he ever liked his job. His satisfaction came from the simple things such as earning enough money to pay for the house, buy us clothes, feed his family – and what's wrong with that as a vocation?'

Graham's career provided a much-needed distraction from his grief and he threw himself into work. He signed a new two-year contract with Channel 4 for an estimated £750,000, but this represented only the tip of his earning potential. He was much in demand for voiceovers for things like disco compilations, and had a lucrative contract to promote McVitie's biscuits. 'Graham is always very busy, he does all sorts of work,' explains Noel Giles. 'He was working for the Australian Tourist Board for ages.' This last one seems somewhat peculiar given that Graham professed to hate Australia. 'I wouldn't go there if it was as close as France,' he once declared. He also chaired seminars on the role of the television presenter in the 21st century and, all in all, he was building up a very healthy bank balance.

Famously generous, Graham was keen to share his newfound wealth with his friends. 'I think you just have to find ways of spreading it around to try and assuage your conscience,' he told the *Observer* journalist Lynn Barber. 'You want money to be a good thing, you don't want it to alienate you from your friends so they start thinking, "Oh we can't ask Graham because we're going to a scuzzy pub." But equally I don't want to feel I can't ask my friends out for dinner because they can't afford it. I'm quite happy to pay for everyone because it's my pleasure. You don't want money to make you a social freak where you can only hang out with rich people.' Neither was he about to move to a trendy area like Notting

Hill, where many celebrities chose to live. He liked the normality of life in East London, he said, and as a non-driver he still travelled to work by tube.

Graham had been determined not to let fame change him. But he decided there was one area of his life that he would have to alter: he had to lose weight, and fast!

Seeing himself in an episode of *So Graham Norton* in 1999, he was appalled to see how fat he had become. 'I was horrified at how I was bulging out of my jacket and sagging over my trousers and how my chin was wobbling about,' he said. 'I was at my worst and had got quite porky.' Like many performers before him, Graham had realized that the old adage of the cameras adding at least ten pounds was cruelly true. 'Television cannot tell you a lie because it will show the big fat arse,' he said grimly. 'With TV, particularly what I'm doing on the show – running up and down the stairs – you do get a genuine reflection so you see how big your arse looks in some-thing. And struggling to get into your clothes is so depressing. You feel humiliated, like your clothes are mocking you.'

One can always rely on one's mother to deliver a few home truths and Rhoda Walker inadvertently put the boot in. 'My mother would ring me and say, "Oh dear, that jacket looked terrible on you. You look as if you're all squeezed in,"' Graham said. And, horrible though the prospect was, he real-ized it was time to do something about it and go on a diet.

By January 2000 he had managed to lose one and a half stone. 'It feels like a lot of weight,' he said in an interview. 'I do feel a lot more spry. But because I don't want to become obsessed I don't weigh myself. If I look in the mirror and think my jeans are baggier then that pleases me. Once you've achieved some sort of result it's very easy to just sit back and think, "Well thank God that's over, back to the cake counter!" ' But he said he was determined not to go down that slippery route. 'If I could keep it off for a year I'd be happy,' he said. 'If I had one slim summer, I'd be thrilled. I've never had a slim summer, not even when I was a teenager. I didn't think about it much, but I was never happy with the way I looked. I suppose I'd like to have been taller and slimmer.'

Although he had never eaten healthily as an adult, he said he had now become 'really good' and was eating lots of vegetables and fish. On some days he would follow a bizarre 'green and white diet', only eating food in those colours. But frustratingly, hardly anyone had commented on his weight loss. That was all right, however, because newspaper feature writers are always keen to write about the rich and famous' battles with the bulge. 'I got into it slowly,' he told the *Mirror*'s Nina Myskow. 'I've never followed a diet, never bought a book, never counted a calorie. I can't make myself that miserable. And I'm not going to cut out booze. Life's too short. And it's not like I've got the potential to be an Adonis.' He liked to drink, especially vodka and tonic or white wine, and couldn't bear to give up his favourite food, potatoes. 'It is absolutely the comfort factor,' he enthused. 'It's almost like I could go to sleep on a bed of mashed potato. It's so incredibly satisfying.'

Graham confessed that he had been driven to lose weight purely by vanity, not for health reasons. 'I'd never have lost weight without television,' he said. 'If I wasn't on TV I wouldn't have bothered because it is so boring thinking about what you're eating and going exercising and all that stuff. I'm 36 now and you sort of think, "Maybe it's just time to let it go," but watching myself I just couldn't bear it.' What had really helped him shed the pounds was enrolling at a gym. 'It's the exercise, really, that's done it,' he said. 'What saved me was they opened a gym right at the end of my street. And because I hadn't been exercising at all, the weight came off really quickly.' For Graham, whom one could never describe as the sporting type, the thing that drove him on was the thought of how slim he would look on television. He went to the gym twice a week, preferring to use the running machines and bikes because he could watch TV while he exercised. 'I'm sure I wouldn't do it if there wasn't a telly in there,' he said. But he didn't do weights. 'I have to accept that it's too late for me to get the body of a Chippendale,' he said sadly.

In the autumn of 2000, his new sleek physique achieved recognition, albeit of a slightly dubious nature, when he was voted Rear of the Year. Although he said it was humiliating having his bum photographed by the paparazzi, he took it all in good part.

Journalists sent to interview Graham often expressed surprise at having discovered him to be much quieter and shyer than he appeared on television. Quite why this should be such a revelation is unclear, as one wouldn't expect Liz Dawn to be exactly like her *Coronation Street* character Vera Duckworth, for instance, or for Barry Humphries to spend his entire life as his alter ego Dame Edna Everage. Comedian Rowan Atkinson is well known to be resolutely serious off screen, and Graham explained that he by now considered Graham Norton almost as a character. 'You would kill me if I was Graham Norton on telly 24 hours a day,' he pointed out. 'I'd probably kill myself. It would be widely annoying.' His theory about being famous was that you started out being wholly yourself, and although the real you changed over the years, the television you remained fixed forever. 'So you start off being yourself and then that becomes the act,' he explained. 'I used to be more like I am on television, but now I am not quite as full on.'

In fact Graham said that success had removed the pressure to be funny in real life, so he was amazed to see the comedian and actor Robin Williams going all out to make people laugh when he met him at a party. Graham considered that Williams clearly felt obliged to put on a permanent show for everybody. 'You think, "For God's sake, you've been nominated for Oscars, how insecure are you?"' he said. 'It was like he was afraid to stop. He was like the Duracell rabbit of comedy.'

Graham was a big hit with the young, high-spending audience that television channels and advertisers so wanted to attract. And he was particularly popular with women. This was a real achievement because Friday late-night viewers were traditionally lads looking for the cheap thrills provided by shows like *EuroTrash*. The 10.30pm Channel 4 slot had even been dubbed the 'tits 'n' trash zone'. But women loved Graham Norton and he liked them. He claimed that gay men generally felt more relaxed around females. 'I prefer women,' he said. 'I suppose it's to do with me not feeling masculine enough. I always feel I'm being judged by men because I don't know about the things they know about: sport, politics, things like that – important things that matter. And I just sort of feel I'll fail them.'

But he was not so popular, it seemed, with certain sectors of the gay community who thought he was perpetuating a negative stereotype. During a newspaper interview with the *Guardian* writer Simon Hattenstone, Graham was informed that one of the journalist's friends considered it depressing that one still had to be like Kenneth Williams or Frankie Howerd to make it as a gay man on telly. Moreover, Hattenstone claimed, most gay men didn't relate to Graham because most gay men weren't like him. 'Well he doesn't bother me because he sounds quite dreary,' snapped Graham, letting his guard drop momentarily. 'I don't really give a shit about his opinion.'

Graham was secure enough in his position as one of Channel 4's brightest stars to be able to shrug off such criticisms. And, during a break from filming his show he decided to return to a spot of stand-up and embarked on a nationwide tour. *Graham Norton Live* was a very different animal to Graham Norton the fluffy television star. For one thing he was much ruder. At the start of his act he appeared just like his TV persona, so much so that it could come as something of a shock to hear him swearing liberally. He would warm the audience up by reading them excerpts from his own teenage diary. Admitting that it was 'a touch pretentious', the 16-year-old Graham appeared to be a cross between Adrian Mole and Jane Austen as he priggishly described a holiday to France. But after the chit-chatting, it was down to business and he warned the audience that things were about to get 'serious'. The gay scene, and in particular the gay personal ads, formed a big chunk of Graham's act. People's various perversions and fetishes were shared with the audience and, on occasion, Graham would even ring them up to have a laugh at their expense.

He also told how being famous had made him a bit suspicious of homeless people. 'I'll be walking along and they'll ask me if I've got any spare change,' Graham explained. 'I tell them there will be plenty when I'm dead, but then they look at me and say, "You're that bloke off the telly!" I mean, how homeless are they! Did someone leave the television in the box they're sleeping in?'

Knowing full well that he had a desirable product that Channel 4 would want to keep on buying, Graham wanted to have ultimate control of his show. He had a highly effective team in his producer Jon Magnusson and series producer Graham Stuart, and couldn't see any reason why the three of them shouldn't make the show instead of United. Taking a leaf out of the book of the big American stars who had set up their own production companies, he decided to form his own company and take control over what was essentially his vehicle. Stuart and Magnusson were keen on the idea and in June 2000 the three men set up So Television. They each became a director and hired trendy offices in Covent Garden which, ironically, lay just around the corner from the restaurant where Graham had worked as a waiter.

As one might expect, Graham's flamboyant aura was much in evidence in his work place. An enormous portrait of him dressed as the Emperor Napoleon dominated the lobby, and there was an eclectic collection of porn in the open plan office. As the captain of his own ship, Graham was happy to go into the office every day. 'I'd hate to be one of those presenters that just comes into the studio and puts on an air of fake ownership,' he said. 'I go into the show with a real sense of ownership so that even if it dies on its arse it's my fault.'

As well as appearing on TV in *So Graham Norton*, Graham starred in a special video diary filmed in Japan. There were also rumours that a 90-minute TV movie was in the pipeline for Channel 4. Hailed as a gay version of the film *Green Card*, it was to be called – what else? – Pink Card, and would apparently be based on Graham and Scott's own experiences. To date, it has not materialised.

Graham was still managing to attract high profile names on to the show, and had even become friends with some of them. One of his favourites was *Home Alone* star Macaulay Culkin, whom he described as 'a really sweet man'. 'I thought he would be a bit weird, but he was lovely, a really nice guy,' he said. Graham had also formed friendships with Carrie Fisher, with whom he was having 'an internet affair' and the daytime TV show host Ricki Lake. He reassured his guests that they wouldn't have to get involved in 'bad things' like the internet porn or the pervy phone calls. But this wasn't strictly true. 'Of course I really do want them to and will hate them forever if they don't,' he added. Cher still proved elusive but Graham lived in hope that she would one day deign to appear.

He said he could cope with guests who turned up drunk – it was the ones who may have been doing drugs that frightened him. 'Drugs are more of a worry because you don't know what they're on and you wonder, are they speeding, are they depressed, are they on the way up, on the way down, where are they going?' he explained. 'Then there are the ones where you can't work out what they are – are they drunk, are they a bit mad, or just eccentric? People like Jane Birkin or Sarah Brightman. They are brilliant interviewees but they are quite other, and you're sitting there thinking, "How did you get to this place? Are you in this place all the time? Or have you just arrived there for the show?" But in the end I don't care, if they are funny and good.' But he clearly didn't hit it off with former Spice Girl Geri Halliwell. 'She arrived with bus-loads of people, her own caterer, all that,' Graham revealed. 'You feel like saying, "You do know you are paying for all these people, don't you? They're not here because they like you." I don't think Geri's quite got that yet.'

Filming his video diary in Japan, he remarked: 'It's amazing how I can just ramble on for hours, isn't it? It's sort of a terrible gift.' Lynn Barber agreed that it was a gift, but said she considered that Graham was 'One of those people, like David Frost or Dale Winton or Richard Whiteley, who seem to have been created for television. Mildly camp, mildly funny, likeable, inoffensive, and able to ramble on for hours.'

Watching him every week on his late night show, Graham's old school friend Julie Forrester was amused to see that he didn't appear to have changed in the slightest. 'He's very much like his TV persona,' she said. 'It didn't surprise me at all to see him on television just being himself. He was just like that at school. He would exaggerate a lot for effect, just to amuse people, not to be malicious.'

By the time the second series of *So Graham Norton* had ended, Graham and spangly clothes had become synonymous. But off-screen he preferred an infinitely more understated look. Although he still dressed expensively, he chose black Gucci jumpers and dark Versace trousers in place of the colourful Roberto Cavalli suits he wore for work. 'Because my job is dressing up, I don't feel the need to do that in life, so I don't,' he explained. 'And I hate shaving, so I get quite stubbly when I'm not working. It's hardly macho though, it's just me with a bit of stubble.'

Where his looks were concerned, Graham appeared to have a bit of a downer on himself. 'It's good to be plain,' he said. 'The plain shall inherit the earth; time is our friend. It's a mantra that gets me through life.' He explained how he had once had a crush on a beautiful man and when he met him a few years later he realized that while the Adonis's looks had already faded, he was thankfully as plain as ever. But conscious of show business' relentless obsession with youth, he did however take pains to look after his skin. 'I do a three-step beauty routine – cleanse, tone and moisturize,' he said in a newspaper question and answer session. 'I scruff too – I use an exfoliation product, but scruff sounds so much more macho.' Like many in his industry, he would be prepared to take drastic action to hang on to his youthful looks. 'I worry my eyes look baggy, so I might have plastic surgery on my eyes one day,' he confessed.

Like all celebrities, Graham discovered that becoming famous altered the way that some people treated him. But an offhand remark he made in a newspaper interview about his home town of Bandon was to ignite a bitter row in the town. Talking about how much Ireland had changed since he'd left, he described it as 'the Sweden of the 21st century'. 'And the weird thing is, my success has forced people to accept the gay thing as well,' he said. 'When I go back, lots of people come up to me in the street and are really nice to me. But I can't help asking myself why they suddenly want to be my friend. If I really fitted in I would still be living there. You see this dilemma going on in their heads. They are thinking, "He is gay but he's on the telly so that makes it ok." In the end, celebrity wins the day. I do find that hypocrisy irritating and I think that if I was a gay bank clerk living in Bandon I would probably be reviled.'

Graham's words were met with indignation and a degree of outrage by people in the town. Local politician Jim O'Keefe hit back. 'I am not from Bandon but I live here with my family and it's a fine town, a very tolerant town and most welcoming,' he told the *News of the World*. 'I see no evidence of any hypocrisy. I am really quite surprised at what Graham has to say. I am quite willing to meet with him and talk over his worries.' And Cork County Councillor Alan Coleman, who also lives in the town, added: 'I don't think bank clerks, whether they are gay or not, are well liked anyway. People in West Cork might have a conservative view when it comes to these kinds of issues, but I think on a one-to-one basis he is treated very fairly. I think to use the word hypocrisy was wrong of him, it's just that we're a little more conservative.'

Even his own brother-in-law thought that Graham was wrong to have said what he did. Noel Giles was dismayed by Graham's comments, not just because he considered them to be untrue, but because in making them Graham had broken a golden rule. 'You do not criticize your own town, it is a heinous crime,' he explains. 'You can attack the government or a multi-national company – even Ireland as a whole. But your own town is sacred. The reason his remarks caused such a problem is that it is one of the few cardinal rules here. We've had nearly 800 years of others trying to trample all over us, so you don't want your own people trampling on your own town.'

Not only was Graham reckless to have overlooked this rule,

he was also, according to Noel, incorrect in his judgement. 'It wasn't just the topic that upset people, but also that there was very little truth in it,' he says. 'There is a lot more tolerance in Irish society that people think. It is out of character for Graham to have talked like that but he is quite capable of making very vicious remarks about people if he feels like it. He can be very cutting, very sharp tongued. But he would never make a bad comment in relation to his guests, only to other people. I don't think you will ever hear him say anything disparaging or badly vicious to the guests. The remarks about Bandon were probably born out of resentment.'

That is also the conclusion that Julie Forrester reached. Julie, who had returned to live in Ireland after several years in London, says that Graham had misjudged people. 'I don't think that's true any more, that he would be reviled,' she says. 'Maybe he has just shored up so much resentment about it that he's taking it out on everyone a bit now. If you asked people, I don't think there would be many people, even now, who would consider Bandon a nice town. It doesn't really have any soul the way other towns do. There are so many different ways of life, and it does make a difference to the unity of the town. When we were at school there were many different religions. One of our friends wasn't allowed to cut her hair or wear jeans – it was some strange Presbyterian thing – and there were several different types of Methodists, all with different rituals and ways of behaving. It was an uneasy town. A bit claustrophobic. Everybody knows everyone and if they don't, they make all sorts of assumptions instead.

'Bandon wouldn't have taken a homosexual to its heart back then, but now it's really different. I think it's very tolerant now and in a way there is even a competitive aspect underlying it all – to see how much you can shock people. I think there has always been a kind of anarchicness in the town, but unless you lived here 30 years you wouldn't know.'

Graham's mother had been embarrassed by the furore that his comments had caused and was particularly upset to find herself the centre of so much attention in the town. Asked by journalists if she had anything to say about her son's remarks, she would only say: 'I am very proud of Graham.' And during a stand-up gig in London in 2001 Graham said that he didn't go home to see his mother very often, 'because she has asked me not to. I have slightly wrecked her life,' he explained to the audience. 'She used to be in the bridge club. Now, women point at her in the supermarket and say, "There she is, that's the woman who spawned the devil child. She's had the devil inside her." My poor, poor mother!'

A third series of *So Graham Norton* began in November 2000 and the question posed by the *Guardian*'s Adam Sweeting was: 'Can he keep it up?' This double entendre proved impossible to resist for journalists and sub-editors and would come to dominate many a headline or intro. The answer was that, yes he could, and it was common knowledge in media circles that the BBC had been scheming to lure him away from Channel 4 with offers of prime-time shows and lorryloads of cash.

'I've certainly been aware that people have been sniffing around,' he admitted. And he indicated that he could well be interested. 'The whole idea of mainstream really interests me, because I think what's considered mainstream is definitely changing,' he explained. 'I don't think people have changed – it seems that TV is just catching up with the people.'

As he should be – having tried so hard to succeed – Graham

was enjoying his fame. Sensitive to the fact that it would be his mother's first Christmas without his father, he invited her to spend the festivities with him and Scott in London. And to celebrate the New Year he took her on holiday to San Francisco and showed her around his old haunts. Being able to treat his mum to expensive hotels and meals out gave him great pleasure, and he realized how lucky he was to have a job that paid so well. 'It's a brilliant job,' he said. 'I'm very satisfied.' Having his own show had even laid his acting demons to rest. Well, almost. 'Doing the show I'm not thinking, "Oh I wish I was in a play," ' he said. 'Although if someone offered me a great part, sadly, I'd take it. But I should be stopped! I'm crap!'

He was happy with his life full stop. The reason he knew this, he explained in a newspaper interview in January 2000, was because of the way he had reacted to a recent household calamity. 'At the moment I think I am very fortunate,' he said. 'What made me realize was that our Christmas tree fell on me. Fully decorated. I was watering it carefully, because it was a living tree. And it fell on me. I realized I must be leading a lovely life because this upset me so much. I was traumatized. The tree had turned on me. It was suddenly an evil tree! It was as if something really bad had happened, like a pet had died or I'd crashed the car. And I thought, "No, Graham, things are going too well in your life if this can upset you this much!" I was livid with the tree. I was so upset with it! So that's how I know I'm leading a charmed existence. Truly blessed.'

But this was all to change soon. Graham's home life was about to be turned upside down as his five-and-a-half year relationship with Scott buckled under the strain of his fame.

Above: Blonde Ambition: Graham camps it up in *La Cage aux Folles*.

Above: So in love: Graham on a night out with boyfriend Trevor Patterson.

Above: Bessie mates: Graham with David Furnish, Sir Elton John's other half, at the Grey Goose Winter Ball at Battersea Power Station in November 2012.

Above: Team GB: Graham with Andrew Lloyd Webber, singer Jade Ewen and songwriter Diane Warren at the press conference ahead of the 2009 Eurovision Song Contest.

Above: Model man: A designer-stubble sporting Graham with Kate Moss at the private view of the 2010 Mario Testino exhibition.

Top: So little girl, would you like to play Dorothy?: Andrew Lloyd Webber puts a contestant through her paces in *Over the Rainbow*.
Above: Graham with four more hopefuls in *Over The Rainbow*.

Top: Finally!: Madonna appears on *The Graham Norton Show*, with James D'Arcy, Andrea Riseborough and Emeli Sande.
Above: So hilarious: Graham with guests Minnie Driver, Clare Balding and Stephen Merchant.

Above: Empty handed: For once Graham failed to win anything at the 2012 British Comedy Awards.

10 THE PRICE OF FAME

Graham may well have been feeling 'truly blessed' with his life, but his boyfriend certainly was not. While Graham's career was going from strength to strength, Scott Michaels' attempts to make a life for himself in England were proving less satisfying. Although he was pleased that things were going so well for Graham, Scott felt that the balance of power between them was becoming more and more uneven. And while he had initially been prepared to play a supportive role in the relationship, he now felt increasingly sidelined. Inevitably, their previously happy partnership began to suffer.

Scott found it particularly hard to cope with the amount of attention that his partner now attracted. As Graham's face was beamed into millions of homes every week, he was a recognisable 'celebrity' and as such his life had changed irreversibly. He and Scott could no longer do the things they had used to, like popping down the pub for a quiet drink. This had become a virtual impossibility, as complete strangers had no compunction about interrupting their conversation in order to talk to Graham, often monopolising him for the entire evening. And it wasn't just the public that was the problem. People in the industry made it clear that Graham was the person they were interested in, not Scott. When he drove Graham to his live gigs or accompanied him to showbusiness events, Scott would be upset to find himself frequently ignored. The sort of people who were only interested in talking to 'the talent', they were not inclined to be friendly or even civil to 'nobodies' like Scott.

All of this might have been possible for Scott to deal with if he had felt happy and fulfilled in his own career. But he did not. In fact he felt the complete opposite: dissatisfied and frustrated. The main problem was that, under the terms of his residency application, he was forbidden to work for 18 months. Denied the opportunity to earn his own money and pursue his own goals, Scott had no option but to rely on Graham's income. This was something that did not sit easily with him. A fiercely independent man who had always stood on his own two feet, he felt distinctly uncomfortable having basically to live off Graham. He was happy to look after him, driving him to gigs and cooking him meals, only because it was the one thing he could do properly to contribute. As he says himself, he went into 'housewife mode'. But being a housewife was not what he wanted to do. He wanted to have his own career, his own money and his independence. This was the major problem that was eventually to undermine their relationship.

Scott was also a foreigner abroad and as such he found it hard adjusting to life in London. 'It was something to get used to,' he explains. 'It is difficult to take somebody who is familiar with their way of life and put them some place totally different. It was a different place and a different world. When I lived in California I used to say I hated it because the weather was so nice and the people were so friendly. And then I moved to Britain and it was completely the opposite. It was a difficult thing to get used to.' If Scott had been allowed to work, of course, he may well have settled in much better, but as it was he soon found himself yearning to return to America.

Graham was aware of his unhappiness and sympathized with his boyfriend's plight. 'I must say, he doesn't particularly like living here,' he admitted in an interview with the *Mirror*. 'It's now his persona, you know, that Britain is crap. But I think that if he went back to America, there would be things about here that he would miss.' Graham had even contemplated leaving Britain and going to live in the States with Scott so that he would be happy. 'Would I dump all this here, and go with him to live in the States,' he mused in February 2000, when they had been together for just over four years. 'What might happen, is here dumps me, rather. In which case, that kinds of frees things up!' But Graham's career, for the time being at any rate, was based firmly in the UK and it would have been reckless for him to have upped-sticks and move across the Atlantic. 'Ideally, what I'd love is if we both had a life both places, so Scott didn't feel so much a prisoner in Britain,' he said. 'I feel badly for him.'

'A lot of the problem about coming to London was that my residency forbade me to leave the country or work for 18 months,' Scott explains. 'So I sat there for a year and a half feeling pretty much like a lump. However, during that time Graham's career was going up, up, up, and it threw the chemistry between us off balance. If you are not allowed to work you end up feeling like a kept person. You can't even pay when you go out to dinner. I have always been very independent so it was a difficult pill to swallow. I figured that eventually it would even itself out, but looking back, it never was going to.'

Scott, talking at length about his relationship with Graham for the first time, says that Graham was sensitive to his predicament regarding money. 'He understood completely,' he says. 'It was just that he had the means to pay for things and I didn't. I had always been independent but that changed by the nature of what happened. If I wanted to do or buy something I was used to just going out and doing it. I found having to ask very uncomfortable. It wasn't a problem for Graham, it wasn't something that was held over my head or anything like that, but I didn't feel comfortable about it. If I was a drone it would have been perfect. But I'm too headstrong.'

When the journalist Lynn Barber was researching an article on Graham, she went to his production company in Covent Garden to ask his colleagues what he was like to work with. To her surprise, no one had a bad word to say about him. 'They all said he's just so nice,' she wrote. 'He never throws a wobbly: the worst that can happen is he'll go a bit quiet some days.' Graham believed absolutely in being nice to people. 'I don't think you should have to try to be nice, I think most people are nice,' he once said. 'I think being cheerful and nice is just a politeness. I think if you can't be nice, you'd better stay at home.'

It was this attitude, admirable though it may be, that was to prove a major bone of contention between him and Scott. For when they found their evenings out gate-crashed by an autograph hunter or thick-skinned hanger on, Graham was far too polite to tell them to get lost. And while Scott was more than happy to do so on Graham's behalf, Graham shied away from the unpleasantness which that entailed. Consequently, the couple would find themselves spending hours on end with people they didn't want to be with, yet another intimate evening out ruined. And because Graham's natural inclination was to be nice to people, it only served to encourage their attentions. All of which Scott Michaels found to be incredibly frustrating and annoying.

'Just as Graham had to learn about being a celebrity, I had to learn to share him with a lot of people I didn't know,' he explains. 'It was weird because you do feel quite possessive of your partner and it wasn't as if we could just go out and have a couple of beers and a laugh like we always had. It became, "Oh, we have to spend an hour with this person," because Graham was too polite to say, "Fuck off." That is a British thing that I couldn't get my head around. I had never spent time around people I didn't like, but Graham would spend whole evenings with people just because he didn't want to say no to them. I don't think I'm being rude, but I will be honest and say, "Go away." And I was happy to do that for Graham. We would end up playing this game – although it wasn't a game at all – where Graham would be the good cop and I would be the bad cop. He would be the good guy and I would be the bad guy who said, "Go away." A lot of times I would just tell them to sod off, but it made Graham very uncomfortable.'

It is entirely likely, of course, that part of Graham enjoyed the attention. The reason most people go into show business in the first place is because they want to be noticed. And they were his fans after all. They liked him and Graham couldn't help but be flattered to be the subject of so much attention. 'I would say it was easier for him than it was for me,' says Scott. And Graham was clearly enjoying his new-found fame. *Times* journalist Clive

Davis had commented upon Graham's evident enthusiasm for the showbiz lifestyle. 'He certainly has a B-list celebrity's appetite for party-going,' Davis wrote. 'Even seasoned revellers on the canapé circuit marvel at his stamina.' Having people come up to him in the pub to ask for his autograph and say how much they liked his show, was most probably not the nuisance to Graham that it was for Scott Michaels.

Earlier on in their relationship, Graham had talked about their cosy evenings in by the television, sharing cups of cocoa before having an early night. 'No more partying around the bars for old queens like us, because we're not wanted there any more,' he said in a newspaper interview. 'I'm not so much drifting into middle-age – in the gay world, you get kicked into it.' This was a very telling quote. At the time Graham was overweight and feeling his age. The gay scene is notoriously harsh on anyone over the age of 30 and Graham knew that if he was to walk into a gay club, young men would probably not be queuing up to get off with him. 'Beauty will always win the day in the gay world,' he noted drily. 'If Gore Vidal and a cute window washer from Croydon walk into a gay bar, you know who's going to pull first.'

But that was before Graham became famous. Next to wealth, fame is the biggest aphrodisiac there is and as a trendy celebrity he suddenly found himself much in demand. When men came over to talk to him, usually pointedly ignoring his partner sat next to him, Scott Michaels was understandably aggrieved. It was as if Scott didn't exist, and it became an increasing source of annoyance to him. 'I was ignored, that's pretty much the downfall of any relationship with someone from show business,' he says. 'People's attitude is, "This is the star, and this is the piece of shit standing next to them." '

But if Scott expected Graham to share his sense of indignity at this, he was to be disappointed. It didn't appear to ruffle Graham too considerably. 'It didn't annoy Graham very much because he saw the big picture,' says Scott. 'He would say to me, "I do this to be able to do the type of things that we do – to have a car and have a nice house." He was very accepting of all that. But I didn't want to be Mrs Graham Norton. We would talk about that jokingly, but that is what it turned into. I was just waiting for the day when it all would even out, but that day just didn't come.'

Scott had to accept the fact that he had fallen in love with one person and ended up with another. When they met, Graham was working as a waiter and had only appeared in a handful of shows on Radio Four. But as he became a famous television star, his priorities altered and his relationship with Scott no longer appeared to be his main consideration. 'Graham changed, he sort of had to,' says Scott. 'His duties, his responsibilities, all became very different. We weren't just a couple of guys who wanted to go out and have a beer any more, things became all about him. Whatever we did was pretty much what Graham wanted to do. And because I was a stranger in England I didn't have a whole lot socially going on myself. I became increasingly isolated.'

Scott also fancied working in television but despite the fact that Graham's connections could have potentially proved useful, this turned out to be more difficult than he had imagined. 'I just couldn't get decent work in telly like I wanted,' he explains. Instead he busied himself by putting plans in place for his internet site, findadeath.com, and looked forward to the day when he would be earning money and could pay his way. He also began work on a book about the cult of *The Rocky Horror*

Show. 'I thought that when my residency came through I would have my own job, my own career, my own friends and that things would get better,' he explains. 'I did get my residency but by then it was too late. Graham and I had other problems by then. It just became too big. Out of control is a bad word to use, but the relationship had run its course. I think my residency came through in June 2000 and I moved out in December.'

Scott says that it was ultimately his decision to end their affair, but admits that he and Graham spent a long time trying to salvage their relationship. 'We did a lot of talking and Graham didn't just dismiss our problems,' he says. 'We tried working it through for a few months but it didn't work out. Eventually I took the bull by the horns and said, "That's it, I'm out of here." Once I'd left it was final – it had to be. Graham doesn't show his emotions very much – I am the more dramatic person – but he was upset. I must say, leaving wasn't the easiest thing I've ever done. It was quite difficult but you've got to do what you've got to do.'

An agent friend of Scott's had warned him early on in their relationship that Graham's career would always come first. Graham was shocked when Scott told him this, because he claims he had never thought of himself as ambitious. But he now admitted that it was probably true. 'I don't feel ambitious, I feel I have just been wandering around with my fingers in my ears and somehow ended up with a show and some money put away,' he said. 'But I know that can't be true. I must have made some decisions somewhere along the line, I must have set some goals.'

Like Scott, Graham knew that it was his fame that was to blame for the relationship failing. 'It was my success and celebrity that came between us,' he said. 'It was very difficult

200

for him because he started dating one person and ended up with someone else. I think Scott would have liked us to have worked at the relationship, but he found what happened to me during the five and a half years that we were together more difficult to accept than I did. Then again, I am the person it's been happening to. At least I had something to deal with. It must all have been wildly frustrating for him.'

Although Scott doesn't consider Graham to be ruthlessly ambitious, he always knew that he wanted to be a star. 'I believe that being famous was his intention all along and he's achieved what he wanted to,' he says. 'I don't think it was "at whatever cost", I think it was just the way things were. Whatever happened between us just ran its course I suppose. But I kind of knew that would happen anyway. I was the longest relationship he has had.' The longevity of their affair was to prove comforting for Graham as well. 'It was the longest relationship I have had, so in my eyes it was a success,' Graham said proudly.

Because they had been so close for so long, Graham and Scott were anxious to remain friends. After an initial cooling off period where they did not see each other, they appeared successfully to have made the transgression. 'There has got to be a time at the end of any relationship where there should be time away, but in any relationship I've ever been in I have always maintained a friendship because I felt they were too important not to have in my life,' explains Scott. 'Graham and I are friends, we meet each other socially and I'm happy with that. I suppose if you devote any sort of time to anybody, it is the least you can hope for. I can't imagine not liking someone enough to never see them again.'

But he admits it has not been easy. 'You definitely have to fast-track the relationship into a friendship if you want to remain sane about anything,' he says. 'You have to put the intimate side of your relationship aside and quickly move into friendship because otherwise it's quite difficult to turn on the television every night.' This last point was one that Graham too understood. 'Scott had to deal with the whole me being on telly thing, and our whole lives used to revolve around what I was doing,' he acknowledged. 'We're still friends and talk to each other most days. It's difficult but Scott was a huge part of my life and it would be very hard to imagine him just disappearing from it.'

However, if living with a television personality was complicated, breaking up with one was no less tricky. 'It's not getting any easier,' Graham was to admit, a full year after the break-up. 'I feel really bad for Scott because difficult as it is to go out with someone off the telly, it's almost worse to split up with them. You see, they just won't go away. I'm still on TV, I'm still in the papers. Scott can't leave me behind. It must be so upsetting turning on the telly and seeing me skipping around laughing. I don't envy Scott.'

Graham, however, appeared fully to have recovered from any heartache he had felt at splitting with Scott. 'I find maintaining a relationship harder than a break-up,' he admitted. 'I came out of it thinking I'm quite bad at relationships and I'm probably better off not being in one. I'm sure I'll change my mind if I meet someone, but I do quite like living alone. I've always been a hard person to be with.' When he had made the remark about him and Scott being old queens who weren't wanted in gay bars any more, Graham appeared to regret not making more of the chances he had had. 'I look back at pictures of myself when I was young and pretty and think, "Damn fool, why didn't you take more advantage of the opportunities that came your way then?"' he said in an interview. Now that he was once again single, Graham realized that he could have a second bite of the cherry.

Having shed a total of two and a half stone by October 2001, he was now a slim 11 stone and a famous face to boot. All of a sudden he cut a glamorous figure on the gay scene. On the subject of his sex life he told Lynn Barber: 'There are occasional developments – let's say my loins have stirred – but normally I'm just too drunk to do anything. I might go to a gay bar and think, "Ooh, he's very sexy," but then by the time it gets to it, I'm beyond it – I'm just wheeled off and put in a taxi.' But it seemed that having a well-known face would only get him so far. 'The annoying thing is that you'd think being famous would mean people would be queuing up to sleep with you,' he said. 'I think gay men are a lot more savvy than women. Yeah, they'll talk to me because I'm off the telly, but when it comes to sleeping with people they go for much more attractive people. How annoying is that!'

Graham had managed to keep the weight off because he knew that if he put even half a stone back on it would show immediately on camera. And he feared that if he had continued being 'Mr Flabby', as he called himself, people would have stopped watching him. 'They would,' he insisted. 'Television is a very visual medium.' But he was also much happier being slim and was justifiably proud of the physique he had honed to perfection in the gym. He had even hired that prerequisite of the showbiz world, a personal trainer. As a result, he was contemplating posing nude for the women's magazine *Cosmopolitan*. 'They do it every year, but I don't think so,' he said. 'There is a terrible bit of me that would like to do it, the vain, pleased with my stomach bit, but I'm not going to.'

But he was happy to be photographed in a vest for a photo shoot with the *Observer*. Well, almost happy. He claimed that he let the photographer talk him into posing in the vest, but within minutes he was worrying how it might look. His body that is. 'Part of me is thinking it will look like shite,' he fretted to Lynn Barber, who was doing the interview. 'But even if the body does look good, what on earth am I doing posing in a vest by a mirror?' The answer of course, was vanity. If you've got it, flaunt it. Having worked so hard to lose the weight, Graham wanted to show off his new look. 'There's a terrible bit of me that wants to do it, that wants to stand around in a vest,' he admitted. 'Because it's new! I do find myself wearing tight t-shirts and things – just because I never could.'

Graham had been relieved that the split with Scott had not caused much sensation in the newspapers. 'One of the great things about being gay and out is that the papers couldn't care less about your love life,' he said happily. '"Gay man in casual sex encounter" doesn't really zing off the page now does it?' He said that the only time the tabloids got interested in his love life was when they thought he was going out with Ben Fogle, the contestant from the television series *Castaway*. But even then, Graham claimed it was only the lure of another potential outing that had attracted the newshounds. 'Ben got door-stepped, it was mad,' he said. 'They wanted him to be gay.'

But as Graham reinvented himself as sexy, young, famous man-about-town, his antics did begin to make the papers. Now a regular at trendy London gay clubs like The Shadow Lounge, he was on one occasion reported to be dating the current Mr Gay UK. As well as having to watch his former partner on TV, Scott Michaels now had to see and hear from mutual friends just how much Graham appeared to be enjoying his single status. He could have been forgiven for thinking that his nose was being rubbed in it, but he was sanguine about the dramatic change in his former partner.

'I'm not sure it surprised me, there's not much that could surprise me anymore,' he says. 'It's been a weird trip for the last few years. Graham's a single guy and he's enjoying his success. Trailing around gay clubs may not be the route to happiness but it's what we all do anyway. It's just the nature of the beast. Graham is very pleased with the position that he's in right now and I hope it continues for him. I don't know what is going to happen in the future, but I hope that he finds somebody and settles down. That would please me. It would really bother me if he was just involved in that gay club scene because I know how shallow show business can be. And he as a human being is not. Everyone who knows him says that he is one of the most sincere people they've ever met in the business. And I think he's got one eye caught to the fact that he's never going to meet somebody – completely trust somebody – right off the bat like he could have before he was famous.'

Scott was right in this respect, but it was not something that appeared to concern Graham unduly. 'I'm not worried when people approach me in bars and clubs because they recognize me,' he told the *Sunday Mirror*. 'You develop a sort of sixth sense. Some people are pretty obviously more interested in your fame than in you. But sometimes, you might be well aware of that and still think, "Oh what the hell, I fancy you anyway, let's get on with it!" Mostly, though, I gravitate towards the people I take on trust as liking me for who I am, rather than what I am.'

Graham's life had become a dichotomy. He was anxious not

to lose touch with his old friends, but at the same time he real-ized that things were now different. 'I make a conscious effort not to be swept away by it,' he said. 'My friends haven't changed, nor has the area where I live, and I still take the tube into work. I think it's important to maintain all that.' He said he had no desire to live in a gated community and travel every-where in a car with blacked-out windows. 'I don't want a life like that,' he insisted. 'I come to work by tube. I put on a base-ball cap and pull it down over my eyes. I get on the train and read. In the morning, people are so wrapped up in the misery of their own lives they don't notice anyone else. By the evening, they're more aware of their surroundings so I usually take a taxi home.'

Only a high-earning showbusiness personality, however, could afford to spend the tens of thousands of pounds on clothes that Graham did. He loved expensive designer clothes and although they were his only real indulgence, he admitted that he found the amount of money he spent on them to be 'disgusting'. 'Sometimes I feel kind of trashy and horrible when I go shopping,' he said. 'I see myself picking up things that I only sort of like and thinking, "Oh well, I'll buy it anyway". That's when I think somebody should be slapping me across the back of the legs.' For the Royal Television Society Awards in March 2001, he went shopping for a suitably flashy outfit to wear. And, like a guilty shopaholic, he was anxious to confess his retail sins. 'The worst one I didn't do but thought about it – and the fact that I thought about it made me feel ill – was in Dolce & Gabbana,' he said in a newspaper interview.

'I bought these trousers and a shirt there and then I saw this jacket and went, "Oh, how about that?" and they said, "Oh, that's quite expensive." And I thought, "God how much can it be?" I mean the trousers and shirt were already almost £3,000 and I was thinking this was as expensive as clothes get. So I asked how much it was and they said, "£35,000." As much a house somewhere – nowhere that I'd like to live, but still! And I tried it on and it fitted like a glove, it was marvellous. And I thought, "I can't do that." But I did go out into the street afterwards thinking terrible, mind-whirring thoughts – "Is there any way I could justify that?" And luckily I did come down on the no side, but it was a bit close.'

As a television presenter, the way he looked was obviously important to Graham. But he was at pains to point out that he would hate anyone to think that he fancied himself. That might damage his carefully crafted image. 'Because what I sell is not sex and patently I am not a sex object,' he explained. 'What I sell is just a friendly, poofy chappie.' Lynn Barber, to whom he made this remark in an interview for the *Observer*, reckoned that this showed a glimpse of a rift between the real Graham Norton and the bloke on the telly. 'The real Graham Norton wants to be fanciable – who doesn't?' she wrote. 'But the bloke on the telly needs to be harmless, caponized, just a friendly poofy chappie, because otherwise how would he get his guests. His show is all about sex… but it relies on Norton being sexless.'

Despite the often-explicit nature of his show, Graham continued to come across as an innocent who was just as shocked by the things people said and did as his viewers were. The BBC certainly thought that he was 'safe' enough to appeal to a more mainstream audience and, in the Spring of 2001, they attempted to lure him away from Channel 4. To the senior executives at Television Centre, the BBC's headquarters in

Shepherd's Bush, Graham filled all the criteria they wanted in a presenter. He was young, trendy and funny and, crucially, he appealed to a very specific target audience. The four million people who regularly watched his show were almost exclusively young and upmarket with money in their pockets. In short, they represented the perfect audience profile that television channels so covet. At the time, Graham's contract with Channel 4 was up for renewal and the BBC offered him a rumoured £5 million to change allegiance. It was an attractive offer, and one which Graham considered very seriously.

It was a tough decision to make, and not just because of the amount of money involved. On the one hand, he knew that going to the BBC would raise his profile considerably and turn him into a mainstream entertainer; on the other hand he enjoyed working for Channel 4 and thought that his show was on a roll. If he accepted the Beeb's proposal it would also mean having less time to focus on his production company, So Television. And he was very aware that he wouldn't be able to get away with the more outrageous aspects of his humour at the BBC. Before making his decision, Graham sought advice from colleagues and friends, including Scott Michaels. 'We talked about the BBC offer but Graham has always been the best judge of himself,' says Scott. 'He will ask people's opinion and he will take them into consideration, but he wouldn't not do something simply because others said so. He listens to opinions but he is definitely his own man.'

In the event, Graham decided to turn the BBC down and remain at Channel 4. At the end of April 2001, he signed a new two-year deal for £4 million – a cool £1 million less than the BBC was prepared to pay for him. 'I know! It's ridiculous!' he said of the BBC's offer. 'It was just that I was so happy at Channel 4 and thought there was still life in the show. I didn't want to kill it off.' Caution had also played a part in his decision to stay where he was. 'It's lovely to get one successful show, the chances of finding a second one are not so hot,' he said. 'It seems too early to be jumping ship.' He appeared to have no regrets. 'It's the sort of thing that could have blown up in my face,' he told the *Sunday Mirror*. 'The papers would have started banging on about the BBC spending the licence fee on this idiot – and I'd have been heading in the opposite direction.'

The following month, with two British Comedy Awards and a Bafta already under his belt, Graham added yet more awards to his trophy cabinet by winning two more Baftas. He won Best Entertainment Performance at the British Academy of Film and Television Arts' annual awards ceremony, beating, among others, the evening's host Angus Deayton. 'I would feel badly, but Angus won Bafta's cash prize this evening,' he quipped, referring to the £50,000 fee Deayton reportedly received for presenting the awards. Graham also picked up the Best Entertainment Programme award for *So Graham Norton*, beating the two biggest-rated shows on the box, the BBC's *The Weakest Link* and ITV1's *Who Wants To Be A Millionaire*?

With these latest awards, Graham was recognized to have made it to the very top of his profession. 'There seems little doubt that Graham Norton has attained the lofty eminence of the bona fide A-list,' wrote Clive Davis in the *Times*. 'If you think that his show is just a saucy, slightly above average outpost of the late Friday night schedules, you are in a distinct minority.' Graham was also voted Personality of the Year at the Television and Radio Industries Club Awards in March, although he was unable to attend the ceremony.

But as his star continued to rise, there came the increasingly hostile attacks in the media. The *Sunday Times* said that, for Graham, 'anything goes and the lower the better. It's all a bit of a laugh, the subtext goes. And the studio audience does laugh, on cue, at jokes that have the cutting edge of a rotten banana.'

Clive Davis of the *Times* considered that one of the low points of the 2001 series of *So Graham Norton* came when Graham persuaded an audience member to show off a holiday snap of a gang of young women urinating in public. 'Not quite what Channel 4's founders had in mind when they launched their great experiment in public service broadcasting,' he noted disapprovingly. 'Once upon a time we used to enjoy a mild chuckle watching documentaries about the down-market inanities of Italian commercial TV. Now we beat them at their own game.' It seemed that once he had started, Davis could go on and on listing what he considered to be Graham's many short-comings. Describing his on-screen look, he said Graham was 'dressed up as if he had been going through old clothes in Elton John's dustbin. It is the laziness of the humour, not the bad taste, that is most depressing,' he continued.

Davis did have some crumbs of comfort to offer though. 'To appreciate just how intelligent Graham Norton can be when he puts his mind to it, you had to catch the live show he took on his first national tour last year,' he conceded. 'With no VIPs to flirt with, he had plenty of chances to open up about the pitfalls of fame.'

But perhaps the most scathing criticism came from the *Sunday Telegraph* writer who described *So Graham Norton* as a show that: 'like a huge, filth-lobbing mortar, tosses into the nation's living rooms the grossest comic possibilities of sex and the lavatory.' It continued: 'Like the whiff of cheap cologne in a crowded room, Norton is horribly inescapable.' Like Davis, the *Sunday Telegraph* writer considered Graham's particular brand of humour to be sadly lacking in effort. 'More than anything it is the arrogance – the sheer laziness – of the Norton concept that makes his success so depressing,' they wrote. 'The bad taste might be acceptable if it was packaged with any hint of imagination, or sufficient humility to accept that not everyone regards bodily functions as the height of hilarity.'

However, it looked like Graham had managed to win round at least one die-hard critic. 'I must be mellowing. I've started to enjoy Graham Norton's show,' wrote The *People*'s outspoken television reviewer Garry Bushell. 'The confessions at the start are still revolting – if Norton ever got a standing ovation he'd ruin it by shrieking: "Now sit down if you've never interfered with next-door's Shih tzu." But watching him and his guests surf the net for nuts and sluts is laugh-out-loud funny – if you get your kicks from laughing at the mentally ill, that is.'

For the fourth series of *So Graham Norton*, which began in early 2001, Graham managed to get Elton John to appear on the show. Sir Elton found himself talking on the phone to a deranged American pervert calling himself Rocket Man, who claimed to be wearing a spacesuit and bringing himself to climax as they spoke. And when Graham interviewed Boyzone star Stephen Gateley, who had just publicly come out as the gay member of the band, he made a point of not mentioning his sexuality at all. Top of Graham's wish list, which had now become his 'hit list', were Madonna and Dame Shirley Bassey. He had had high hopes of getting Bassey, he said, but had heard that she had been rather put off after seeing Elton John's appearance. 'I think she worries I might embarrass her,' he concluded.

But his biggest coup came early on in the series when he persuaded country and western singer Dolly Parton to come on the programme. He presented her with an embroidered pillow in the shape of an enormous bosom and she appeared genuinely touched by his gift. Laughing and relaxed, the famous gay icon was clearly enjoying herself. She later told how Graham had behaved like an ardent suitor, wooing her with telephone calls and flowers. 'I must admit that I did feel a little nervous before I went on the *So Graham Norton* show,' she confessed. 'I felt a little worried because people had told me that it was really raunchy and so different to the things I normally do. It was not in my original schedule when I came over to the UK but Graham was so sweet. He sent me flowers every day and people told me that he really loved me. I thought, "What the hell – if he is going to all this trouble to get me on the show he must be a fan."'

He certainly was. Graham adored Dolly and once he had actually met her, his adoration only intensified. 'I was always a fan, but now it's like I'm almost in love with her,' he gushed. 'She's just really lovely.' The feeling appeared to be mutual. 'When we met we clicked at once,' said Dolly. 'We were just like two little naughty cartoon kids. I love him to death.' In fact the two of them got on so well that the singer invited him to make a television show about her kitsch American theme park, Dollywood. Graham travelled to Pigeon Forge, Tennessee, in October to film the show, which was to be a Christmas special.

That too was a roaring success and the two days they were together were spent talking non-stop. 'She's really special,' Graham said. 'But I don't think you can say she's a friend – she's very busy being Dolly Parton. Dolly has to be Dolly all the time. I'm not like that. I don't have to be Graham Norton all the time – I would find it just so exhausting.'

The highlight of *Graham Goes To Dollywood* was to be Graham and Dolly singing a duet. The song Graham wanted to sing was 'Islands In The Stream', the record that had been a big hit for Dolly and Kenny Rogers. There was only one problem: Graham couldn't sing. Yet here he was, about to duet with the most famous country singer in the world. He needed help, and he needed it fast. With a flash of inspiration, someone suggested contacting the Spice Girls' singing coach Pepi Lemer. Could she teach Graham Norton to sing in less than a month, Pepi was asked by Graham's office? She said she would have a go, and privately thought that it would be quite nice to spend time with someone so handsome. 'I didn't even know who he was,' she admits. 'I thought he was an actor who was in one of those wonderful period costume dramas – Jeremy Northam – and I was so excited because I think he's wonderful. So when I opened the door and saw Graham I was disappointed. But then I realized how wonderful he was.'

Pepi soon forgot her disappointment and fell under the famous Norton charm. 'He was brilliant,' she says. 'He was absolutely wonderful. He's not a natural singer and he was the first one to admit he had never sung before in his life. He was completely frightened so we had to start from scratch. To begin with I had to place his voice. He had no idea if he was a baritone or a tenor or what he was because he had never sung

213

before. In fact his voice is quite gruff and quite deep and because it was pretty powerful and strong I had to teach him how to control it. It was coming out like a train and he kept saying, "I don't know what to do with it, how do you get up there, how do you get down there?" He was panicking and asking me to teach him what to do.

'But in the end he knew where to place his voice and he was completely brilliant. 'Islands in the Stream' is quite a difficult song to do because of the harmony, but he was wonderfully open to all the teaching. He literally had to learn the song line by line and word by word but he was a real trouper – an extraordinary trouper considering it wasn't that natural for him. He didn't want to go on to become a big pop star, he just wanted to be able to sing the duet with Dolly Parton. And we only had about three weeks to do it. Because he was away filming a lot I only saw him three or four times. He had to do a few strange exercises, which made him laugh. I got him to make a big "Hey!" sound and when he did it he was so loud that he actually frightened himself. But we didn't really have time to do exercises; that was the brilliant thing about working with Graham. He didn't have the time to learn how to sing; all he had time for was to learn how to sing that song.

'It was a crash course. He came to my house and also to the Pineapple Studios in Covent Garden. When the time came to record his part of the duet I thought we would have to be there all day. But Graham was flying off to Dollywood that morning so we literally only had a couple of hours to do it in. But he got it down and recorded it and then went straight over to America.'

When Pepi saw her pupil singing with Dolly Parton on

Boxing Day she felt extremely proud of him. 'He actually sounded all right when he did the duet,' she says. 'His voice is quite country and in the end he did the accent quite well. And he managed to keep in tune. To go from never having sung before to singing with one of the biggest country singers in the world within three weeks – and to keep in tune – is quite an achievement. It was a lot of pressure and it was nervous-making for him, but I think Graham has got such an ability to adapt. It was not the sort of thing he is so brilliant at – the wonderful gift he's got where he can do ad-libs at the drop of a hat and feed off other people. This was foreign to him. It was just him and his voice, and me in the studio saying, "No, no, no, a bit higher, a bit lower."

'I told him that he should go on *Celebrity Stars In Your Eyes*. He still needed some training to get to grips with his voice, but I said if he enjoyed it he should go on from there. I think he was thinking about it, but he is so busy. It was such a joy to teach him because he was very enthusiastic and very humble. He doesn't act like a star. He's a human being, he's lovely – a sweet man. He's got a wry look at stardom: you've got to take it all with a pinch of salt because you're here one day and gone tomorrow. If you have a long life-span you're very lucky in this industry.'

Dolly Parton, however, was less flattering about Graham's lyrical efforts. 'Boy, he sure cannot sing,' she laughed. 'He's no Kenny Rogers!' The two of them were filmed in Dollywood's newly opened water park and Dolly told how she allowed her usually immaculate image to go to the wall. 'We sat in inflatable rings in wet suits,' she explained. 'I had no make-up on and my hair was all wet. I wouldn't do that for anybody but Graham. I told him there was no way he would get me on any of the rides. I'd get on the roller-coaster, be sick and my wig would end up lodged in the trees!'

The weird and wacky world of Dollywood made for entertaining television. A bizarre theme park that combined thrill rides with the story of the singer's life, it even had its own currency. Visitors had to exchange their money for 'Dolly dollars' to spend in the park. These looked similar to the US dollar bills, but in place of George Washington's dignified profile was a picture of the buxom Dolly. Oh, and they were pink. Graham brought a few of the notes home with him as souvenirs for his nieces and nephew. His sister Paula had three children from her marriage to Noel Giles: daughters Helsa and Guenael and a son called Dylan. Graham often brought them back quirky little gifts and mementos from his travels.

Graham did quite a bit of travelling in 2001. As well as going to Tennessee, he flew to Mexico to film *Si Graham Norton*, a special programme for New Year's Eve. But when he and the team arrived in Central America, things began to degenerate into the kind of horror stories usually told by his studio audience. 'We all had galloping diarrhoea and the house that Graham was staying in had poor plumbing,' revealed his producer and friend Jon Magnusson. 'He was a bit tense about that. We all were. In fact, one day our cameraman was filming in a waxworks museum and he actually had an accident in his pants.' But the sanitary arrangements paled into insignificance compared to what came next. 'We visited a cove of witches, who told Graham's fortune and wanted to cleanse him,' Magnusson explained. 'To do that, they stripped him off and rubbed potions into his chest, before spitting tequila all over him. He wasn't happy. He let us know he really wasn't amused.'

The *Sunday Telegraph*'s television reviewer did not approve of the end result. 'Presumably Norton knew in advance that the magic wouldn't work, for were he serious about being cleansed he could start by having his mouth sandblasted,' they wrote scathingly.

In March, Graham had visited Africa as part of that year's Red Nose Day. Comic Relief, the charity co-founded by writer Richard Curtis, had invested some of the money raised the previous year in a small herd of cattle for a village in flood-ravaged Mozambique. They sent Graham and television vet Trude Mostue along to deliver the cows. The pair travelled through Maputo, where they met people who had lost their homes in the floods, and even found themselves chipping in with the hard work of farming. Attempting to plough a field with the help of one of their new cows, Graham discovered a hidden talent. 'My rows were s-shaped while Graham's were dead straight,' noted Trude. Graham did, however, manage to plough someone's mobile phone into the ground when they accidentally dropped it.

In December 2001, Graham received the ultimate showbiz accolade when Madame Tussaud's unveiled a waxwork of him. Posing obediently with his dummy for a press call, he revealed how going to the London attraction as a four-year-old was one of his earliest memories. 'I came with my parents but wasn't allowed in the Chamber of Horrors,' he said. 'I was so upset!'

By the end of 2001, rumours were rife in the television industry that Graham was about to be given his own nightly talk show. He had made no secret of his desire to go five nights

a week but the big question was – the one so beloved of newspaper writers and sub-editors – could he keep it up? He was
about to find out.

11 THE HOLY GRAIL

When the fifth series of *So Graham Norton* began at the end of 2001, Graham found himself facing stiff competition in the form of Jonathan Ross's much-hyped new BBC1 chat show, *Friday Night With Jonathan Ross*. Both went out in the same slot, and as Ross was an experienced chat show host and his programme was on a major channel, many people – Graham included – expected viewers to choose him over *So Graham Norton*. But, in the event, Graham gave his rival a run for his money and on the first night that they were pitted head to head it was *So Graham Norton* that emerged the winner in the ratings war. He was magnanimous in his victory, generously describing his success as a 'fluke'. 'We won't continue to beat him,' he said. 'He's really good at what he does. And he's on BBC1.' Graham did feel cross with the schedulers though. 'I do think it's mad putting Jonathan head to head with my show,' he said. 'It just seems rude to the viewers.'

Graham considered that one of the reasons his show trumped Ross's that first night was because he had finally managed to secure that most prized and elusive of guests:

Cher. After three years and literally dozens of telephone calls, faxes and bouquets of flowers, Graham had persuaded the singer to appear on his show. Once she had said yes, Graham immediately started to fret that the famous diva might not fully understand the humour of his show. But he needn't have worried. Cher appeared relaxed and at ease and looked as if she was enjoying herself, all of which came as a huge relief to Graham. 'I love Cher, she's just her own special creation,' he effused afterwards. 'You kind of worry that this is a woman who is used to being treated in a very certain way, and for her to let all that go is brilliant.'

It was Graham's speciality to get stars to do and say the most unlikely things. He cajoled former *Baywatch* actor David Hasselhoff to join him in a spoof *EastEnders* sketch. In the skit, David was designated the decidedly unglamorous role of Jim Branning, while Graham hammed it up as Dot Cotton. And when American actress Cybill Shepherd appeared on the show in March 2002, she caused a sensation. Announcing to a bemused Graham that she had twice slept with two men at the same time – she referred to this as a 'Cybill sandwich' – she proved to be one of the most outrageous guests he had ever had on the show. Boasting of her wild sex life, she talked about how she had known Elvis 'in the biblical sense' and could vouch that he had an impressive manhood. She went on brazenly to describe how she had persuaded him to perform oral sex on her, adding that he was 'a quick learner once he'd got the hang of it'.

She said her *Moonlighting* co-star Bruce Willis could not kiss and 'had a tongue like a camel'. One of Graham's other guests that evening was Cilla Black, who was clearly shocked by

Cybill's extreme candour and ended up calling her a 'loose woman'. At one stage Cybill pressed Cilla to reveal her own sexual fantasies and when she primly refused, Graham cried excitedly: 'Cat fight! Cat fight!' Cilla did, however, admit that her favourite cocktail was called Shag in the Grass. Channel 4 was delighted with the media attention that Cybill's appearance received. 'Anything can happen on Graham's show and on this occasion it certainly did,' said a spokesman. Cilla's son and manager Robert Willis obviously considered that the show had been audacious, even by its usual standards. 'Graham Norton's shows are known to be more than a little risqué and this was livelier than most,' he acknowledged.

At times, even Graham was surprised by the level of outrageousness that the Independent Television Commission tolerated. 'I can't believe what we get away with,' he admitted. 'We had a woman on the internet sticking a flute up herself and playing "God Save The Queen". Actually, that one got quite a few complaints and we thought, "Fair cop, we did push it a bit." But then the ITC ruling said, "No, it's in the nature of the show – people know what to expect." But, as the *Express*'s TV reviewer Jeremy Novick pointed out, Graham's sexuality went in his favour. 'Gay men have long had a free rein to go places and say things that a straight man could never get away with,' he said. 'In the grand tradition, each has pushed the boat a bit further.'

Graham's other guests that season included Gareth Gates, runner-up of the hit TV show *Pop Idol*. Graham admitted to having a soft spot for the spiky-haired 17-year-old, whose battle to overcome a stutter had won him the public's heart. 'I voted for Gareth because he's so cute,' Graham said.

221

'Hopefully his stuttering might stop now.' Thanks to intensive speech therapy, by the time he appeared on *So Graham Norton* Gates did indeed appear to have his stutter licked. Speaking fluently, he talked non-stop, prompting Graham to quip: 'Ooh! Look at Chatty Cathy. He gets his voice back, and now he won't shut up!'

Throughout the series, Graham continued to give Jonathan Ross what one critic described as 'a meaty punch on the jaw'. The only times Ross managed to beat Graham in the ratings was when his show was preceded by a blockbuster movie. Delighted with Graham's early success over the rival BBC show, in January 2002 Channel 4 announced that he was to present a new show that would go out five nights a week. The nightly chat show, typified by the successful US hosts Jay Leno and David Letterman, was every television presenter's dream and Graham was no exception. 'For me this is the Holy Grail of entertainment and I am delighted to be doing it for Channel 4,' he said. The station's bigwigs were equally pleased. 'A project of this scale and ambition could only be undertaken by a performer with equally large amounts of talent,' said Danielle Lux, Channel 4's Head of Entertainment and Comedy. 'Graham is perfect and will enter into the spirit and rigours of five nights a week with all the energy and wit that has made him one of Britain's best loved entertainers.'

The new show was to start in May and Graham was reported to have received a £1 million bonus for agreeing to the five-night format. A second series was already lined up for autumn 2002. Announcing its new schedule, it was clear that Channel 4 was pinning much of its ratings hopes on Graham's show and the third series of *Big Brother*. But there were immediately concerns that five episodes a week might prove to be four too many. 'Graham Norton has been given five nights a week, but many people are wondering just how long it will be before viewers tire of his arguably rather tiresome brand of toilet humour,' said *Sunday Express* writer Andrew Stewart.

Even critics who liked Graham's show were unsure if it was a wise move. 'Like currants in a vast but rather stale teacake, the schedules are now strewn with that most tired of formats, the talk show,' wrote Rachel Cooke in the *Observer*. 'The yacking begins early, on the sofa at GMTV, and winds up late at night with Frank Skinner and Jonathan Ross. In between, there's Ruby Wax on BBC1, *This Morning* on ITV1 and Richard and Judy's truly awful show on Channel 4. Watch all of these – or any combination of them – and you will almost certainly see the same guest twice. By bedtime, you will feel as if you've been to a particularly bad party, the kind where you nobly circumnavigated the room, only to find yourself stuck with the same red-faced bore over and over again. All of which makes Channel 4's decision to broadcast Graham Norton's successful chat show five nights a week bewildering to say the least. Lots of people think Norton is the ant's pants of light entertainment – and I am one of them. But five nights a week? Haven't Channel 4 executives heard the saying: "If it ain't broke, don't fix it?"'

Graham was understandably anxious about his new project. 'I am feeling quite nervous about it because I don't know how it will be received,' he confessed. 'We might do better things on one night and not another, so we will have to try things out first and see what works.' He still occasionally suffered from stage fright. 'Obviously, I'm not as cool as a cucumber before a show,' he said. 'I still get jittery.' But when his friend and former mentor visited him in London, Graham appeared to be pretty laid back about the new challenge. 'We didn't talk much about TV but he did say that the show was going five nights a week,' says Niall MacMonagle. 'He didn't have any concerns about it, I think he was just very excited by the whole idea. Graham's very energized. He works hard. He doesn't stay in bed in the morning, he's up and going for things.'

Series producer Graham Stuart had no misgivings. 'Going five nights a week is not a negative thing,' he insisted. 'It's not about dilution, it's about a cumulative effect. It's a risk, but also a logical progression. We regard doing a show five nights a week as the Holy Grail of television. Do you know how unbelievably talented Graham is? Of course the show's going to be a hit. We're properly resourced, we know how to land the right guests and Graham is a major star. I believe we are going to change the landscape of the schedules for ever.'

In April 2002, Graham won yet another Bafta award – his fourth to date. For the third year running he picked up the award for Best Entertainment Performance. This did not go unnoticed at the BBC, where plans were being put in place for a sufficiently powerful opponent to pit against his new show. The Beeb decided on the former *Big Breakfast* host Johnny Vaughan, whom they announced would be presenting a nightly football chat show during the World Cup. Vaughan, a Channel 4 defect who had reportedly gone to the BBC for the same money they had been offering Graham, had been hosting the *Johnny Vaughan Tonight Show* since January. His new World Cup show would be going up against Graham's show at 11pm but the Norton camp was supremely confident of their star.

'We think Johnny is a major talent,' said Graham Stuart. 'But we're very happy to go head to head with him.'

They knew that Graham would have a head start because his show, *V Graham Norton*, was to begin on Monday May 6 and Vaughan's World Cup show wasn't starting until May 31. 'I'm going to be with you five nights a week all summer,' Graham announced to his audience on the first night. 'A bit like thrush, but it'll take more than a pot of yoghurt to get rid of me.' Visibly nervous, he rather woodenly read his lines from the autocue. His first guest was an old favourite, Grace Jones, who had appeared on his show several times before. She was in the UK to sing at the Party in the Park, Graham explained, and she appeared alongside singer Ronan Keating, whose latest single was conveniently 'out today'. The second night featured Petula Clark, whose new CD had also just been released, and so it went on. It was plug, plug, plug all week. Jilly Cooper came on to promote her new book, from which Graham made her read saucy extracts aloud, and American actor Josh Hartnett appeared to promote his latest film.

From the very beginning it was apparent that people appearing on the show all had something to sell. This was in marked contrast to Graham's weekly show where, as he had originally envisaged, guests came on mainly to have a good time. On *So Graham Norton*, the guests were people whom Graham genuinely wanted to meet, but with five half-hour slots to fill he could no longer confine himself to his own childhood idols. The bald facts of the matter were that Graham needed at least five guests each week, preferably more, and to be able to sustain that number he had to take who was available. As the series progressed it was inevitable that the majority of people who appeared on the show had a CD, film, book or show to promote. Famously, down to earth actress Kathy Burke told it like it is. 'That's why I'm here,' she said, talking about her new play. 'I'm plugging really, in I?' 'There's no shame in that,' Graham replied quickly.

British television executives might be obsessed with the idea of emulating the successful nightly chat shows hosted by Letterman and Leno, but there is a crucial difference between the US and the UK. 'What they seem to forget, is that those shows are rich as Midas and employ celebrity bookers who are as fierce as sabre-tooth tigers and can draw on a fairly vast pool of A-list Hollywood stars,' pointed out Rachel Cooke in the *Observer*. 'British TV executives have exceedingly short memories: does anyone else remember Jack Docherty's ill-fated Channel 5 series or the embarrassment that was *Wogan* as it dripped its way across the evenings like a soggy dishcloth?'

Because of the plethora of chat shows on British television, competition for guests had become extremely fierce. Where once a bunch of flowers was enough to secure a famous name, professional celebrity bookers now had to bend over backwards to secure big names. Many guests now commanded thousands of pounds – sometimes tens of thousands – before they would deign to step out under the studio lights. Others demanded private planes to fly them to London, or for their dressing room to be specially decorated for their visit. A television producer revealed how one TV show had even paid for a Hollywood film star's pet to be sent away to a health farm for the weekend while they appeared on a show. Many of Graham's previous guests had been American stars, but in the aftermath of September 11, many Americans were reluctant to fly. This meant that Graham now had increasingly to look to home-grown talent for his guest list.

But Graham said he was not worried about finding enough material for his new show. 'I love celebrities, so we will have celebrities on, but the beauty about going five nights is that we will have room to have some of the people and items we haven't got room for on *So Graham Norton*,' he said. One American who was willing to fly was the famously dotty singer Mariah Carey. La Carey apparently demanded that 26 bottles of Evian, 12 boxes of bendy straws and pots of Honey Bear honey be placed in her dressing room. And she informed producers that she planned to bring along her own eight-piece tea service and her own sofa.

Graham was quick to play down any suggestions that his new schedule might prove exhausting. 'People go to work every day and I'm not digging for coal,' he rightly pointed out. However, by the end of his first week, he was feeling a bit pooped. 'This is the first time I have ever had a proper job, so I'm looking forward to the weekend,' he confided to his audience. And he simply could not wait to boast about his plans for the weekend. 'I'm going to David and Victoria Beckham's party!' he announced joyfully. 'Tune in on Monday for all the gossip.'

Posh and Becks, Britain's alternative Royal family, were hosting the show business party of the year to celebrate the upcoming World Cup. Anybody who was anybody was there, many of whom had been guests on Graham's show at one time or another. They included Sir Elton John, Joan Collins, Lulu, Sir Richard Branson, Cilla Black, Jamie Oliver, Ben Elton and most of the England squad. The party, hosted at the couple's

Hertfordshire mansion Beckingham Palace, cost a reputed £350,000 – including £15,000 for security alone. A Japanese garden had been created in the grounds, crammed with decking, bamboo and a half-mile long flowerbed. Victoria had imported 60,000 orchids and bamboo to decorate the marquee in keeping with the Oriental theme. Three hundred and fifty guests, including well-heeled businessmen who had paid up to £3,000 for their tickets, dined on sushi served by geisha girls in red costumes with the England cross emblazoned on their chests. While they ate and quaffed champagne, they were serenaded by opera singer Russell 'The Voice' Watson.

Celebrities had not been asked to pay for their tickets, on the understanding that they would bid generously at the charity auction that followed the meal. This was hosted jointly by Graham and the television presenters Ant and Dec. Among the lots were two tickets to all the England games in the World Cup, which Jamie Oliver bought for his pals, and a pair of David Beckham's old football boots, also bought by Oliver for £29,000. In all, the auction raised more than £200,000 for the NSPCC.

True to his word, Graham shared the inside gossip with his viewers the following night. He regaled them with stories of how he had been caught staring at the pregnant Posh's ample bosom by her husband. 'David said, "I don't mind,"' said Graham, showing his talent for mimicry with a brilliant impersonation of David's famously effeminate voice. Talking about the food that the Beckhams had served, he said: 'Japanese feast – two words which don't go together. I was quite hungry in the car on the way home.' He wasn't the only one. Fellow

228

guest George Best confessed that he and his wife Alex were left similarly famished. Upon leaving the biggest, grandest, most ostentatious party of the year, the Bests decided to call into McDonald's for a Big Mac and fries, but realized they didn't have any money on them.

At the end of the first week of *V Graham Norton*, the critics delivered their verdicts. The *Independent on Sunday*'s headline did not bode well. 'Ooh, er – Graham can't keep it up for a week' it blazoned. 'As a weekend, post pub diversion, it worked,' said their television reviewer Matthew Sweet. 'As a Monday to Friday fixture, regular as Paxman and Michael Fish, the host of *V Graham Norton* is – so far – failing to keep his end up… The set is now bargain-bucket Bollywood and – after an unsuccessful first night attempt to accommodate Grace Jones and Ronan Keating on the same stage – guests have been rationed to one per night.' Sweet then went on to review each episode before concluding that, 'an assiduous editor might have been able to juice enough good material from this week's run to fill, say, one edition of the old weekend show.'

The *News of the World*'s Ally Ross was harsher. 'Stats from the first week of *V Graham Norton*,' he wrote. 'Graham has: Held up three guests' crap CDs. Ripped off 2,382 David Letterman ideas. Had zero decent guests. And tried to stretch one show over five days.' He then made a joke at Graham's expense. It was, he admitted, 'a puerile, predictable, past-its-sell-by-date gag. So, do I get a job as Graham's chief scriptwriter?' The *Sunday People*'s Garry Bushell was of a similar opinion. 'I'm enjoying *V Graham Norton* – it's fun to see the smug little munchkin fall flat on his face,' he sniped. 'Norton is sharp-witted but he's a limited performer and his appeal is too flimsy to sustain five shows a week. He hasn't got the guests or the gags.'

But the viewers seemed to like it. The series got off to a strong start, with 1.7 million people tuning in the first night. Within a few weeks this had grown to just under three million an episode, an impressive figure for Channel 4 at that time of night. *V Graham Norton* had secured a 19 per cent audience share – which included satellite channels – and Channel 4 and Graham were rightly delighted with the figures. But the show was given a further boost when the third series of *Big Brother* kicked off at the end of May. Channel 4 moved Graham's show forward half an hour to 10.35pm so that it would follow *Big Brother* and viewers would hopefully stay tuned. This meant that Graham never got to go head to head with Johnny Vaughan after all. By the time *Vaughan's World Cup Extra* kicked off at 11.20pm, *V Graham Norton* had finished.

According to Jon Rogers of *Broadcast* magazine, the television and radio industry's bible, *V Graham Norton* picked up an extra half a million viewers as a direct result of *Big Brother*. 'The show has been very successful and Graham should be pleased with both the ratings and the audience share,' said Rogers. 'Channel 4 will be very happy too. His weekly show averaged 4.1 million, so to get over three million every night is excellent. One night in July, 4.4 million people were watching. *Big Brother* has definitely been a factor, but to what extent it is hard to gauge. I would say that he's picked up around 500,000 extra viewers as a result of *Big Brother*.'

As well as bringing Graham more viewers, *Big Brother* also

provided him with a rich seam of material for his show. Knowing that many of the people tuning in had just been watching the housemates' latest spats, Graham filled the opening minutes of his show by talking about what had gone on. Near-the-knuckle jokes about the royal family, particularly those lambasting Prince Edward, were also a favourite opener for Graham.

Other guests on *V Graham Norton* included *X-Files* star Gillian Anderson, singers Debbie Harry and Lulu, and *EastEnders* stars Lucy Speed and Kacey Ainsworth. Kacey, who played battered wife Little Mo in the soap, proved to be a particularly good sport, good-naturedly entering into the spirit of things by donning a pair of giant rubber pants on top of her clothes. She and Graham really seemed to hit it off, but Graham is extremely good at putting people at their ease. When eighties singer Gary Numan came on looking particularly nervous, Graham instinctively patted his arm and said soothingly, 'You're all right, aren't you?' But there were undoubtedly occasions when Graham was simply too nice. When Naomi Campbell appeared on the show Graham failed to take the mickey out of her at all. By all accounts, the supermodel is not popular with the public – she was voted the most reviled person in Britain in an online poll – but Graham missed a prime opportunity to have a giggle at her expense. No doubt with an eye to the many episodes he would have to fill during the next series, Graham seemed keener on pandering to her than raising a few laughs.

But guests were often left bewildered by the zany nature of the show. When he was talking to Ben Elton, for example, Graham suddenly jumped up and dashed into the audience to ask them if they had ever been sent an obscene message on their mobile phone. 'Sorry!' he called over his shoulder to Elton, realizing too late his rudeness. 'It's your show, Graham,' Elton replied, looking totally bemused. The audience confessions were as revolting as ever. A woman who described how she had had faeces down her leg was warmly congratulated by her friends for her admission. And some of the 'games' Graham dreamt up plumbed new depths of bad taste. Perhaps the worst moment of the series came when the audience was asked to guess the colour of someone's pubic hair. One member of the audience walked out after Graham teased her once too often. 'I'd been having a dig at her because she hadn't moved her bag out of my way, but she didn't like it and ran out in tears,' he said, seemingly unrepentant.

Betty, Graham's geriatric mascot, retained her position as chief stooge. Graham admitted he was hoping to launch her in a twilight career. 'Stairlifts and incontinence pads need advertising, and Dame Thora can't last for ever,' he quipped mischievously. Betty was frequently the butt of Graham's jokes, cropping up in various disguises ranging from elderly hooker, to legendary rock crazyman Ozzy Osbourne in a skit of his hit US show, *The Osbournes*.

Many of the guests were the same old faces: Sophia Loren, Grace Jones, Bo Derek, Mo Mowlam, but that's not to say that the show was any the worse for it. As they had been on the programme before – in some cases more than once – they knew exactly what to expect and were therefore more relaxed than many of the first-timers. Bo Derek, for example, had been far from chatty when she went on *So Graham Norton*, but appearing on *V Graham Norton* in July, she talked openly about how Jane Fonda had telephoned her and begged Bo to date her husband Ted Turner.

Mo Mowlam was tickled pink when Graham presented her with a roll of toilet paper with Peter Mandelson's face printed on it. 'He doesn't rub off on your bum, does he?' she asked anxiously. Hollywood star Dennis Hopper proved to be particularly good value, willingly joining Graham in a ridiculous *M*A*S*H* spoof. But US comedienne Sandra Bernhardt simply did not get Graham's particular brand of humour. 'You're totally gay and no-one cares!' she told Graham incredulously. 'You really are an island. No-one knows what goes on here!' But the maddest guest of all had to be the Australian crocodile wrestler Steve Irwin, who appeared on the show in July to promote his movie *The Crocodile Hunter*. Irwin, sporting the broadest Aussie accent you will ever hear, managed to make Graham look shy and retiring with his maniacally over-the-top behaviour.

One of the best things about having a nightly show, of course, was that Graham now had an excuse to buy even more clothes. Determined to wear a different outfit every night, Graham and his team of stylists took their shopping baskets around London's top designers. He became a regular customer at the capital's most exclusive shopping streets and was spotted staring wistfully at a velvet devoré jacket in Paul Smith. When the guy who was looking at it noticed Graham's interest he gallantly handed it over. Graham placed a bulk order at his Soho tailor, Mr Eddie's. 'He's making me some suits for my show,' he said excitedly. 'One is a sort of snake-skin velvet. Another one, I'm going to look like a yak in. It's sort of brown silk, with gold hair. I don't think you could wear it on the tube! It's show business. If you go to the trouble of wearing a big shiny suit, then you've done half the work.'

Every fortnight he had his hair cut at London's Fordham White Hair and Spa salon in Soho. While the barber did his hair Graham liked to have a manicure as well. But his flamboyant image wasn't to every style guru's taste. In March 2002, he was voted sixth in *GQ* magazine's Worst-Dressed Man list, coming after fellow Paul Smith aficionado Tony Blair but ahead of Jamie Oliver and Lawrence Llewelyn-Bowen. Graham had managed to keep his weight down and in May he finally agreed to get his kit off for the women's magazine *Cosmopolitan*. Quite why women would be interested in seeing Graham in the buff is anyone's guess, but the photograph was certainly dramatic. Wearing only a crown – well it was jubilee year – a strategically placed Dalmation dog innocently spared us Graham's blushes. 'I thought I'd have a shot at it so I can look proudly back when I'm a 90-year-old butterball,' he explained.

Graham had remained on friendly terms with Scott Michaels and occasionally called him for advice when he started the new show. 'Graham would still phone me up and say, "Do you know anything about this person or that person," because that's kind of my speciality,' says Scott. 'Weird facts about weird people. Sometimes I was a help to him. He has a network of people who find the internet sites but we used to do that together as well. I did watch the new show and I thought it was perfectly fine. It is the perfect show for watching with a cup of cocoa when you get home after the pub. It is what Graham has always wanted to do. He would have been happy hosting a Ricki Lake-type show. His dream was to have a talk show period. He wanted to become a boring part of every day, where everyone would say, "There's Graham on telly again." ' Graham paints a cosy analogy. 'I want it to be as comfortable as putting your jammies on before you go to bed,' he said of his new show.

Despite the impressive ratings, the view persisted that five doses of Graham Norton a week was too much. 'A lot of people came up to me and said, "I can't stand him on my television five nights a week," ' says Scott Michaels. 'That is the typical response of people who ring up Channel 4 to say that they find something particularly offensive. But I think it's a waste of time. Why not just change channel? I think it's pointless to complain about someone being on television too much because the power is in your hands. If you don't like it, don't watch it.'

And that, in the end, is what Michaels himself chose to do. Despite his initial desire to stay friends with his former love, seeing him on television night after night eventually proved too much for him to handle. In June 2002, he quit Britain and returned to America. He admits that his main reason for leaving was to put some distance between him and Graham. 'That was certainly one of them,' he says. 'It was just a little bit less hassle. I'm going back to Los Angeles to re-establish myself, to hopefully write more books and possibly get the death sites tour going again.' He is adamant that there is no chance of him and Graham getting back together. 'I can't even entertain that thought,' he says. 'If I had a problem, I could call Graham. Absolutely, there's no doubt about that. And I know that because of his work he will end up in America quite a bit so I'm sure we'll see each other quite often. I liked his friends, we've all maintained a really good friendship. I was in London for about seven years and now I quite miss it. But it is fresh starts all round.'

Leaving the country was a drastic move, but a big problem for Scott Michaels was that Graham was never out of the papers. When he wasn't winning trophies at award ceremonies he was presenting them, and his face often peered out of glossy magazines like *Hello!*. Graham was enjoying life as a showbusiness A-lister and as well as attending Posh and Becks' World Cup party he was a guest at Liza Minnelli's wedding. Along with seemingly half the celebrity population of England, Graham was invited to the famously troubled diva's wedding to producer David Gest in New York. Opting to travel in style, he decided to go on Concorde. But as the plane started to pick up speed on the runway, an engine misfired and it lurched violently to the right, forcing the pilot to abort take-off. No one was hurt and Graham and the rest of the passengers left on another Concorde, four hours late but still in time for the wedding at New York's Marble Collegiate Church on Fifth Avenue.

Graham later played down the plane drama, which had naturally made newspaper headlines. He told *Sunday Times* columnist Jeremy Clarkson that Concorde was doing around 4mph when the engine went wrong, and that a small dog could have pulled it safely to a halt. The showbiz wedding of the year, however, was another matter. It would have taken a whole team of huskies to restrain Miss Minnelli from going wildly over the top with her nuptials. Singer Natalie Cole sang 'Unforgettable' as the thrice-divorced bride was given away by her friend Michael Jackson. The star-studded guest list included Elton John, Kirk Douglas, son Michael Douglas and his wife Catherine

Zeta-Jones, Anthony Hopkins, Joan Collins, Andrew Lloyd Webber, Liam Neeson and wife Natasha Richardson, Gina Lollobrigida and property tycoon Donald Trump. Michael Jackson also acted as best man, while Minnelli's matron of honour was none other than Elizabeth Taylor. The many brides-maids included ex-*EastEnder* Martine McCutcheon, singers Chaka Khan and Petula Clark, and actress Mia Farrow.

The photographs, when they appeared in glossy *OK* magazine, had to be seen to be believed. Actor Stuart Manning, star of the daytime soap *Night and Day*, admitted that he and Graham had spent much of the ceremony convulsed in fits of giggles. 'At the church we sat in the balcony to get a good look at everyone,' he said. 'We reckon Michael Jackson had got the wrong ring. Halfway through the ceremony, he opened a box, walked over to Elizabeth Taylor, got something from her and walked back to where he'd been sitting, me and Graham just looked at each other and started giggling. And his best man's speech was the funniest thing I've ever heard. He said, "I got these guys together... " that kind of thing for half a minute, then, "Congratulations", and walked off. Everyone was shouting, "Michael! Sing!" But he just disappeared.'

Graham was even less discreet. 'If anyone wants to ask me questions about the freak show, sorry wedding ceremony, feel free,' he bitched afterwards. And hosting the Royal Television Society Awards four days later, he said: 'I told the RTS I wouldn't swear, but it has to be said – fucking hell, I was at Liza Minnelli's wedding!' But if Liza had heard what he said about the ceremony, she didn't hold it against him. She hired Graham to open for her when she made a comeback appear-ance at the Albert Hall the following month, and later appeared on his show.

But as the summer rumbled on, Graham's show began to run into difficulties. The concerns that people had raised when the new format was announced back in January, namely that they wouldn't be able to get enough guests to sustain the show five nights a week, now appeared to be coming true. The show was recorded at 5pm for transmission later that evening but, according to the *Mirror*, by 4.30pm on one Tuesday in July there still wasn't a guest for Graham to interview. 'Camp star's TV show runs out of guests,' trilled the *Mirror* headline. 'It's No Graham Norton.' After ten weeks and 50 shows, the researchers were apparently finding it increasingly hard to secure decent celebrity guests. The *Mirror* told how, after some 'frantic calling around', the show managed to land actor Jimi Mistry, the star of movies *East Is East* and *Guru*.

They quoted a source on the show as saying that the team was facing a daily struggle to get people on. 'The guests they are trying to bring in now are becoming more obscure,' said the source. 'On Tuesday everybody was literally tearing their hair out. A couple of guests fell through at the last minute and with just half an hour to go they still had no idea who they were going to get. If Jimi hadn't agreed to come on, who knows where we'd be. It's all they can do to stop Graham himself getting on the phone and calling people up.' A spokesman for the show played their troubles down. 'I don't think they're having any more difficulties than any one else,' they said.

But with a new series planned for the autumn, and in the knowledge that *Big Brother* would not be on air then, one could be forgiven for wondering if Graham really could keep it up after all.

12 MR SATURDAY NIGHT

By the time of the 2002 Bafta awards in February, Graham was feeling tired and emotional and confiding to friends that he thought he had hit his professional ceiling. 'I think it's realistic to say that I've peaked,' he said the night before the ceremony. 'I'm glad I walked away from the Friday night show with people loving it, though I know a lot of people thought it was rubbish.' But 24 hours later, having picked up his fourth Bafta, his spirits were considerably restored. And in December he was voted Best Entertainment Personality at the 2002 British Comedy Awards while the *Daily Mirror* readers decided to vote him Biggest Prat on the Box.

Worries persisted that he was in danger of becoming over-exposed. 'Friday night for 40 minutes is about enough, I think, but every night of the week people will just get fed up of him,' said Steve Lount, who gave Graham his first professional gig as a stand-up. 'Terry Wogan did it three nights a week in the Eighties and he became a bore.' These fears appeared to be borne out by the viewing figures for the second series of *V Graham Norton*, which failed to live up to the success of the first. Monday night in particular proved to be something of an Achilles heel, attracting only about two million viewers. More disappointing for Graham and Channel 4 were the figures for the Friday night shows. One Friday in December 2002 they managed to pull in only 1.9 million. 'That is particularly bad as you would expect Friday to be a popular night for the programme and it was also following *The Osbournes*, which does well for the channel,' explained Jon Rogers, of *Broadcast* magazine. 'The show's ratings have fluctuated, perhaps depending on the guest, and have been significantly down on the first series.'

Graham was starting to become seriously disillusioned with the treadmill of making five shows a week. He toyed with the idea of going back to the weekly format, but thought – probably correctly – that it would be seen as an admission of failure. Still, the prospect of having to continue to work so hard on the same format for another two years was a prospect he found increasingly daunting. He'd made no secret of the fact he'd love to host a mainstream game show, and when Cilla Black sensationally quit *Blind Date* live on air in January 2003 his name was one of the front runners to replace her.

Even having his name mentioned in the same breath as Cilla's would have been enough to send Graham into paroxysms of joy. 'She is so much the governor,' he gushed. 'I remember once seeing her live. She walked on stage and it was like a light going on. She's just the best.' He would of course have been more than capable of stepping into Cilla's shoes. People instantly respond to him. 'His charm is being Mr Everyman,' says Scott Michaels. 'That's his gift. People just like him.' But, in the event, London Weekend Television announced that it was to scrap the show after eighteen years.

As Graham approached his 40th birthday in April 2003, his obvious next career move was to try his hand in America. To make a life for himself Stateside had been his dream since he'd been a little boy watching US television shows at home in Ireland. 'Do I have ambitions there? Not particularly to be big there,' he'd said early on in his career. 'My only ambition is to live there. I don't care who pays me. If someone paid me to be there, I'd be quite happy with that.' By October 2001 he had become seriously intent on trying to crack the States. *So Graham Norton* was being shown on cable on BBC America, being beamed into 37 million homes, and he'd had a number of approaches from American producers. 'I'd like to give it a whirl,' he said in an interview with the *Observer*'s Lynn Barber. 'I love America and I think American television is the best in the world. It does make ours feel like amateur dramatics. I never expected to get where I am but now I guess I've set my sights even higher.'

He appeared to have fallen into the English way of believing that the grass is always greener on the other side. 'Americans like success, whereas people here are suspicious of it,' he said. 'But I'd be happy presenting America's funniest home videos for the rest of my career if it meant working there. It's my dream to make it in the States. Winning the Emmy was my proudest moment. To be recognized in America is wonderful.' And with it goes big money. America's 'Big Two', the talk show hosts Jay Leno and David Letterman, each earn in excess of £20 million a year.

By the start of *V Graham Norton* in May 2002, Graham claimed that he was 'less and less bothered' about the States, and just wanted his new show to be a success. But, as the year progressed, he was spending more and more time in New York. In the autumn he did a two-week stint of low-profile stand-up gigs at St Clement's, a 150-seat theatre just off Broadway, and – tellingly – he bought himself a permanent base in Manhattan, a £1.5 million 1850s townhouse previously owned by supermodel Claudia Schiffer.

And all the while, in the background, was the increasingly attractive proposition of working for the BBC. In January 2003, the Corporation made renewed attempts to lure him away from Channel 4, offering him a rumoured £15 million. One of the reasons its previous approach had failed was that Graham did not want to give up his production company, So Television, but the Beeb's new offer included the proviso that he could use it to make the shows – an arrangement which could be worth as much as £10 million to the company. The BBC promised him a prime-time chat show, the opportunity to present one-off documentaries and a revamped version of the *Generation Game*. It was an appealing package and the subtext to the BBC's offer was simple: join us and you can name your own price.

He considered the proposal very seriously and, it is fair to say, it caused him a certain amount of stress. On the one hand, it was the chance to go mainstream and become a major household name, but he had his loyalty to his friends and colleagues at Channel 4 to consider. He also knew that timing is key in showbiz, and that if he rejected the BBC's offer and stayed at Channel 4 he could ultimately miss the boat completely. It was a tricky dilemma.

Showbiz veteran Nicholas Parsons, a friend of Graham's, explains why he needed to be judicious about what projects he took on at that important stage in his career. 'Like everything in showbusiness, once you gain your professional confidence and you know the audience loves you, it gives you the assurance to go out there and become even better,' he said at the time. 'He is established now and, providing he doesn't get over-exposed, I think that he'll carry on for a very long time. But once you become very successful you have to plan your career very carefully. I think he's found a niche at Channel 4 and I don't think they'll let him go easily.' Again, Graham rejected the BBC.

Ever conscious of his looks, he then embarked on a vigorous diet to get in shape for his milestone birthday. 'I'm well aware that my 40th birthday is looming but I am soooo trying to forget about it,' he said. 'Everyone asks me what I'm going to do but I haven't thought about it. One thing's for sure, I don't feel like someone who is nearly 40, I still feel like a 21-year-old.'

And despite getting older he certainly hadn't lost any of his talent for being provocative. He persisted in making tasteless remarks about Sir Paul McCartney's then-wife Heather Mills losing a leg, and enraged singer Robin Gibb by cracking a joke about the death of his brother Maurice (he said his heart monitor was 'singing the tune of *Staying Alive*' while he was on a life-support machine). Calling Graham 'scum', the *Bee Gee* threatened to 'rip his head off' if the two ever met. Graham immediately apologized, protesting somewhat lamely that he'd never intended to cause offence, but Gibb said he would never forgive him for laughing about his brother's tragic death.

Gladiator star Russell Crowe provoked a particularly vehement reaction from Graham. 'I hate him, I hate him,' he declared. 'There's something really smug and annoying about him. I've never met him – and hopefully I never will now that I've said that.' He also had a pop at Tom Cruise. 'He should sack his publicist for letting him appear on the cover of *Vanity Fair* without a shirt on the month after Brad Pitt,' he bitched. 'Brad

Pitt looks soooo much better.' And he sufficiently ruffled the feathers of the ever-sensitive George Michael that the singer decided to have a go back. 'Graham Norton is very funny and talented and deserves his TV profile but, let's face it, he's only two steps away from John Inman and that's 30-year-old stereotype stuff,' sniffed George.

But what about America? How did Graham see his future? He spent such a large part of 2003 there that it looked as if he was bound for the States. He performed a series of stand-up gigs in New York in May, and secured a rumoured £5 million deal with Comedy Central to make 13 episodes of a new show called *The Graham Norton Effect*. But newspaper reports that he was leaving Britain for the US were wide of the mark. Unbeknown to all but his closest circle, the BBC had made yet another attempt to persuade him to leave Channel 4. And this time Graham was listening.

In December the Corporation triumphantly announced that he had signed an exclusive two and a half year contract in a deal allegedly worth £3.5 million. 'We've made no secret of our admiration for Graham Norton and I'm thrilled he feels that we could offer him the space to grow creatively,' said BBC1 controller Lorraine Heggessey. 'I'm convinced he will delight viewers of all ages at the heart of the Saturday night schedule.' BBC entertainment controller Jane Lush added that it had long been her ambition to work with Graham, and admitted they had spent a 'lot of time and effort' getting their man. His contract would begin the following April when his Channel 4 deal expired. In the meantime he was concentrating on his American show and was penning his memoirs, *So Me*.

But being the BBC's shiny new star was one thing; actually

getting on-screen quite another. Suffice to say, Graham's new career did not exactly get off to the most promising start. By May 2004, a month into his new contract, media rumours had begun to circulate that the BBC didn't know what to do with their hot new talent. He made a pilot show for a new series, but the idea was aborted without being aired. And although the *Radio Times* had declared him the most important person in comedy, there was no sign of him actually appearing in a mainstream show for the BBC.

Outwardly at least, Graham didn't appear too concerned, saying airily that his British television career was only Plan B (Plan A being his American career). However, *The Graham Norton Effect* was not well received by American critics when it aired on Comedy Central in June that year. The influential *New York Times* called it 'a freak show', and the channel was reported to have rejected the option of a second series. Middle America, it appeared, had not warmed to Graham. 'I'm sure the bags under my eyes held me back more than my being gay,' he said later. 'That, and the fact that I'm from Europe. It was a bit of a wake-up call.'

Things didn't look much more promising back home. At the BBC's autumn launch in July, Graham's name was conspicuously absent from the line-up. *The Graham Norton Effect* was going to be shown on BBC3, but it transpired that the BBC had to pay extra for it because it was purchased before his new contract was signed. Lorraine Heggessey faced increasingly pressing questions from the media about how and when the BBC were going to find a use for its expensive new purchase, and was forced to admit that he might not make his debut until the following year. By August – a full eight months after he'd agreed to join the Corporation – neither side had come up with the format for a new show.

Little wonder, then, that Graham didn't appear all that optimistic about his new job in an interview he gave later that month. 'I actually think we should just do any old shit because whatever it is will be doomed to failure, because it will please no one,' he said, adopting an uncharacteristically pessimistic tone. 'The BBC audience will just be sniffy, like, "Why is this filth merchant on our television?" and the Channel 4 audience will be like, "Why is he all squeaky-clean now?"' The hiatus in his on-screen television career was obviously getting to him – so much so that finally he felt the need to announce the exact date he would begin work at the Beeb. 'September 18,' he promised. 'Relax everyone – I am not running off with your licence fee. I only get paid if I turn up!'

Even so, he spent most of 2004 in New York. There was another, more personal, reason why the city held such an allure for him. Having remained single since his break-up from Scott Michaels, he had begun to despair of ever finding someone special. 'The upside of being a celebrity is you get a higher quality of casual sex,' he said in the summer of 2004. 'It does make it easier to have sex with way cute boys that are out of my league, but it makes it harder to have a relationship. I've been through a rash of ridiculously young guys, and it's stupid. I'm desperate for an age-appropriate boyfriend.'

And within a short time of making those remarks he had fallen for American singer Kristian Seeber. And while at 19 years Graham's junior the 22-year-old Seeber could hardly be said to be 'age-appropriate', the two embarked on a relationship that would endure, on and off, for the next few years. By March 2005 they had been together for almost a year, although they had already broken up once – a trauma that left Graham devastated. Back in London to promote *Strictly Dance Fever*, his debut show for the Beeb, two things were obvious. He was clearly besotted with his young lover, and he was finding maintaining a transatlantic love affair extremely hard. 'It was weird being on my own when I got back,' he said. 'I want to stay here more than ever, but it's hard. I really miss Kristian. I have thought about moving over there but this is my home. I want Kristian to shift his nice ass over here for a while.'

It was, of course, not the first time that Graham had found himself an ocean away from his boyfriend. It had been the same in the early days when he was dating Scott. 'This one isn't domestic bliss at the moment, it's fun,' he said. 'We're dating. The thing is I would like a little more domestic bliss. I think he would too. But because one of us is always on holiday when we meet, there is always a slight party atmosphere going on. If he does move here, I wonder what will happen when the music stops. I don't know, but I think we'd both like to find out.' But at the same time, having already been hurt by their brief split, he was desperately trying to rein in his emotions. 'I really like him, but I've no idea where it will go,' he said honestly. 'I enjoy it for what it is.'

Strictly Dance Fever was billed as a cross between *Strictly Come Dancing* and *Pop Idol*, and involved members of the public learning different dance moves and being eliminated by viewers' votes until one of them was left to claim the £50,000 prize. 'Though, sadly, it is *Pop Idol* without Simon Cowell and *Strictly Come Dancing* without the celebs,' noted Lynn Barber. The show was not Graham's idea and he admitted he wasn't crazy about the title, but he said he'd agreed to do it because he thought it was a show he'd like to watch. 'I also liked the fact that for my first big foray into BBC land, it wasn't *The Graham Norton Show*,' he added. 'It's not about me, it's about the dancers.'

The fact that there weren't going to be any celebrities involved was also something of a blessing for Graham as he had – shock horror! – begun to tire of dealing with the monstrous egos and delicate dispositions of showbusiness folk. Whereas in the early days he had been genuinely thrilled to meet his childhood heroes, his excitement had waned in the intervening years. 'It slightly wears off because it's quite hard work having to deal with people on that level,' he admitted. 'I mean, they aren't normal and that's how they got to be stars. If they were ordinary they wouldn't be there. And so you have to sort of "deal" with them, and if you are a genuine fan, then you are quite willing to do that, but when you are doing five shows a week and meeting a lot of them… God, it's exhausting.'

He was later to admit that he had been 'nervous as hell' presenting his first major show for the BBC. Conscious of the criticisms that he was too expensive and too outrageous for the mainstream channel, he curbed his natural exuberance and, as a result, some thought he failed to shine. The series was followed in August by *The Bigger Picture*, a late-night, 30-minute BBC1 show that was an ambitious attempt to mix humour and serious current affairs. It was the first programme produced by Graham's own team and, in the show's defence, it was not an easy brief to pull off – particularly given events such as the July 7 suicide bombings in London that were then dominating the headlines. As Graham put it: 'Our problem is that there's slightly too much news. And of the wrong variety. It doesn't yell comedy. Not a lot of laughs at the moment.'

He wanted his new show to be a bridge between his old persona and a newer, slightly more mature persona. 'I'm trying to find a way of evolving into – oh God, it sounds ridiculous to say more mature, but you know, I'm 42, I can't run up and down stairs in a shiny suit any more,' he said. But the critics were not convinced. The *Observer*'s Kathryn Flett hated the show, although she said it pained her to say so because she 'adored' Graham. '*The Bigger Picture* was meant to inspire laughter but instead made me put my head in my hands and sniffle at the sheer awesome wrongness of it all,' she said. She criticised the 'predictable' format – in which Graham and three guests sat around on sofas talking about topical events – and questioned who on earth was choosing the guests. 'Nothing wrong with Richard Wilson, Jo Brand or Jane Moore individually – but all together on the same sofa at 10.35pm?' she wrote. 'Including one person under 40 might have added a frisson of dewy freshness to proceedings, but instead it was like eavesdropping on a quiet Monday night at the Groucho Club.'

By the following February, Graham's private life was once again in turmoil following the latest – and this time seemingly permanent – split from Kristian. For a while Graham held out hope for a reconciliation, but admitted it didn't look likely. 'I don't know what's happening with Kristian at the moment,' he said sadly. By April the couple were still apart, with a rather forlorn-sounding Graham announcing that he was now 'too old' to be attractive to gay men. 'People don't ever throw themselves at me,' he complained to *Closer* magazine. 'They come over and say hello but they're not going to waste their time having sex with you when you're an older man. That's just how the gay world works. I'm normally single so it's not really that weird being on my own now. By and large I've always lived my life as a single man, but there are definitely moments when I wish it was different.'

Although Kristian was far younger, Graham's relationship with the American had been more than a dalliance. Indeed, their break-up left him with a badly bruised heart and he confided to friends that it would be a long time before he fell in love again. 'I don't think you date people unless you think that it might be a possibility you'll be together forever,' he explained ruefully. 'Everyone is a bit romantic when they fall in love. You do hope it will be forever and always. I never understand people who just go on lots of dates. In the past I would have pursued some-thing just for sex. But now I can't be bothered.'

Part of the problem with their relationship was that some thought Kristian was only after Graham for his money. 'A lot of people thought he was a gold-digger because he's younger than me, but he so wasn't and I felt really bad for him,' says Graham. Initial attempts to remain friends failed and, for a while, the two weren't even on speaking terms but, by September, they had begun seeing each other again – albeit just as friends. 'I think if we got back together we'd take it much more slowly than we did,' Graham said. 'It was all a bit of a whirlwind.'

Having given up, for the time being at least, being part of a couple, Graham turned to man's best friend. He rescued a dog, Bailey, a nine-month-old labradoodle (a cross between a Labrador and a poodle) from an animal charity and was besotted with his new pal. He even had a picture of his pooch staring out from his mobile phone. 'I love having him,' he enthused. 'Although he is a very naughty dog. He's chewed up some really expensive shoes and he chased a little girl who was scared of dogs. We've been to dog training classes and he knows all the commands. He just chooses when he wants to obey them. I used to go to clubs to meet people, but I haven't been in one for ages because I have to go home to let the dog out.'

April 2006 saw a second series of *Strictly Dance Fever*, with judges Arlene Phillips, Ben Richards, Wayne Sleep and Stacey Haynes sifting through the contestants to find a winner. Travelling around Britain auditioning hopefuls for the programme, Graham claimed to be shocked at the lengths some people went to. 'We've seen a 78-year-old woman do the splits, and a random woman in Cardiff who did the flamenco and when she lifted up her skirt for the stamp she didn't have any knickers on,' he laughed incredulously. 'There have been some who are borderline mad. One woman dressed up as a cat, with fur, to perform a dance from *Cats*. We're looking for raw talent, but some of the people we've seen are so raw they're beyond sushi.'

All good camp fun of course. But the same month, in a documentary for BBC3 entitled *The Trouble With Gay Men*, he launched an astonishing attack on his TV bosses, accusing them of making him 'too gay'. 'I am surrounded by scores of straight producers making sure I am as gay this week as I was last week,' he complained. He said he was under pressure to act more flamboyantly, and revealed he was not happy at having to make constant gay references and double entendres in his shows. 'So you say, "I don't want to do this really gay joke," and they say basically, "you think of a better joke". And then you say, "Alright, I will be taken up the arse one more time",' he groaned.

It wasn't until July 2006 – more than two years into his contract – that Graham finally found his niche at the BBC with the reality series *How Do You Solve A Problem Like Maria?*. The prime-time Saturday night BBC1 show, in which unknown female singers auditioned for the lead role in an upcoming West End production of *The Sound of Music*, became a massive hit, attracting six million viewers and making a star of winner Connie Fisher. But while Graham's skill at fronting the show proved that he could indeed be the respectable face of main-stream Saturday night television, the indiscretion and irreverent sense of humour that propelled him to fame (and which made him such a juicy interviewee for journalists) was far from gone. It seems to be against his nature to go too long without putting his foot in it and, sure enough, in September 2006 he provoked complaints from viewers after making a comment about Princess Diana's death.

And the following month he caused Middle England to erupt in fury after admitting in an interview with *Marie Claire* maga-zine that he had taken 'loads of drugs'. Drug rehabilitation groups were furious at his description of the potentially fatal Class A drug ecstasy as 'fantastic' and 'fun'. 'We're appalled,' said a spokesman for the National Drug Prevention Alliance. 'It's mind-blowing that somebody has said that. He's in the public eye and influencing young people. It's irresponsible. We know that people die randomly from ecstasy.'

Graham had indeed appeared effusive in his praise for the drug. 'The only time I took ecstasy was years and years ago,' he said. 'It was absolutely amazing. It was just fantastic – really, really fun. I think that coke is quite middle-aged stuff. It's quite a slow drug that involves coffee tables. It's the middle-class drug of choice.' And he added: 'The downsides of drugs are buying them and the people you end up doing them with.'

Conservative MP Ann Widdecombe joined in the condemnation. 'Unfortunately, the message going out is that if you are poor, black and living on a council estate you will get busted, but if you're Kate Moss or Graham Norton you'll get away with it,' she said. Other high-profile BBC personalities had lost their jobs after being exposed as drug takers – people like *Have I Got News For You* presenter Angus Deayton and *Blue Peter*'s Richard Bacon – but on this occasion the Corporation stood by its man. 'The issues that Graham discusses in this interview are aimed at an adult audience and reflect the frank and open nature of his personality,' said a BBC spokesman. All the same, it was a lesson to Graham that he was now Mr Saturday Night and, as such, he needed to be judicious about what he said to the media.

The row didn't stop the BBC from renewing his contract – in the face of ardent overtures from ITV his pay was reportedly doubled to £7 million. But at the same time it was obvious that he needed an outlet where he could be his wickedly outrageous self without the worry of shocking the licence payer. And as far as the Beeb is concerned, that means a slot on BBC2. Traditionally the home of more cutting-edge, contemporary comedy, artists can get away with much more than they can on the premier channel. *The Graham Norton Show*, planned for the following year, would give him far more scope for the near-the-knuckle stuff that made him a star. In short, it would be more like his Channel 4 show.

The 13-part series began in February 2007 and was sufficiently successful for the BBC immediately to extend its run for an additional six weeks. A mix of celebrity guests, comic monologues and stories about the eccentricities of the great British public, it was undeniably Graham Norton – albeit a slightly toned-down version. 'I haven't shed that rude skin,' he insisted. 'But now our main concern is always "Is it funny?" rather than "Is it outrageous?"'

Graham was also in the midst of hosting *Any Dream Will Do* on BBC1, the Saturday night follow-up series to *How Do You Solve A Problem Like Maria?*. This time the search was on to find someone to play Joseph in a new Andrew Lloyd Webber production of *Joseph And His Amazing Technicolor Dreamcoat*, due to hit the West End that summer. It was the job of the judges – including actor John Barrowman, producer Bill Kenwright and TV presenter Denise Van Outen – to pick the winner from the 12 finalists, and Graham's to provide a sympathetic shoulder for the rejects to cry on. 'With *Maria* everyone had quite a fixed idea in their minds that they wanted this young girl with hints of Julie Andrews – whereas with *Joseph* the playing field is wide open,' he said. 'However, our new *Joseph* needs to be hugely likeable and a bit of a heart throb – people must fancy or want to be him. It's no accident that he is normally played by pop stars because the guy playing *Joseph* needs to be special.' In the event 25-year-old Essex-born singer Lee Mead won the competition.

The show was pitted against the ITV1 talent contest *Grease Is The Word*, in which Simon Cowell and judges Sinitta, David Gest and choreographer Brian Friedman searched for youngsters to play Danny and Sandy in a new London production of *Grease*. Unsurprisingly, Graham was backing his own show to win the Saturday night ratings' war. 'Cowell is a TV talent, but Andrew is a phenomenon,' he said. 'He wrote his first musical at 18. The man is a genius. Simon is just a good businessman.' Sure enough, by May the 10-week show was riding high in the ratings, beating *Grease* by pulling in 6.1 million viewers to 4.1 million. A triumphant Graham couldn't resist taking a pot shot at his rival. 'Simon is a huge TV talent – I admire his work ethic,' he said. 'But he's got all the money he needs – he should pack it in and enjoy himself.'

255

13 SO GROWN UP

Now well and truly into his stride at the Beeb, 2008 saw Graham cement his position as one of the UK's most bankable TV talents. His success with the two previous Andrew Lloyd Webber shows – and in particular the surprising on-screen chemistry he'd developed with Lord Lloyd Webber (described by one television critic as Britain's 'most unlikely screen double act') – led the BBC to commission a third show for the pair in 2008, called *I'd Do Anything*. Thousands of youngsters auditioned that spring, desperate for the chance to be picked for the show and win the chance to play Oliver and Nancy in a West End Production of *Oliver!*

But this time Graham had a tough battle on his hands in the face of stiff competition from ITV1's *Britain's Got Talent*. With each programme desperate to win the highest Saturday night ratings, the rivalry inevitably led to a war of words between Graham and *Britain's Got Talent* judges Simon Cowell and Piers Morgan. Graham kicked it off by mocking the other programme's 'shameless use of sob stories' – such as 13-year-old contestant Andrew Johnston admitting that he had been bullied for wanting to be an opera singer. Cowell said Graham should shut up and keep his opinions to himself, whilst Morgan said he personally had been incredibly moved by Johnston's story. 'For me, the most poignant moment came when young Andrew revealed he had been bullied at school for pursuing his dream of being a chorister,' he said. 'Pick on someone your own size Norton, you mincing, talentless little fool.' *I'd Do Anything* was ultimately the loser in the reality TV ratings war, with the final part of the competition attracting just over 5 million viewers compared to *Britain's Got Talent*'s 11 million.

In the autumn *The Graham Norton Show* returned for a new series, pulling in a relatively modest 1.37 million viewers in week one, but being welcomed back like a favourite old friend by most newspaper critics. Guests included Goldie Hawn, Ricky Gervais and actress Thandie Newton, whom the ever-mischievous Graham persuaded to read out a porn script – which she did with style. One of Graham's great gifts is his ability to persuade people to do the unlikeliest things, and since the start of *So Graham Norton* in 1998 his guest list has read like a roll call of Hollywood's best-known names.

And yet one person continued to prove frustratingly elusive. Madonna, the ultimate showbiz diva, remained stubbornly out of reach. 'We hear she has seen the show and loves it,' said Graham. 'Hopefully one day she will think, "What the hell, it looks like a laugh, I'll do that." ' In the meantime he had to make do with gazing at her picture. He shelled out £10,000 at a charity auction for a photo of her eyes, saying it was worth it just to hang it in his bedroom and know that Madonna was watching his activities. 'Well I did put the picture above my bed,' he said in his best nudge-nudge-wink-wink manner. 'So whatever's happened there, she's seen.'

Graham has built up an impressive property portfolio over the years, and as well as his townhouse in Manhattan, he owns a luxury seafront pad in Cape Town, South Africa, which he likes to visit during the winter months. But his main home remains his four-bedroom Georgian terrace townhouse in Wapping, East London, where he lives with his two dogs. In 2007 he rescued a second pup, an eight-month-old terrier cross, from canine charity Dogs Trust and named her Madge – short for (what else?) Madonna. And the same year, he purchased an empty warehouse behind his Wapping home for £680,000 and set about converting it into a party pad for himself. Four tiny rooms were knocked through upstairs to create a 40ft living room and separate home office.

He is, say friends, extremely house proud but has, so far at least, resisted the lure of the glossy magazines to be featured At Home in return for a large cheque. When he decided to have his bathroom renovated, he was shocked when a friend suggested he telephone *Hello!* magazine. 'I was horrified,' he explains. 'For the first time in my life I could afford to have it done. I didn't want to pose by my bath for some living magazine!' It is more his style to be photographed, grinning like the cat that's got the cream, on the front cover of the *Gay Times*, surrounded by half a dozen semi-naked, hunky musclemen. There are times when Graham simply can't believe his luck, and the day of that particular photo shoot was, one imagines, one of them. 'My dreams have come true,' he said not long after he became famous. 'I do cool things, I get to meet the people I always wanted to meet – and I do get paid very well for it.'

In the absence of an At Home spread, his friend Niall MacMonagle offers an intriguing glimpse into what it's like Chez

Norton. And he reveals that Graham's taste in interior design is dramatically at odds with his flamboyant on-screen image. 'I stayed with him one November in his wonderful house,' says Niall. 'He has done it out beautifully. It is just plain white, with one beautiful Habitat sofa, a plain white vase with tulips in it, and that's it. Understated elegance. There is a shelf on the way up the stairs, which is seriously laden with awards.'

There is, MacMonagle adds, also an impressive array of books on display. 'When he was at school Graham was a voracious reader and he still is,' he explains. 'He's got a shelf-load of books in his house. He likes the American writer Laurie Moore. She's got a wicked sense of humour and she's very, very clever. I imagine that if Graham ever writes he will write like Laurie Moore. I have kept the letters I have had from him over the years and they are so entertaining and wonderful. He is hiding that literary side of himself on the television, but I'm convinced he will come around to it some day. He's very quick and very intelligent. The television programme doesn't do him justice at all.'

Graham and his dogs are a regular sight in his neighbourhood – indeed, he has lived in London for so long, he seems to consider himself British rather than Irish. But having had a rather ambivalent attitude to his homeland for many years, he has managed to lay a few ghosts to rest. In 2001, after being away for Ireland for many years, he bought an apartment in Cork, and in 2004, he forked out £1.1 million on a near-derelict house on the Sheep's Head Peninsula in West Cork, which he spent two years renovating. For Graham to have even considered buying a home in Ireland is an indication of how confident and secure he now feels in himself. He returns to his holiday home in West Cork to relax most summers and, touchingly, hinted that he would like to be invited back to his old school to present the prizes on speech day.

After going through some difficult patches in his relationship with his mother during his younger years, he is extremely close to and protective of Rhoda, who is now 80. So much so that when he published his autobiography in 2004, he made her promise that she wouldn't read it, and instructed those who had not to bother telling his mother what was in it because, he said, 'she doesn't want to know.' He is similarly caring towards his sister and when her marriage broke down in 2001 he was there for her. 'Graham is supportive of Paula, they are fairly close,' says Paula's estranged husband Noel Giles. 'The children live with me but Graham is in contact with them. To be fair to Graham, his relationship with the three children is the same as if Paula and I were still together. He is generous at Christmas; he always gives them a good present. They don't see a lot of him because he is frantically busy. There are spells where he comes back frequently, and then not at all.'

Amazingly for one who is at the top of a notoriously cutthroat profession, Graham's success does not appear to have been at the expense of his ethics. He still, charmingly, believes in being 'nice', and whilst he may occasionally be provoked into being less than polite, he is usually repentant. Not for him the petulant showbiz tantrums and diva-like behaviour of some big stars. It seems that Graham Norton is as agreeable off screen as he is on. 'He is one of the nicest men in the business, which is quite surprising, I can assure you,' says theatre producer Mark Goucher. 'To be one of the top television personalities in this country and still be one of the nicest men in the world is quite something.'

This is an opinion that is echoed by many of the people who have worked with him over the years. 'I have often noticed with performers that those who are far more mechanical in their comedy – those who actually have to work far harder to be funny – are often more of a pain in the arse,' says a senior television producer. 'Graham could never be accused of that. He works enormously hard, but he has an innate talent and he is as funny off screen as he is on. There are many comics who have to switch it on, but he isn't one of them. He is an intrinsically funny person and that's what he uses. He's certainly not blasé about it and he works hard at whatever he does but, without naming names, there are comedians who God knows whatever gave them the idea they should be comedians. It's as if they have gone to some sort of careers office and decided that they are going to be a comedian. It's something they've worked out and they've honed, but it is mechanical and often rather charmless. But with Graham, what you get on screen is a version of what you get off screen. He's not a constant joker off screen of course, but it is inherent in his nature to be funny.'

As a result he is popular with his crew. 'Graham is an enormously easy-going performer because he, quite rightly, has confidence in his ability to deliver,' says a television producer who knows him well. 'He has always been very aware that fame has a finite life and while he may end up continuing to do well, his pitch of fame might only last for a certain while. He always did have a very mature response to it and that's why, charmingly, he will still do *Just A Minute* on Radio 4 because he enjoys it. He said it is his retirement, and I rather like that. He likes doing other stuff. And he's still flattered that he's asked to do so. I'm sure fame has altered the way he conducts his life, but I don't think it has altered him inherently as a person because he knows how fickle it can be.'

But no-one can be nice all of the time and Graham can be outspoken and even cruel when the mood takes him. A woman phoned a newspaper, claiming that Graham had called her a c*** in a nightclub. 'The dreadful thing is, it was true,' Graham sheepishly admitted. 'She was bothering me. I tried everything to get her to leave me alone. I was drunk. She pushed me too far.' He also confesses to getting fed up with people asking him continually to speak on their mobile phones. 'It does get really annoying but I've had a few glasses of wine now so I can deal with it,' he said at London's Mardi Gras concert. Mostly he is fine about people asking for autographs, 'But, just occasionally, by the end of the day I'm bored with being Graham Norton,' he explains.

And despite being one of the most famous gay men in Britain, it appears that some poor innocent souls still haven't got the message. 'Even now, camp and well known as I am, I will meet someone at a party who will ask, "Are you married, do you have children?" ' he says. 'And I'm embarrassed for them. I think, "Dear God, how thick are you? I've been talking to you for five minutes, and you've taken nothing on board." '

Perhaps inevitably, over the years Graham has lost touch with the majority of his old friends. When he left Ireland in 1983, it was the last that many of them were to see of him. 'When I saw Graham on television in *Father Ted* it was like someone returning from the dead,' says former school friend Colin Bateman. 'He had completely disappeared. When he left, he left. We didn't know where he went afterwards. All of us bar Graham have kept in touch and meet up occasionally. We get together for a few beers even though we are scattered around. But Graham was the mystery man. He did a complete evaporation and we lost track of him. I suppose if he's got a career to follow and he's out of the group here it's easier to stay away than to try and face the ghosts of home. It's only a 50-minute flight, which is one way of looking at it, but in another way it could be a big jump.'

As time went on, more people were shed. 'He hasn't got any friends from that time, none that I'm aware of anyway,' says Harry Moore, who knew him at university and shared squats with him in London in the mid-eighties. 'I don't think he wants to acknowledge that time in his life.' That also seems to hold true for Graham's former lover, Obo. The hippie had no idea that the friend he knew as plain Graham Walker had gone on to become one of the biggest TV stars in Britain. 'I didn't realize he was famous,' he says. 'I had no idea that in the years since I have spoken to him he has achieved so much success. But I can't wait to see his show next time I am in Britain and maybe catch up with him again.'

Of course it is not always the celebrity who changes. Sometimes it is the way others see them that irreversibly alters the relationship. This certainly happened with Helen Dean, who knew Graham when they were pupils at Bandon Grammar School and continued their friendship for many years. 'For years after we left college we used to see each other once a year but about four years ago it fizzled out,' says Helen, who is now called Helen Redmond and teaches at their old school. 'Now he has gone beyond us I suppose. It is very difficult if you're not used to meeting stars. I would find it very difficult to treat him in the same way. I only know one star and I think that if I saw him now it would probably be awkward.'

Graham's oldest friends now are the people he met at the Central School of Speech and Drama. 'Graham still has the friends he has had since drama school, and he sees them quite often so he's grounded in that department,' says Scott Michaels. Graham has also stayed in touch with his former teacher and mentor Niall MacMonagle. 'I think it's pathetic when teachers try to be friends with pupils,' MacMonagle admits. 'But years later when they've crossed over the threshold into adulthood, then you can meet them as adults, not as teacher-pupil. I think the best thing about Graham is the energy inside his head. He is just so alive to everything: to ideas, to people, to books especially. And music. He strikes me as someone having a very good time on planet Earth. He laughs with people rather than at them. He just sends up the absurdity of certain situations, social or sexual or whatever. He pokes fun but he is just naughty and mischievous rather than cruel. And he is extraordinarily kind. He's so good to his mother. When I last went over he had just taken his mum to Paris for the weekend. And he took her with him to Los Angeles where he was given some award. He is very good to his family.'

Like so many who pursue a career in show business, Graham is afflicted by agonies of self-doubt – and never more so than where his appearance is concerned. A female interviewer once described him as being more insecure about his looks than any woman she'd ever met, and he agonizes daily about how fat/old/wrinkled he looks on camera. Even when he was young he never felt particularly slim or attractive. 'That's the tragedy,' he said shortly after turning 40. 'You live with constant self-loathing, and the terrible thing is that as you get older you look at old pictures of yourself and go, "God, I looked really good then. What was I thinking?" He said he wouldn't rule out having cosmetic surgery, although when a magazine once rang his agent to say they'd heard a rumour he'd had a face-lift in America, he was incensed.

'Don't you think I would have sued a plastic surgeon if this is how I looked after my plastic surgery?' he cried. But he admitted he would love to have the 'huge bags' under his eyes removed – if only he could pluck up the courage to go under the knife. 'I'm hoping if I wait long enough they'll develop a non surgical procedure,' he said.

He forces himself to visit the gym at least three times a week, the payoff being that he can then enjoy a few guilt-free glasses of wine in the evening. 'I love drinking,' he says. 'It's a social thing though and I'm a happy drunk. If I were worried then I'd stop. Drinking is my vice because it's easy and convenient.' Nonetheless, he has – one imagines jokingly – described himself as a 'borderline alcoholic', and in the past he has confessed to enjoying a small tipple before he goes on camera. 'Before I do a show I always have a glass of wine,' he says. 'I still need that little bit of Dutch courage but I wouldn't dare have any more than that. It would be a very slippery slope if I did.' He also admits that – *quel surprise* – many of his more outlandish outfits are the result of what he calls 'drunk shopping'. 'I tend to buy clothes after lunch,' he says. 'You know, have a few glasses of wine and you hit the shops.' Which, no doubt, goes a long way towards explaining his perennial appearance at the top of Britain's Worst Dressed list.

Graham enjoys splashing out on expensive designer outfits – creations that on occasion have cost as much as a house in some parts of the country (although as he points out, 'Not anywhere I would want to live.'). But he is generous with his time and his money and supports a number of charities. And despite his cracks about the homeless, he is not as callous as he makes out. He designed a glittery T-shirt for a homeless persons' charity, and created a personalized Valentine card for another charity. He customized a pillowslip for the Fashion Acts, and in March 2002, he was part of a group of celebrities that took part in a powerboat race off the Isle of Wight to raise money for a children's hospice.

'When the Comedy Box came to a temporary close in November 2000, I approached Graham's agent to see if he would be interested in doing our final night,' says Steve Lount. 'I wasn't going to advertise him, I was going to have him as a surprise guest. He was one of the biggest names we'd ever had in our six-year history, although obviously he wasn't a big name when he first appeared. I thought there was no way he would agree to it but his agent phoned me and said, "He's said he will do it if he's available." But as it turned out, our date coincided with the start of that autumn's series of *So Graham Norton* so he couldn't do it. But I thought it was nice of him to have agreed in principle.'

Graham has also maintained his links with the Edinburgh Fringe. 'He loves coming back to the festival,' says Karen Koren. 'He feels that the festival made him, which it did really. He's very sentimental about it. He has compered our talent competition, *So You Think You're Funny*, for the past four or five years. He has stayed very down to earth. He's kept his realness and he's not affected in any way. I think he's very mature about his fame. He's enjoying all the things he does but he's not precious about it.'

But he has on occasion taken a swipe at the festival. 'I've said it before and I'll say it again: something that drags limping and sweating on for a month cannot be called a Festival,' he said in his *Pink Paper* diary in 1998. 'Forget all those mink, there are thousands of performers trapped up here that need to be freed.' On the subject of mink, and the plight of little furry animals in general, Graham remained unmoved. 'Fur campaigners are so dull,' he has said. 'Why don't they just lighten up? No one really cares about all that. Sure, it might once have been alive, but it probably had little beady eyes and nasty sharp teeth. I wish that these people would find a new topic to bore us all about.' Quite how Graham would feel about being electrocuted up the bottom and made into a hat, though, is anyone's guess.

Rather surprisingly, given his status as one of our most popular and well-paid presenters, Graham is always saying he doesn't expect his TV success to last. Indeed, he appears remarkably self-deprecating about what he has achieved. Maybe it's his way of not tempting fate. 'God, I'll be lucky if I last ten years,' he said in 2001. 'Ten years is a long time in television. But there's always *Just A Minute*. It's nice. It gets you out of the house. You have to wash. And I love doing it. I think of that as my retirement fund.'

This pleases *Just A Minute* host Nicholas Parsons enormously. 'We are delighted that he loves doing it and if he's free he will always be a guest on it,' he says. 'As with all the regulars on *Just A Minute*, it's a case of if they're free. Radio doesn't pay – it's not like television – and we are invariably calling round people to see who's available on the date. He's very careful not to push the boundaries because on Radio 4 you can't go too far. He's a bit cheeky, but never suggestive or vulgar. He can be most circumspect and correct and still be just as funny. I think that shows that he doesn't need to rely on his outrageousness.'

Parsons is a huge fan of Graham and effusive in his praise of him. 'He is one of the most popular people we have on *Just A Minute*,' he says warmly. 'He is also one of the most charming and delightful people I have ever met. My granddaughter Annabel is a big fan of his and when he was on the show she asked if she could meet him. I took her backstage and he was sweet and adorable to her. She was absolutely thrilled because she thinks he's the best thing on television. People love him. It is that loveable quality that he has in real life that comes over in his work. And it cuts right across all age groups. He is the kindest sweetest man you could meet, and it makes you realize that the comedians who think you have to be very crude and offensive in order to have success are approaching it the wrong way. Those who achieve most success are those whom the audience loves and warms to.

'You can't be successful in our business without really liking people. He is naturally a very charming, unassuming person. He hasn't got any inflated idea of his own ability, or his own personality or his own position. He is very natural and unpretentious and a most engaging personality. I'm sure it helps if you get your success later in life. If you struggle very hard, like Graham has done, you know how fragile things are. But I also think that he is at heart an extremely kind, gentle, loving human being.'

However, Graham has implied that life as a famous television star is not always all it's cracked up to be. 'Success is a weird thing because you stop living,' he said in an interview with the *Guardian* in 2001. 'All my interesting stories are from before I was on television. Nothing interesting has happened to me since then. Maybe it's because the most interesting thing in my life is the show and that's on telly. So I can't go up to people and say "You'll never guess who I met last week, Ricki Lake." They'll just say, "I know that, you twat, I saw you." ' Bizarrely, he has said that one of the best moments of being famous was when a supermarket in Ireland opened a checkout for him. 'That it made me truly happy caused me quite a bit of soul-searching,' he said.

His inability to find lasting happiness in his private life was also something that, for many years, caused him much introspection. 'It's hard to have everything I guess,' says his friend Niall

MacMonagle. Undoubtedly, Graham's fame came between him and previous boyfriends, including Scott Michaels, and Graham recognizes that it makes it difficult to find someone new. 'I tell kids if they want to get into TV they'd better get used to the fact that they'll never get laid,' he complained. 'I never get picked up. It's so depressing. Everyone thinks I have men throwing themselves at me but it's so not true. Going out with me is so uncool. Imagine telling your friends, "I'm going out with Graham Norton." I mean, it's ridiculous!'

Nonetheless, he is an enthusiastic member of London's gay nightclub scene and although he is aware that some people might want to have sex with him simply because he is famous, he generously says, tongue in cheek, that he doesn't mind. 'I make a decision about how much I care,' he says. 'Everyone sleeps with someone for some reason. If you have an interesting job or you have money or are on the telly, people might find that attractive. That's OK.'

His failed affairs led him to conclude that he was probably not cut out for a live-in relationship. 'I don't think I'm difficult to live with but I find it hard to live with other people,' he said candidly. 'At the beginning I don't set any boundaries. It's almost like I'm a guest in my own house and give it over to them, and then grow to resent that over time. All my day is spent dealing with other people. When I come home I like it to be empty. The presence of others in my house kind of annoys me.'

Warming to his theme, he continued: 'Finding someone you want to spend your life with is hard. As you get older your checklist of what you're looking for gets longer, but the checklist of what you're offering gets shorter. You become fussier but you've no right to be that way.' Even if he were to find a life partner, he said, he wouldn't be inclined to go through a civil ceremony such as that undertaken by Sir Elton John and his boyfriend David Furnish. 'I have no interest in gay marriage,' he says, 'It's fine for those who want to.' His mother's words upon learning that he was gay – that it was 'such a lonely life' – ring in his ears to this day, yet he publicly rejects her gloomy prognosis. 'I'm sure my mum would not describe me as lonely now,' he insists. 'These days it's not just about the family unit. It's about extended family and your relationships with your friends, so I'm not lonely – whatever else I may be.'

Proving that he is game for a laugh, Graham announced in November 2008 that he would join the West End cast of the musical, *La Cage aux Folles*, playing the temperamental drag queen, Albin. The leading role, which involved donning a blonde wig, high heels and red sequinned frock, was a dream come true for Graham, who had seen the original Broadway production on tour in 1984, and had wanted to play Albin ever since. He was to take over the role from actor Douglas Hodge in January 2009, but had to step into his supersized stilettos three weeks early when Hodge and both his understudies fell ill. Ever the professional, Graham took to the stage at the Playhouse Theatre despite his preparation time being cut short. He was, he confessed, 'fantastically frightened' by the prospect. 'I haven't felt like that in years – probably not since my first couple of stand-up gigs,' he said. 'And it's quite nice to feel like that. It's like self-harming, I suppose – you feel alive. I just think this is a fantastic show, so if I don't destroy it in some sort of terrible Godzilla-in-heels crashing through a terrible jungle way, then I'll be really pleased. When you watch the show, you'd have to be such a curmudgeonly, horrible person not to leave the theatre in a good mood.'

The *Telegraph*'s theatre critic Dominic Cavendish agreed. Despite describing Graham's contribution to the performance as 'a theatrical car crash,' he said he defied anyone to see the show and depart 'without a smile on their lips, a song in their heart and a spring in their step.' Graham proved a huge hit with audiences and was clearly revelling in the opportunity to camp it up night after night. 'It's not the first time I've worn a dress,' he admitted. 'But it's the first time I have been this glamorous in a dress.'

He was unprepared, however, for the amount of sheer toil involved. 'It was really hard work – eight shows a week,' he acknowledged afterwards. Indeed, when he hosted *Over The Rainbow* in 2010, the fourth of BBC1's talent competitions to find a new West End star (this time to play Dorothy in Andrew Lloyd Webber's theatre production of *The Wizard of Oz*) he expressed surprise that anyone would actually want to win. 'I could not help thinking, 'Jesus, this is the prize?" he said. 'All it really taught me was that the prize that these girls are fighting for is very tough, the prize being on a television show; the hard bit is when you win because it is gruelling what you have to do.' Asked by an interviewer if he would consider doing it again, he replied: 'Erm, no.'

The beginning of 2009 saw Graham in ebullient mood, seemingly determined not to tone down his own television persona following the fall-out from Sachsgate. The scandal, which centred around the broadcast of prank telephone calls to actor Andrew Sachs by Jonathan Ross and Russell Brand on Brand's Radio 2 show the previous October, had morphed into an ongoing row about broadcasting standards and perceived bad taste. The pair originally rang Sachs, who is best known for playing the hapless waiter Manuel in *Fawlty Towers*, as a guest to interview on the show, but after he failed to answer the telephone they left lewd messages on his voicemail, including comments about his granddaughter, Georgina Baillie.

It led to a record number of complaints and harsh criticism of Brand, Ross and the editorial decisions of the BBC. The two presenters were criticized by a number of MPs, including Prime Minister Gordon Brown. Ross was suspended by the BBC, while the BBC and media regulator Ofcom launched investigations. Both Brand and Lesley Douglas, the Controller of Radio 2, subsequently resigned and Ross was suspended without pay for 12 weeks. The BBC was also fined £150,000 by Ofcom.

Hardly surprising, then, that the Corporation had rather got its knickers in a twist over the whole sorry debacle. In January it stood accused of failing to learn from its mistakes after Graham made offensive remarks about Britney Spears and Gordon Ramsay on his chat show. Referring to the chef's affair, he quipped that 'women were enjoying two fingers of Gordon's,' whilst the singer's intimate parts were compared to turkey giblets. 'In view of the controversy, the BBC should have learned their lesson,' opined John Beyer, director of Mediawatch-UK. The BBC, meanwhile, trotted out its customary response, 'Graham is known for his irreverent presenting style,' a spokesman said.

The man himself insisted he wouldn't be watching his words. 'You're aware of the mood, but at the same time I just get on and do my job,' he said. 'You can't do your job if you're desperately trying to second-guess things the whole time. What nobody says is, "Look, the BBC has four TV stations, seven or eight radio stations, 24 hours a day, 365 days a year – it was a blip." They police the output incredibly rigorously. On the chat show the script gets shown to the lawyers, lawyers and executives come to the recording and they go to the edit.'

Money was also in the news following Sachsgate – in particular the enormous amounts the BBC was paying its biggest stars like Ross. Scrutiny, inevitably, turned to Graham's own lucrative deal with the Corporation and he admitted he didn't know why he was paid so much. 'I can neither defend nor explain the money I'm paid,' he says. 'It's baffling to me, but, equally, if the market forces have decided I'm worth that – and I'm not saying I am, I've no idea – but if they have decided that, then of course I'm going to take it. Who wouldn't? Compared to the vast majority of people I'm ridiculously well paid, and I'm sure people resent that. I would too.'

Within months, though, he was publicly offering to take a pay cut if it was required. Whilst on the face of it one could be forgiven for thinking he had taken leave of his senses – after all it was usual when the time came for renegotiation of contracts for stars to aim for a pay increase – Graham was actually being exceptionally shrewd. With the spotlight focussed firmly on how the BBC was spending licence payers' hard-earned cash, and with the country in the grip of recession, 'tightening one's belt' and 'reducing the deficit' were the buzzwords of choice. As an intelligent businessman, Graham was sensible enough to know when he was well off. As he would later admit, he was not about to risk his career by flouncing off in a huff to another channel.

Besides, the BBC was continuing to demonstrate its commitment to him. In May he took on the role he was surely born to do – taking over as host of that most sought-after of camp TV spectacles, the *Eurovision Song Contest*. Terry Wogan, who presided over the show for an astonishing 35 years, quit in 2008 in protest at the 'political voting' of that year's final (some Eastern European countries were accused of voting tactically to ensure Russia won.) Saying that it was no longer a music competition, Sir Tel said the prospects for Western European acts were poor because of Eastern Bloc countries voting for each other. 'I don't want to be presiding over yet another debacle,' he complained.

Having twice presented the spin-off *Eurovision Dance Contest*, Graham was the obvious person to take over the iconic event. 'Sir Terry is nothing less than a legend and it is an impossible act to follow but somebody must and I just couldn't say no,' he says. The 2009 competition took place in Moscow, and despite the problems that have afflicted the contest in recent years, Graham was full of enthusiasm. 'I can't imagine being that upset by it [the block voting],' he said. 'It is a singing competition you know. We're not looking for world peace here. I can't wait to get to Moscow. With a combination of cheap vodka and a language barrier, what could possibly go wrong?' Killjoy bookies were already offering odds of 4/1 that he would quit after his first year. 'Replacing Sir Terry Wogan is a huge task for Graham Norton,' said Nick Weinberg, a spokesman for Ladbrokes. 'We think that he will quit sooner rather than later.' Anyone who took out those odds, however, would have lost out as at the time of writing he is still hosting the show.

Britain's entry was performed by 21-year-old Sugababes singer Jade Ewen with 'It's My Time', a song written by Andrew Lloyd Webber who accompanied her on the piano. Lord Lloyd Webber, Graham confessed, would be the more anxious of the two. 'Our girl Jade is very impressive,' he said. 'She is an incredibly self-contained person. Andrew will be more nervous than she is.' In the event, Britain came fifth but, Graham being Graham, the night did not pass without controversy. The BBC was forced to apologize after he managed to offend thousands of Albanians by poking fun at their entry – 17-year-old Kejsi Tola who danced with a masked man in a blue spangly jumpsuit. Graham told viewers: 'The bad news is you are about to see Albania. Whenever you see *Eurovision* there is a moment where you go, "What?" Maybe you've had that already. Trust me, you haven't.' His comments led the nightly news bulletins in Albania and an Internet petition, calling Graham 'very rude and insulting' and demanding an apology, attracted 1,200 signatures. The BBC received 117 complaints and was, once again, forced to defend its man. 'Graham's commentary was in his own inimitable style,' a spokesman said.

Neither did Graham get to enjoy any Russian vodka – cheap or otherwise. After a late night hosting the BAFTA awards in London in April he had fallen down the stairs at home and broken a couple of ribs. He was taken to hospital, prescribed strong medication and – to his dismay – told to abstain from alcohol for the duration. 'When I opened my pain medication it said to avoid alcoholic beverages for four to six weeks, so I'm going to be sober in Moscow,' he wailed.

In June the BBC announced his chat show would be moving to BBC1 in the autumn – a decision that immediately led to media speculation that he was being lined up to replace the still-very-much-in-the-doghouse Jonathan Ross. BBC1 Controller Jay Hunt, in a mind-boggling piece of BBC management-speak, denied the switch was a threat to Ross. 'I can see how it seems that way,' she said. 'But the Graham Norton strategy is part of something I feel strongly about, which is that he is a unique talent. My decision to move Graham across does not affect any decision about Jonathan going forward.' The change, she said, would mean there would now be 'two compelling performers who will be regularly on at 10.35pm.' Graham's show was to screen on Monday evenings, with Ross's continuing in the more prestigious Friday night slot.

However, Ross's contract would be up the following year and, according to media reports, he had not begun talks with the BBC over a new package. Ms Hunt told the *Mirror* that he would be getting considerably less in his new contract. 'We are pushing very hard on talent, telling them we can't go on like this,' the *Mirror* quoted her as saying. 'Is Jonathan immune from that? Absolutely not.'

Graham, meanwhile, was set to have five major BBC projects on the go by the end of 2009. Added to that, his television production company So Television had posted another fantastic year, netting him £500,000 in fees and dividends according to accounts filed at Companies House. But his next BBC1 project, the family show *Totally Saturday*, would bring him back down to earth with an unpleasant bump. The BBC hoped the show would be its answer to ITV's successful Ant and Dec's *Saturday Night Takeaway*, but it was to prove a spectacular flop. DJ Chris Moyles led the criticism, telling his Radio 1 listeners that *Totally Saturday* was 'appalling television.' 'Imagine *Saturday Night Takeaway* with no budget,' frothed Moyles. 'If everybody had been away for a week and hadn't come up with any ideas and they'd got to the office three hours before the show went live on air – it's like that.'

Damning words indeed. Jonathan Ross had a pop at his rival too, describing the show – in which members of the public had their belongings 'borrowed' and then made the centre of attention – as 'not good enough'. 'Poor Graham. I feel for him when I watch that show,' he said. Crocodile tears perhaps, but the critics agreed, deriding the show as 'a new low'. Launched at the beginning of June, *Totally Saturday* was axed by July 6, a week early, after slumping from 4.3 million viewers to only 2.5 million.

Added to Graham's previous less-than successful projects such as *When Will I Be Famous?*, *Strictly Dance Fever* and *The One and Only*, the show's failure inevitably reignited speculation that the BBC didn't know what to do with their highly paid star. In July, an article in the *Guardian* accused Graham of 'staggering from one dud to another,' and asked who was to blame – Graham or his 'hapless' employers. 'There was a moment on Graham Norton's *Totally Saturday* show recently when I swear I saw him die a little outside,' wrote their man Stuart Jeffries. 'Is there nobody… on the BBC payroll – a security guard, ideally – who can stop this sort of thing? It's as though the BBC isn't sure what to do with the man who cost them so much. His bosses have repeatedly fired him from their cannon at the wall of Saturday night TV and, more often than not, Norton seems to have landed with a splat and slid down that wall unedifyingly.'

Graham was pragmatic about the show's failure, although it clearly concerned him. 'I'm aware that you don't get to do that many *Totally Saturday*s before people start saying, "Let's not get him to do our new show",' he said. 'Nobody likes making big turkeys but you have to take it on the chin. That's the nature of the beast. It's very hard to get it right.' He also revealed he had made another pilot in the summer that had failed spectacularly too. 'It was a physical game show which went hilariously wrong on the night because no one got any points at all,' he admitted. 'Every time we looked at the scoreboard there was just nothing on it. The people playing the game did it so stupidly it failed.'

His flops seemingly consigned to the dim and distant past, Graham signed a new BBC deal in the autumn – albeit for a rumoured £500,000 (20 per cent less.) He had seen it coming and appeared sanguine about his reduced wage. 'Unless the BBC finds oil, I fully expect my pay to be cut,' he'd admitted the previous September. 'Either I refuse to work for less and they tell me to bog off or I go "OK," and work. It's my job to say I'll take a pay cut and it's my agent's job to make sure it's not very big. Market forces dictate. I could go to the BBC, "I refuse to take a pay cut, I'm worth this." They'd say, "That's very interesting, Graham, but no, you're not. And now you're not working at all." The fact that I'm paid at all for wearing shiny suits on a sofa is a miracle.' He didn't, however, feel it was right for presenters' salaries to be made public knowledge. 'When it comes to specifically how much I earn, I prefer that to stay private,' he said.

As the sixth series of *The Graham Norton Show* prepared to air on its new home BBC1 at the beginning of October, it was increasingly clear that Graham – and the BBC – were operating in a completely different climate. Freshly reprimanded by his bosses, who had upheld a complaint against him for 'reinforcing a potentially offensive stereotype' by making a homophobic joke about the haircuts of lesbians on a previous show, Graham and his team had been given an official warning to watch what they said. 'The programme team were reminded of the need to avoid any possibility of being seen to endorse offensive sexual stereotypes,' said a BBC spokesman. But Graham insisted the move to BBC1 would not mean compromises. 'In my head, we're not going to tone the show down at all,' he said. 'They moved it to BBC1 because they liked it, not because they wanted to change it. As far as we're concerned they like the show so that's what they're going to get. *Little Britain* survived BBC1, the world didn't end, and that was on earlier than us.'

But the *Sunday Mirror*'s acerbic TV critic Kevin O'Sullivan reckoned he'd spotted a change for the worse when the new series kicked off. 'How come BBC2's excellent *The Graham Norton Show* wasn't as funny after switching to BBC1?' he asked. 'Less swearing, more mainstream… not so entertaining. So dull it hurt.' However, there was praise from the *Observer's* critic. 'Graham makes it look easy when it isn't… Mr Norton is entirely at home on BBC1,' they said.

Graham's big fear – irrationally – is that he will end up out of work and have to appear on a reality TV show such as *I'm A Celebrity… Get Me Out Of Here*. 'It'll end one day, I understand that,' he says matter-of-factly. 'But there are any number of digital channels who are always looking for someone to stand in front of a camera. Hopefully, one of them may want me so there will be lots of work on the way down.' In any event, the stabbing that almost took his life means that he doesn't allow himself to become overly concerned with things outside of his control. 'In the long term it made me less afraid of things,' he explains. 'I suppose my little mantra is, "It's only TV". I'm lucky; I didn't find success until my mid-thirties. Fame for the young is cruel. Hopefully, if God is good, I'll hit rock bottom just when I'm ready to retire. I've already had more than my share.'

At the age of 46, he was already starting to think about retirement. 'I've started thinking recently that when I'm 50 I'd like to work less,' he confided. 'I've never really had a plan or a goal. I'd just read books and walk the dogs. I've already beaten the odds. I've been on telly longer than most people manage. They normally last three or four years and then slip away, and you see them when you flick though all those Sky channels.' Still single, he appeared to have become resigned to being alone. 'I'm a great one for looking at other people's relationships and thinking, "I'm glad I'm not in that",' he said. 'I'd prefer to be miserable alone than miserable in a relationship.' It did seem a tad sad, though, when he admitted shortly after Christmas that he had spent the festive period alone in Ireland 'getting drunk'. 'My family were supposed to come and join me for Christmas but the weather was too bad,' he explained. 'So I spent a week absolutely by myself and turned into a recluse.'

In January 2010, what had been expected ever since Sachsgate finally happened when Jonathan Ross announced he was leaving the BBC. Graham lost no time in throwing his hat into the ring for Wossy's former berth. 'It is a very good slot, so if they asked us to do it, I imagine we would say yes,' he told the *Sunday Mirror*. 'But I wouldn't want to do an hour. I think an hour is too long for a chat show.' As if to underline that he fully understood the responsibility that would go with the flagship Friday night slot, he revealed he was ready to tone down his comedy. 'Now you do a really disgusting joke and the audience don't like it,' he mused. 'It's interesting how gentler humour is doing well in this time.'

He went so far as to say he was pleased to have left the smut behind. 'You know what? I really don't miss it,' he claimed. 'If I missed it I would still do it. And that was the point, we took it as far as we could and now the show is still fairly irreverent and it is still fairly out there but it's not that rude.' Speaking more recently, he claims television audiences have become more illiberal since he began working in the industry. 'There are things we can't say and do on TV or radio that ten years ago we absolutely could have said or shown,' he explains. 'I think that's the BBC reading the mood of the audience – the audience don't particularly like cruel jokes, and I think they did.'

Ross would not be leaving until his contract expired that summer, however, and in the meantime Graham was kept busy presenting *Over The Rainbow* in March, and the *Eurovision Song Contest* in May. The same month he sat in for Chris Evans on his Radio 2 Breakfast Show when the presenter took a fortnight's leave. Holidays – or at least trips to the seaside – were very much on Graham's mind too that summer as he enjoyed weekends at his latest new home in Bexhill-on-Sea, East Sussex. Opening a local care home's summer fete, he admitted he loved the area, 'but not as much as my dogs – who don't understand why we ever have to go back to London.' He also found time to visit his holiday home in Ireland, where he opened a new cancer care unit at the local hospital. 'If you told me when I was 18 that each year I would voluntarily come back for two or three months, I would never have believed it,' he confided to the *Irish Examiner*. 'I would have thought you were mad. When I finished school I ran away. I couldn't wait to get out of here. But I love West Cork now.'

That October he fulfilled a wish when he was invited to present the prizes at his old school's Speech Day – the first time he had been back in 30 years. As his *alma mater*'s only famous ex-pupil he provided a more glamorous attraction than in previous years, such as the time during Graham's final year at Bandon Grammar School when the celebrity guest was the inspector from the local artificial insemination station. 'It's a rural thing,' he explains. 'But I always felt a bit miffed they could invite the AI man and not me.'

On the work front, Graham was branching out. His stint at Radio 2 had led to the offer of a permanent Saturday morning show of his own at the station, replacing the one soon to be vacated by – ta dah! – none other than Jonathan Ross. Graham, however, was still playing down the likelihood of taking over his old adversary's Friday night BBC1 timeslot. 'I think if they wanted me to they'd have asked by now,' he said in May. 'Friday night is a very nice slot and if they offered it I'm sure we'd say yes. But it's doing well on a Monday night so it's that awful thing of, if we moved and bombed then there's no canoe, no paddle, no river, nothing. At least now we've got half a paddle and a canoe. So we're keeping our heads down and just being grateful we've got a show.' By October, though, he had been offered – and accepted – it. For his part, Ross could have been forgiven if he half expected to return home to Hampstead one evening, and find Graham ensconced in his armchair drinking his wine.

The Graham Norton Show ended the year on a high, pulling in its biggest audience to date on Christmas Eve, attracting 4.52 million with guest appearances from Matt Lucas, David Walliams and Matt Smith. The following spring, So Television recorded profits that were up by more than 9 per cent. Companies House records show Graham received a £500,000 dividend and £1.5 million in production fees and royalties. At the same time it was revealed that So Television was in talks with ITV, who were keen to buy the growing company. It would be unusual, but not unprecedented, for an ITV-owned production company to make shows for the BBC (others include *University Challenge* and *The Royle Family*.)

But the big news of 2011, was that after clocking up (in his own words) 'a heroic number of rubbish relationships', Graham was in love again. The object of his affections was handsome Canadian businessman Trevor Patterson, 20 years his junior. Graham met the 29-year-old software designer in the autumn and, according to his friends, was 'head over heels'. 'Things are moving really fast,' said one. 'Trevor has a playful sense of humour and is young at heart which suits Graham perfectly. I think this one could go the distance.' Indeed, within weeks of meeting Trevor, Graham was even musing on the subject of fatherhood. 'Part of me would like to have kids, but I'm 48 now and have left it a bit late,' he confided in an interview with *Woman's Own* magazine. 'I think you want to bring up your child with someone. There are lots of great single parents out there but I'm lazier than they are so I'd quite like to share the responsibility.'

The pair celebrated Graham's 49th birthday in April 2012 together, spending two weeks at the luxurious One & Only Reethi Rah resort in the Maldives. Graham also showed his new love off at various film premieres and after-show parties in London. By October the couple were living together and Graham was telling friends he was happier than he'd ever been during his 15 years in showbiz. His new love even shared his passion for pet pooches Bailey and Madge. 'When Trevor moved in, I thought: "He had better like dogs!" It is quite a difficult house to live in if you don't like them,' he laughs. 'But if I met someone who did not like dogs, I probably would not like him.' At the time of writing the couple are still together, although Graham has thus far ruled out wedding plans. 'When I hear about people getting married quickly, saying stuff like: "Yeah, after seven months we got engaged," I think: "Really?" they must be very young,' he recently told *Closer* magazine. 'I am 50 next year and I kind of think it is very soon in the relationship for something like that. I would be very cautious about going down that road. At the moment we really enjoy spending time together.'

By the end of 2011, Graham seemed to have forgotten all thoughts of retirement, as viewing figures for his chat show topped the 4 million mark. 'I am chaining myself to that show and hopefully

I'll still be doing it in another 15 years,' he laughs. As well as his newfound domestic bliss, 2012 saw two other significant events. The first, in January, was when Madonna, having proved elusive for so long, finally agreed to grace his sofa with her presence. Having pursued her for so long, expectations were high but the diva did not disappoint. Appearing relaxed and comfortable, she made an entertaining and chatty guest. Speaking about her new album and upcoming tour, Graham – cheeky as ever – asked her how she could be 'arsed' to do it, to which she replied smilingly: 'a girl has to make a living.'

Whilst his earnings may not be quite in Madonna's league, Graham was about to enjoy a financial windfall when the ongoing talks with ITV came to fruition. In August 2012 the company bought So Television in a deal rumoured to be worth up to £17 million, comprised of a £10 million lump sum and the incentive of a further £7 million if the company achieves profit targets by the end of July 2016. 'So Television has been our baby for 12 years, so I'm thrilled that the ITV family has decided to take it under their wing and help it blossom,' said Graham.

Despite his admission (which surely must come under the heading of 'Tell Us Something We Don't Know, Graham') that he promotes 'terrible' films in order to get celebrities to appear on his programme, *The Graham Norton Show* has become an entertaining mainstay of BBC1's Friday night schedule. In October the *Sunday Express* hailed him as 'Britain's best chat show host' and claimed Jonathan Ross was 'now a distant memory for BBC1 viewers, having just registered his lowest viewing figures yet on ITV1.'

There is still the odd upset, of course, such as when Russell Brand accused Graham of making his mum cry. The comic appeared on Graham's show in June, just a week after his estranged wife

Katy Perry had been on. Graham, believing it would be strange if he didn't mention the coincidence, asked him about the failed marriage. Ignoring the question, Brand looked at his 65-year-old mother Barbara, who was seated in the audience, and fumed: 'My mum is here. She got upset when you dragged up my marriage. I saw her cry Graham. That's the reality because it's real people, Graham, that's my real mum. I have come here to promote a film and you have made my mum cry. I don't see you as that sort of person, Graham.' Graham tried to apologize, saying: 'I don't see myself as that kind of person...' but Brand continued to berate him. 'What I would have done, mate, in your position is to come up to me before the show and gone, "Eh, listen it's a bit odd your ex-missus was on last week. I might mention it, is that OK?" '

Graham exited 2012 on a high when his New Year's Eve chat show achieved its biggest-ever audience of 4.51 million. Featuring an impressive line-up that included Hollywood A-listers Tom Cruise and Hugh Jackman, the show secured 26.9 per cent of the audience share. Rival comedian Alan Carr's *New Year's Specstacular* (correct spelling) on Channel 4, meanwhile, attracted only 1.78 million. Having learned, perhaps, from his tongue-lashing by Brand, Graham stayed well away from the delicate subject of Cruise's recent marriage split from Katie Holmes. The actor may well have been happy to have been spared an inquisition, but Graham's reticence did not go down well with the *Sunday Mirror*'s Kevin O'Sullivan, who slated 'grovelling Graham' for 'an epic display of crawl-arsing to Hollywood's top weirdo Tom Cruise.'

As Graham prepares to enter his sixth decade in April 2013, he knows he has much to be thankful for. 'Even I am surprised at how sanguine I am,' he says. 'I suppose it's because I'm feeling pretty good and settled. I like my job and where I live, I've got my dogs and I'm seeing someone. I didn't like 40 at all. Turning 40 hit me like a ton of bricks, but my life is much more settled and happy now. I will be celebrating the Big Five-O!' Indeed, so content is he these days, he has even decided against the plastic surgery he'd always promised himself. Having been to see a man about having his 'hideous' eye bags removed, he says he now plans to learn to live with them. 'Every time I had an appointment something would come up,' he says. 'In the end I took it as a sign that maybe it's not meant to happen. Maybe I've grown into them.'